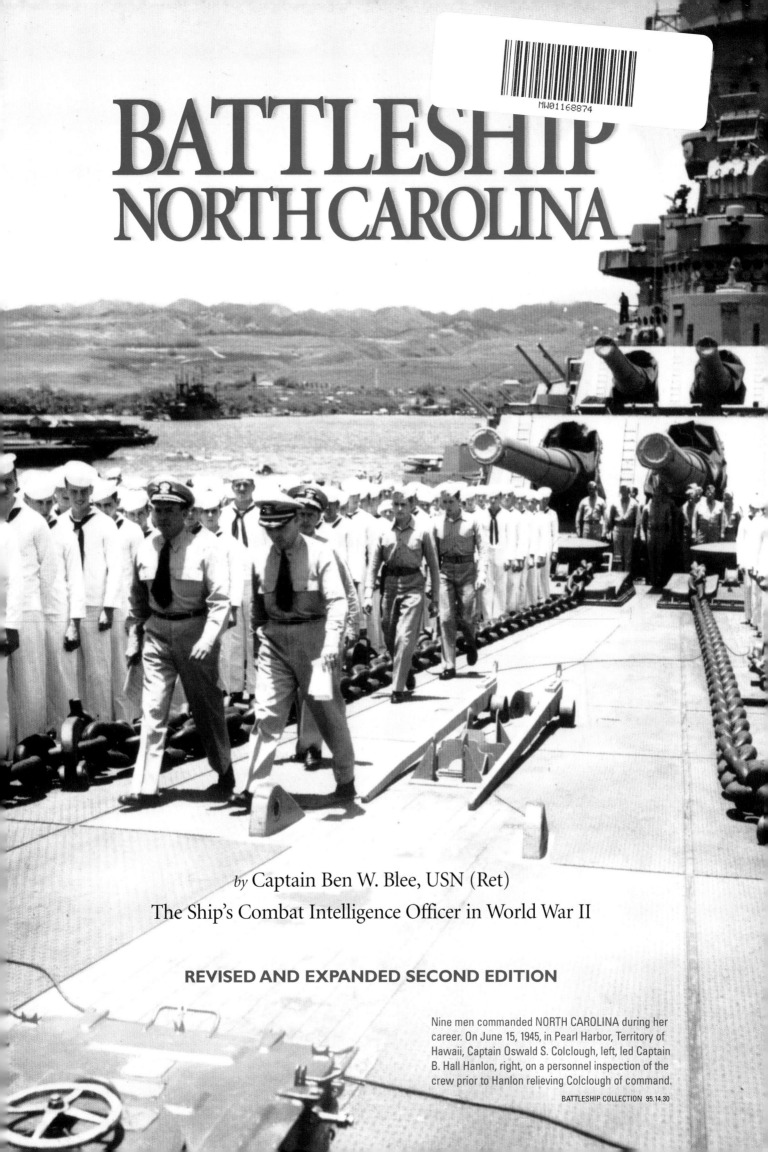

BATTLESHIP
NORTH CAROLINA

by Captain Ben W. Blee, USN (Ret)

The Ship's Combat Intelligence Officer in World War II

REVISED AND EXPANDED SECOND EDITION

Nine men commanded NORTH CAROLINA during her career. On June 15, 1945, in Pearl Harbor, Territory of Hawaii, Captain Oswald S. Colclough, left, led Captain B. Hall Hanlon, right, on a personnel inspection of the crew prior to Hanlon relieving Colclough of command.

BATTLESHIP COLLECTION 95.14.30

In Memoriam

of TEN SHIPMATES KILLED IN ACTION DURING WORLD WAR II

George E. Conlon
AUGUST 24, 1942, BATTLE OF EASTERN SOLOMONS

Albert S. Geary
SEPTEMBER 15, 1942, TORPEDO ATTACK

Ingwald N. Nelson
SEPTEMBER 15, 1942, TORPEDO ATTACK

Leonard E. Pone
SEPTEMBER 15, 1942, TORPEDO ATTACK

William O. Skelton
SEPTEMBER 15, 1942, TORPEDO ATTACK

Oscar C. Stone
SEPTEMBER 15, 1942, TORPEDO ATTACK

Eldon E. Means
APRIL 6, 1945, AIRCRAFT RECOVERY ACCIDENT

Edward E. Brenn
APRIL 6, 1945, FRIENDLY FIRE

Carl E. Karam, Jr.
APRIL 6, 1945, FRIENDLY FIRE

John M. Watson
APRIL 6, 1945, FRIENDLY FIRE

May they rest in peace.

BATTLESHIP
★ ★ ★ ★ ★ ★ ★ ★ ★ ★ ★ ★ ★
NORTH CAROLINA

PUBLISHED BY BATTLESHIP NORTH CAROLINA

PUBLISHER
USS North Carolina Battleship Commission

DIRECTOR
David R. Scheu, Sr., CAPT, USN (Ret)

MUSEUM SERVICES DIRECTOR
Kim Robinson Sincox

CURATOR OF COLLECTIONS
Mary Ames Booker Sheret

GRAPHIC DESIGNER
Alice Whicker Heitchue

COPY EDITOR
Patti S. Borda

INDEXER
Roberta Engleman

FRIENDS OF THE BATTLESHIP INTERN
Carrie A. Davenport

WEBMASTER
Randy Drew

PROOFREADERS
Charles M. and Sue K. Paty
Dr. Henry S. and Terry G. Falkowski

FIRST PRINTING , SECOND EDITION,
BATTLESHIP NORTH CAROLINA, 2005

ISBN 0-9608538-2-0

Copyright held by
Battleship NORTH CAROLINA
PO BOX 480
Wilmington, NC 28402-0480
910.251.5797 telephone   910.251.5807 facsimile
ncbb55@battleshipnc.com
www.battleshipnc.com

FOREWORD

BY CAPTAIN DAVID R. SCHEU, SR., USN (RET)
Director, Battleship NORTH CAROLINA

This volume is a revised and expanded second edition of the book, *Battleship NORTH CAROLINA*, authored by Captain Ben W. Blee, USN (Ret), at the request of my predecessor, Captain Frank S. Conlon, USN (Ret), that was first published in 1982. When the third printing was exhausted the time seemed right for revision, and octogenarian Captain Blee remained the best-qualified person to author the new edition due to his long personal association with the battleship.

Having served through most of World War II in the Pacific Theater, Captain Blee witnessed or participated in much of NORTH CAROLINA's war experience. From his ship, heavy cruiser PENSACOLA (CA-24), he witnessed NORTH CAROLINA's dramatic entry into Pearl Harbor when she first arrived there to reinforce our hard-pressed Pacific Fleet on July 11, 1942. Later, PENSACOLA operated with the battleship during the Guadalcanal Campaign. While on watch as officer of the deck, he observed in stunned disbelief the torpedoing of the NORTH CAROLINA and two other ships. In April 1944 then Lieutenant Blee reported on board NORTH CAROLINA for duty and served in her until July 1945, just one month before hostilities with Japan ended. This 16-month period encompassed most of the fighting participated in by the battleship. As combat intelligence officer and assistant officer-in-charge of the combat information center, he observed firsthand the ship's extraordinary war service. Most significantly, his primary duty was to keep the commanding officer and other senior officers of the ship briefed on enemy activity as well as the current operations of our own forces. His experiences provide him with a unique, authoritative perspective from which to undertake this project.

Of particular note in this edition is the expanded treatment of the Japanese side of the torpedoing of the U.S. aircraft carrier WASP, destroyer O'BRIEN and NORTH CAROLINA September 15, 1942. This action was a disaster for the U.S. Navy because the first two ships were lost, and the battleship was knocked out of the war for nearly three months for repairs, while the Japanese suffered no loss or damage whatever. Questions regarding which Japanese submarine or submarines were involved and how the action occurred have baffled historians and naval experts on both sides of the war for 40 years. In 1984, Captain Blee located in Japan several surviving submariners who had taken part in the attack. Inviting them to Wilmington for a reunion with battleship crewmembers in 1986, Blee presided over presentations and a roundtable discussion of the event, which enabled him to solve the mystery.

Captain Blee served in the Navy for 27 years; he commanded three ships and concluded his service as Fleet Intelligence Officer, U.S. Pacific Fleet. Retiring in 1967, he settled with his family in Jacksonville, North Carolina, which gave him the opportunity to renew association with an old love, the battleship. From 1974 to 1977, and again from 1985 to 1989, he served as chairman of the USS NORTH CAROLINA Battleship Commission, responsible to the governor for overseeing management of the battleship. While in that position he wrote the original script for the documentary, *SHOWBOAT, A Battleship at War.* He also assembled an extensive collection of valuable historical records, correspondence, photographs and personal memorabilia comprising the beginnings of the ship's official archives and initiated the invaluable oral history program.

Publication of this new edition has provided an opportunity to update and expand information to complement Captain Blee's narrative by including interesting oral history extracts, charts and many additional historical photographs donated by the ship's officers, crew and their families or collected by my staff over the years. I commend the book as the definitive history of the Battleship NORTH CAROLINA.

Dedicated to

Joe Warren Stryker

REAR ADMIRAL, UNITED STATES NAVY, RETIRED
1904-1980

★ ★ ★ ★ ★

As Navigator and later as
Executive Officer of the ship,
he demonstrated extraordinary
skill and courage in battle,
inspiring by his example the
superb spirit and character
of the ship's company.

★ ★ ★ ★ ★

PREFACE

BY CAPTAIN BEN W. BLEE, USN (RET)
The Ship's Combat Intelligence Officer in World War II

I have loved the NORTH CAROLINA from the first time I saw her on her arrival at Pearl Harbor when we desperately needed her, July 11, 1942. Thus, when I was asked to undertake the revision of this book, it was a pleasure to resume my dedication to keeping her story alive. And yet, the task remained a difficult one, not because of any lack of material, but due more than ever to tough decisions on what had to be left out. Left out, for instance, are the names of hundreds of her crew who manned her guns in battle, swabbed her decks, stood endless watches on her bridge, at her guns or in her steamy engine rooms; prepared thousands of meals, or cared for her sick and wounded; in short, men in a wide variety of roles who sweated, endured, risked their lives, agonized and exalted with her, making all her victories possible.

On the other hand, scattered throughout this book the reader will find a feature new in this edition called *"Life Aboard,"* consisting of personal recollections of scores of named individuals of all ranks and ratings. They are quoted here to provide a closer look at what it was like to serve in a battleship at war. I hope those quoted will not find fault with me in cases where I have condensed or paraphrased their statements where necessary for brevity or to avoid repetition. Other major additions include over 200 recently unearthed official Navy photographs of NORTH CAROLINA and her crew during World War II, plus a score of charts illustrating the major World War II campaigns and battles in which NORTH CAROLINA fought.

Less significant combat encounters are barely mentioned and some omitted entirely to avoid repetition. In more technical sections I was challenged to translate naval parlance into language everyone can understand. I trust my purposes have been achieved without departing from accuracy.

Neither I nor anyone else could have authored this work without help. I am indebted first to Arnold S. Lott and Robert F. Sumrall, authors of the 35-page booklet *Ship's Data 1,* the forerunner and inspiration for the first edition of this work. For help with details of the ship's operations before I reported on board April 6, 1944, I owe particular thanks to retired Admiral A. G. Ward; retired Rear Admirals J. W. Stryker, J. E. Kirkpatrick and J. T. Burke, Jr.; and to retired Captain R. J. Celustka. For help during the period after I was detached from the ship July 5, 1945, until the Japanese surrender September 2, I am indebted to retired Rear Admiral Kemp Tolley and Commander A. P. Oliver. For advice on countless particulars of Showboat lore best understood among the ship's enlisted men I owe special thanks to former Boatswain's Mate First Class Paul A. Wieser.

To retired Captain David R. Scheu, Sr., Director of Battleship NORTH CAROLINA, I owe my deep appreciation for his recognition of the need for an expanded edition, for his steadfast support of the project, and especially for his technical expertise in explaining more clearly the fine points of battleship gunnery and fire control. A 1967 graduate of the Naval Academy at Annapolis, Captain Scheu devoted most of his naval career to duty in surface ships, including two years (1981-83) in USS NEW JERSEY (BB-62), as Operations Officer. Since NEW JERSEY's original armament was nearly identical to that of NORTH CAROLINA, Captain Scheu's experience and counsel were of enormous help to me in this writing.

To Museum Services Director Kim Robinson Sincox and Curator of Collections Mary Ames Sheret, I owe my thanks for their tireless work in assembling the oral history quotations and newly acquired World War II photographs. Kim's idea of the *Life Aboard* series to enliven the narrative was a stroke of genius. I am indebted to the battleship's official Webmaster Randy Drew for his painstaking research in national photograph repositories, and for his ever generous assistance in solving photographic and computer problems. I extend my thanks to retired English teacher Mrs. Walter W. (Harriet) Stegemerten, who helped me with punctuation. I owe special thanks to Alice Heitchue for the overall graphic design of the book and for her skillful rendering of my many newly added charts and diagrams. To Patti S. Borda and Roberta Engleman, copy editor and indexer, respectively, I am indebted for the professionalism with which they improved the book's literary quality and its usefulness as a World War II research reference. Many reference works, all listed in the bibliography, were essential to the corroboration of my memory, particularly of the events related in Part Three. Principal among my sources were NORTH CAROLINA's official *War Diary* and *Action Reports,* plus Rear Admiral Samuel Eliot Morison's 14-volume *History of United States Naval Operations in World War II.* The latter was my chief reference for placing the story of NORTH CAROLINA in perspective within the overall context of the war against Japan.

Many other gallant ships defended America along with NORTH CAROLINA in World War II, and this is also their story. However, my goal has been to preserve the story of this great man-of-war and her magnificent crew.

To the Crew...

May the memory of your patriotism and your courage in battle long endure to inspire future generations of Americans.

CONTENTS

PART TWO, A Typical Wartime Day at Sea

PART THREE, World War II Operational History

INTRODUCTION

The USS NORTH CAROLINA of this book, 55th in the long series of battleships laid down for the U.S. Navy, was the first of 10 "fast" battleships to join the fleet in the World War II era. Now a state war memorial in Wilmington, North Carolina, she is immaculately preserved almost exactly as she was in her prime during nearly four years of distinguished service in World War II.

Her name was borne proudly by several predecessors, and her origins go back through many centuries of naval history. Countless evolutions of warship design are distilled in her, with the famous Civil War ironclads, MONITOR and VIRGINIA (ex-MERRIMACK), among her direct ancestors.

Her commissioned service lasted only a little more than six years, but much of that short lifetime was spent at sea in the combat area of the western Pacific, where she battled enemy forces on more than 50 separate occasions.

World War II produced revolutionary changes in naval warfare, with the aircraft carrier and its planes replacing the battleship and its big guns as the main offensive arm of our Navy in most situations. Nevertheless, battleships were indispensable members of the team because of their tremendous firepower, particularly in the roles of air defense and shore bombardment.

Although NORTH CAROLINA will never sail again, she will endure for hundreds of years, not only as an authentic World War II battleship, but also as a symbol of courage and sacrifice of our country's citizens, during what was arguably the most significant period of the 20th century, to inspire generations of Americans yet to come.

On the proud occasion of the ship's commissioning, April 9, 1941, in New York Navy Yard, Secretary of the Navy Frank Knox congratulates Captain Olaf M. Hustvedt on becoming the ship's first commanding officer.

EARLIER AMERICAN WARSHIPS OF THE SAME NAME

The first USS NORTH CAROLINA, completed in 1820, was a 74-gun ship of the line, or "line-of-battle ship." She and others of her class were considered the heavy capital ships of their day mounting 42-pounder and 32-pounder cannon. She was a three-masted square-rigger with an overall length of 196 feet 3 inches and beam (width) of 54 feet. Displacing 2,633 tons, she carried a complement (wartime crew) of 820.

Pride of the Navy and envy of foreign navies, this first USS NORTH CAROLINA was such a magnificent sailer that command of her was considered a prize assignment. For nearly half a century she and her sister ships, because of their impressive bearing, superior sea-keeping qualities and powerful armament, were the undisputed master warships of the world.

During the Civil War the Confederate States Navy built a 174-foot ironclad NORTH CAROLINA at the William and Benjamin Beery shipyard, also called the Confederate Navy Yard during the war, which was located on Eagles Island near the battleship NORTH CAROLINA. Her main battery consisted of four 8-inch guns, and she was protected by canted armor above the waterline. Displacing 600 tons, her complement was 150. Due to structural imperfections and unreliable machinery, she was usually kept at anchor near the mouth of the Cape Fear River, where she served as a guard ship to help keep the port of Wilmington open for Confederate blockade runners. Unfortunately, she developed leaks and sank in September 1864 near Southport, North Carolina.

The second U.S. Navy ship named NORTH CAROLINA was Armored Cruiser 12, which joined the fleet in 1908. She had an overall length of 504 feet and a beam of 73 feet. Partly armored with up to nine inches of plate, her displacement was 14,500 tons and her designed speed 22 knots. Armored

The 74-gun ship of the line NORTH CAROLINA carried a cloud of white canvas and full broadsides of muzzle-loading cannon.

The second USS NORTH CAROLINA, Armored Cruiser 12, joined the fleet in 1908.

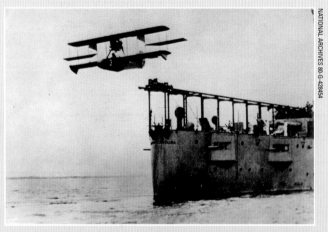

A World War I veteran, ACR-12 was the first ship of the U.S. Navy to launch an aircraft by catapult while underway.

Artist Rose Stokes's conception of a ship intended to become BB-52, but never completed.

Cruiser 12 carried a formidable armament consisting of four 10-inch guns in her main battery, plus sixteen 6-inch and twenty-two 3-inch rapid fire guns in her secondary battery. She also carried a number of smaller caliber guns and four underwater torpedo tubes. Her complement was 38 officers and 821 enlisted men.

ACR-12 operated in the Caribbean, the North and South Atlantic and the Mediterranean. She became a pioneer of naval aviation when an AB-3 Curtiss flying boat was launched from her stern by catapult while underway on November 5, 1915. During World War I she performed convoy escort duties, making six round trips to Europe.

Next came Battleship 52, which was to have been called NORTH CAROLINA, but was never completed. Laid down in 1920, all work on her was halted three years later under terms of the 1922 Treaty for the Limitation of Naval Armament, commonly called the Washington Naval Treaty. This treaty not only limited naval armament, but also established a 10-year "holiday" during which no new battleships could be built. In compliance, the United States sold the uncompleted hull for scrap in 1923. Designed to displace 43,200 full load tons — a monster for that era — she would have had a length of 684 feet, beam of 106 feet and a speed of 23 knots. She was to have mounted twelve 16-inch guns, plus other smaller caliber guns and two torpedo tubes. This NORTH CAROLINA and her five sister ships, had they been completed, would have been the largest and most heavily armed capital ships in the world as of the 1920s.

DESIGN BACKGROUND OF NORTH CAROLINA–CLASS BATTLESHIPS (BB-55 and BB-56)

When the U.S. Congress approved the building of new battleships in the early 1930s, the limitations of the Washington Naval Treaty of 1922 remained in effect. In order to meet the treaty's requirements, U.S. naval architects were compelled to accept a number of painful compromises in ship design. The most important requirements of a battleship were armament, armor, speed and endurance. Any one of these features, if optimized, increased weight or displacement at the expense of the others.

The Washington Naval Treaty limited capital ships to 35,000 tons standard displacement — the weight of the volume of water a ship will displace fully manned, loaded, equipped and ready for sea. However, standard displacement excluded by definition fuel and reserve feed water for the boilers. Excluding these items from the displacement limit was an attempt at fairness. It recognized that different navies had different range requirements. It allowed them to carry whatever fuel and water was needed to reach convenient fueling stops. The navies of countries with short ranges or many available ports did not need to carry as much fuel as those traveling great distances between ports. For instance, Italy was concerned primarily with short-range operations within the Mediterranean Sea. Great Britain enjoyed a world-wide network of bases that provided ample fueling opportunities. The United States had to be prepared to send its fleet across the vast Pacific to support its interests in the Far East. Therefore, the United States needed long-range battleships, which required more fuel and reserve feed water for the boilers.

Making allowances for extra fuel and water sounded reasonable, but it adversely affected other desired design features. For instance, extra fuel and water required a larger hull, meaning more steel, thus more weight, leaving less tonnage for armament, armor or engines. Moreover, a ship with a large fuel capacity had a greater displacement and deeper draft. Thus, she would need greater engine power to propel the heavier hull. Heavier machinery required even more compromises in armament, armor and everything else.

These were just a few of the dilemmas designers of NORTH CAROLINA (BB-55) and her sister ship, USS WASHINGTON (BB-56), faced as they began their work in 1933. ("BB" stands for battleship, the numerals for the 55th and 56th battleships of the U.S. Navy.) The effort put into the design of these two ships was staggering. Over 50 design variations were prepared and evaluated over the next two years before the Navy's General Board (an advisory committee of senior admirals) agreed upon a basic plan. This plan included a main battery (largest guns carried) of twelve 14-inch guns in three quadruple turrets, a speed of 27 knots and armor to withstand the impact from an enemy's 14-inch shells. Eventually meeting these specifications proved possible, but unavoidable compromises resulted in less than optimum design, particularly in terms of speed, armor and underwater protection.

The intention of the Navy to provide twelve 14-inch guns in three quadruple turrets as the main battery pre-dated the London Naval Treaty of 1936, which was the next attempt at naval arms limitation after the Washington Naval Treaty of 1922. It reflected a judgment on the part of the Navy's General Board that the 14-inch shell was adequate. The Navy already had an improved 14-inch gun ready for installation. Its use would provide 12 barrels, an advantage of numbers, and its 1,500-pound projectile was expected to create sufficient destruction once it penetrated armor.

DESIGN INNOVATIONS OF NORTH CAROLINA-CLASS BATTLESHIPS

The overall design of the two ships was largely pre-determined by a combination of treaty restrictions and what was deemed most appropriate placement of the three main battery turrets and the four main propulsion spaces. Nevertheless, the designers of NORTH CAROLINA and WASHINGTON were able to incorporate many radical improvements over the designs of earlier U.S. battleships, including the following:

■ A sweeping flush deck, unbroken from bow to stern, made these ships more seaworthy and more graceful in appearance than their predecessors.

■ A massive superstructure, surmounting the hull amidships like a medieval castle, replaced the tripods and cage masts of earlier ships. A sturdy tower, resembling a castle keep, dominated this structure forward. The tower loomed to a height of 120 feet above the waterline. It provided superb platforms at seven different levels for yardarms and halyards on which to run up signal flags; for battle lookouts, searchlights and automatic antiaircraft weapons; for a secondary conning station; for gunfire control stations and equipment; and for radio and radar antennas.

■ The two main battery fire control directors and four secondary battery directors were ideally

Note the clean lines of the ship as revealed in this early photograph.

mounted aloft with commanding fields of vision for their purposes: i.e., to locate targets, ascertain their movements and feed that information to computers in the gunnery plotting rooms far below decks, in order to generate aiming orders for the guns.

■ In earlier battleships the secondary battery occupied old-style casemates (small openings in the hull below the main deck) with limited arcs of fire to each side. The guns of NORTH CAROLINA's secondary battery were clustered on or above the main deck in rotating armored mounts, positioned for widest possible fields of fire, and obviously intended to endow the ship with a superior antiaircraft gunnery capability.

■ The hull shape forward featured a bulbous bow at the keel designed to reduce resistance and increase hull efficiency by as much as five percent at high speed. The hull then rises sharply to the waterline and into a forward flair up to the main deck.

■ The ship mounted four propellers and two rudders. The rudders were 10 feet off centerline, positioned behind the inboard propellers. The inboard propellers were attached to twin skegs (streamlined supports protruding from the hull), another design innovation. Where the hull began to slope upwards toward the stern, the twin skegs extended straight out along the same plane as the keel. These identical fin-like shapes together formed an inverted U-shaped tunnel intended to reduce resistance and increase fuel efficiency (unfortunately a theory that didn't prove valid). Since the skegs were on the same plane as the keel, they helped support the ship in drydock.

■ The two 85-foot stacks with their raked caps conveyed an impression of superior engine power, which these ships certainly had, with 115,000 shaft

horsepower and a top speed six knots faster than any of their predecessors.

■ The four engine rooms were arranged one behind the other lengthwise in the ship and separated by strong watertight bulkheads, designed to limit flooding from torpedo or mine damage.

Overall, the effect of these innovations was to give NORTH CAROLINA and WASHINGTON a formidable, state of the art bearing, which served warning to any potential enemy of their advanced capabilities as fighting ships.

In the two classes of new battleships that followed the NORTH CAROLINA-class, design was similar in many respects, but with important improvements. First came four 35,000-ton SOUTH DAKOTA-class ships, BB-57 through BB-60: SOUTH DAKOTA, INDIANA, MASSACHUSETTS and ALABAMA. Although these ships were 50 feet shorter than the NORTH CAROLINA-class, they packed the same firepower and were slightly faster. Next were the four IOWA-class ships, BB-61 through BB-64: IOWA, NEW JERSEY, MISSOURI and WISCONSIN. These magnificent ships, built without the constraints imposed by naval arms limitation treaties, were superior in armament, speed and armor. With a full load displacement of 57,500 tons, length of 887 feet and 212,000 shaft horsepower, these great ships — the overall best battleships ever built by any navy — could steam at 33+ knots. However, as forerunners of the fast battleship breed, it fell to NORTH CAROLINA and WASHINGTON to cope first with most of the innovations and set the pace for the eight battleships that followed. All three classes were limited in beam to 108 feet; barely narrow enough to pass through the Panama Canal.

Watch for these **"Life Aboard"** memories and stories from the battleship's oral history program, which the reader will find scattered throughout this book. They are intended to provide a closer look into the lives of the men who served on board the NORTH CAROLINA; men who made her the pride of the Navy, who served her guns in 50 battles, and who either loved her at first sight or learned to love her and trust her with their lives. Although most of the quotations date from long after World War II and some of the men quoted went on to much higher naval rank, for simplicity the position and rank or rate given for each man quoted are the highest held while serving on board NORTH CAROLINA.

"I fell in love with her when I first saw her. I am talking about the ship, not my wife. I don't know. There was just something about it to see that huge thing sitting in the Navy yard. It was love at first sight, really."

— Jackson Belford, Signalman Third Class

"During my 27 years in the Navy I served full tours of duty in six different ships, commanding three. I liked every one, but the NORTH CAROLINA I loved."

— Author

War veterans travel thousands of miles to visit the battlefields where they risked their lives in combat. For the crew of the NORTH CAROLINA, all their battlefields are in Wilmington, North Carolina, where their ship rests in honored glory.

"My first thoughts on seeing the NORTH CAROLINA for the first time since I was discharged [after World War II]... was to have a lump in my throat which kept swelling until I nearly choked and I could hardly speak, and the tears were flowing down my cheeks. I would like to be remembered as a sailor who loved the NORTH CAROLINA with all his being."

— Leo Drake, Chief Fire Controlman

"I wasn't married until I was 35, so I had a lot of girl-friends around the world in one place or another. I've gone back to those ports and they're still there, but they don't look quite the same. They're a little older. But when I went back aboard the NORTH CAROLINA, she was just as young and beautiful as she ever was."

— Commander Kemp Tolley, Navigator

After years of studies, designs and changes, the keel is laid for the first U.S. battleship to be built in 16 years.

CONSTRUCTION BEGINS

As of June 3, 1936, when an act of Congress authorized construction of NORTH CAROLINA and WASHINGTON, the Navy had not constructed a new battleship in 16 years. A few new cruisers and destroyers had joined the fleet in the late 1920s and early 1930s, but on the whole the Navy was a fleet of old if not obsolete ships. Ships are not built in a day or even in a year. In the case of NORTH CAROLINA, four years were spent designing her, and another three years and eight months elapsed before she was ready to join the fleet, thus proving an old saying: "When you need the ships, it's too late to build them."

Building a major warship is an immensely complex undertaking, involving a much more massive and intricate structure than is apparent to the eye. For instance, it may be difficult to believe that there is more of the ship under water than is visible above the surface. Even though NORTH CAROLINA was built of thousands of tons of steel, some of it as much as 16 inches thick, she floats because inside her hull is a vast honeycomb of air-filled compartments. NORTH CAROLINA's hull was so immense by the standards of her time that before construction commenced, the building ways at the New York Navy Yard had to be lengthened and strengthened.

Construction of such a ship begins with laying an enormous steel I-beam lengthwise between the building ways, the pair of inclined slides leading into the water. This I-beam is called the keel and serves as the ship's backbone. The keel of BB-55 was laid at the New York Navy Yard, Brooklyn, New York, on Navy Day, October 27, 1937. Smaller I-beams are attached to the keel at right angles to form the ribs, called transverse frames. The longitudinal frames are I-beams that run bow to stern the full length of the ship and are attached to the transverse frames. The ship's hull or outer skin is created when steel plates are riveted or welded to the transverse and longitudinal frames. The ship is divided into decks (floors), and each deck is comprised of compartments (rooms) formed by bulkheads. Bulkheads are walls extending athwartships (crosswise) as well as fore and aft

This photograph, taken June 27, 1939, shows the ship under construction on the building ways of the New York Navy Yard. Note the circular forms of the barbettes (armored supports) of the two forward turrets.

(lengthwise). The decks, bulkheads and much of the ship's equipment are made of steel plate of various thicknesses, depending on the stresses, strains and impacts they may be required to endure.

The main deck of NORTH CAROLINA is surfaced with teak, which helps absorb shrapnel, sound and heat. Below the main deck, in order, are the second deck, third deck, first platform deck, second platform deck and the inner bottom. A platform deck is one that does not run the ship's full length. That part of the ship rising above the main deck is called the superstructure, with elevations upward called, in order, the 01 level, 02 level, 03 level, etc. NORTH CAROLINA's navigation bridge, for example, is located in the forward superstructure on the 04 level. "Sky Control," the control point for air defense, is located in a tub-like structure near the top of the tower foremast at the 0-10 level, 15 "stories" above the inner bottom.

GENERAL ARRANGEMENT AND BUILT-IN STRUCTURAL PROTECTION

The general arrangement below decks is shown in the diagram below. The three large circular forms are the non-rotating armored barbettes of the 16-inch turrets. They enclose and protect the ammunition handling machinery and provide the support needed by the extremely heavy turrets and guns. Grouped around the barbettes are the 16-inch

powder magazines. The turrets are numbered I, II and III, in order from bow to stern. (Navy practice was to identify main battery turrets with Roman numerals, secondary battery mounts with Arabic numbers.)

Extending over 200 feet between Turrets II and III, the main propulsion plant is contained in four separate combination boiler-engine rooms, with two boilers and a steam turbine in each. Each of these four power plants was capable of functioning independently of the others, driving its own propeller shaft. The barbettes, ammunition magazines, main propulsion plant and certain other key stations are enclosed within a box-like structure known as the "citadel."

The citadel refers to the portion of the ship below the second deck containing vital components, surrounded by armor and other protective features. The citadel was designed to protect against three main threats: the shells of opposing battleships, torpedoes and bombs. Due to obvious limitations on size, weight and cost, criteria had to be established to govern the extent and thickness of the armor. The Navy's rationale was that a battleship's armor should be adequate to withstand hits at the most probable ranges by the enemy's equivalent of the ship's own main battery. Thus, NORTH CAROLINA's armor protection was designed to withstand 14-inch, 1,500-pound projectiles at ranges between 19,000 and 30,000 yards.

Of course, it was not feasible to encase the entire ship in armor, so the vitals were grouped as compactly

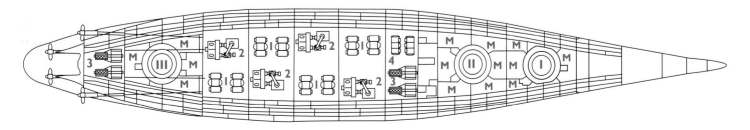

GENERAL ARRANGEMENT
Principal main battery gunnery and machinery spaces below the second deck

LEGEND

1 –	Boilers
2 –	Turbines/reduction gears
3 –	Diesel generators
4 –	Evaporators
I, II, III –	Turret barbettes
M –	16-inch magazines

Waterline length – 713 feet
Waterline beam – 104.5 feet

As evidence of the painstaking effort that went into the designing of the ship, this full-scale wooden mockup of Secondary Plot was created ashore in the New York Navy Yard to test the installation's workability.

and centrally as possible in the citadel, or "raft body." In NORTH CAROLINA this area was protected by a main side belt of 12-inch plates inclined 15 degrees from the vertical with the lower edge inboard. The lower portion of this side belt tapered to a thickness of 6.6 inches at its bottom edge, 9 feet below the waterline. The belt extended longitudinally from forward of Turret I to a point aft of Turret III.

A series of three hardened steel decks protected vital spaces from bombs and high-angle long-range gunfire. The main deck armor (1.45 inches) was thick enough to activate contact fuzes and detonate the projectile. The second deck (5 inches), also called the armor deck, was designed to absorb the full explosion of the armor piercing weapon whose delay fuze would be activated as it penetrated the main deck and exploded in the space between decks. The third deck (.75 inches), also called the splinter deck, provided the last layer of protection for the vital spaces. It was designed to stop any flying structural pieces of the second deck which the force of the explosion dislodged.

The ends of the armored citadel were shielded by 11.1-inch transverse armor bulkheads. Equally heavy transverse bulkheads protected the steering engine room, shielded by side armor of 14.9 inches. Main battery turrets had 16-inch faceplates with 9.8-inch sides, 11.8-inch backs and 7-inch tops. The barbette armor ranged from 16 inches at the main deck down to 11.5 inches above the armored second deck and 4.42 inches below that deck. The 5-inch gun mounts were enclosed in gun houses of

1.95-inch plate affording limited protection against fragmentation damage and strafing. Extending upward from the citadel to the conning tower was a communications tube of 14-inch armor. The thickness of armor surrounding the conning tower varied from 16 inches on the sides to 14.7 inches on the front and back, 7 inches on the top and 3.9 inches on the bottom.

In addition to armor, the citadel's sides had other protective elements, which gave the underwater hull limited defense against torpedoes, gunfire, mines and the near misses of bombs. This side protective system was designed to resist the explosive force of 700 pounds of TNT. The system was comprised of a honeycomb of watertight spaces that ran the length of the citadel and underneath the ship, protecting and buoying her like a life jacket. For most of the ship's length the honeycomb was five compartments thick. Two layers were kept filled with fuel or water while the others were empty. Also extending the length of the citadel was an empty "blister" which bulged outward directly under the armor belt, helping to support it. Protecting the bottom of the ship, the outer hull and two inner bottoms created a structure totaling five feet nine inches deep, with the lower layer liquid-filled and the upper empty.

The concept of watertight integrity is integral to the ship's construction below the main deck. The many decks and bulkheads within the hull of a large warship divide it into literally hundreds of compartments, most of which are watertight. Thus, if there should be flooding from damage by a bomb, shell, mine, torpedo, grounding, collision or as a result of firefighting or other causes, the flooding will be limited. Should underwater damage flood compartments on one side or near the bow or stern of a ship, the added weight will make that side or end settle deeper into the water. If one side tilts downward, the ship is said to "list" to that side; if either the bow or stern settles deeper, the ship is "trimmed down" by the bow or stern. Compensation for list and trim — "stability control" — is accomplished by counterflooding; by deliberately pumping water or oil into empty tanks, either on the opposite side, or at the opposite end of the ship, in order to restore it more closely to its designed equilibrium.

"Damage control," as prepared for and practiced by NORTH CAROLINA's crew, went well beyond stability control, to include all measures taken to limit or repair any type of damage. Whenever the crew was called to battle stations, well-equipped repair parties assembled at various points in the ship, ready to proceed at once to the scene of damage. They were capable of fighting fire, shoring (bracing with heavy timbers) weakened bulkheads, repairing equipment and machinery and caring for the wounded through assigned medical personnel. Control of damage and stability were under the overall direction of the damage control officer in Central Station, located below decks in the armored citadel.

PROPULSION AND MACHINERY

The NORTH CAROLINA–class battleships were the first U.S. Navy capital ships to combine powerful armament and strong protection with moderately high speed. They were designed to make 27 knots, as opposed to the 21-knot maximum of their fastest U.S. Navy predecessors. In the 18 years between the completion of WEST VIRGINIA (BB-48) and NORTH CAROLINA, battleship displacement had

increased only 10 percent while power had increased 300 percent. This increase was due primarily to rapid advances in marine engineering, making it possible to equip the NORTH CAROLINA with more efficient boilers and machinery.

The main propulsion plant consisted of four steam turbines, each located with two boilers in a separate combination boiler-engine room, and each driving a separate propeller shaft through reduction gears. This plant arrangement permitted full power operation on any shaft, entirely independent of the others, a valuable asset in the event of battle damage. In addition, cross-connecting steam lines and other interrelated systems permitted any desired combination of boilers and engines. In other words, boilers from one room could operate the turbine in another, if necessary, adding to the plant's capability to function despite damage.

The eight Babcock & Wilcox boilers were of a new superheated double-jacket type in which the air required for combustion was drawn directly into the boilers from outside, rather than through the firerooms as in older plants. This eliminated the

Photograph shows the front of Number 7 boiler in one of the ship's four combination boiler/engine rooms. The large circular gauges at upper left showed steam pressure in various parts of the system. Extreme care was necessary to ensure that pressure never exceeded safe limits. "Navy Special" black fuel oil (NSFO) was burned in the boilers.

problems of pressurized firerooms, saving weight and space and reducing the noise level. The boilers operated at a pressure of 575 pounds per square inch and temperature of 850 degrees Fahrenheit.

Under normal conditions, the four sets of General Electric geared turbines delivered a maximum of 115,000 shaft horsepower, enough for a designed speed of 27.5 knots. In an emergency, a maximum overload shaft horsepower of 121,000 could be generated and sustained for a period of up to two hours. In actual service, NORTH CAROLINA's maximum recorded speed was 27.3 knots in 1941. Subsequent increases in weight of armament (primarily the addition of fifteen 40-mm gun mounts) reduced top speed such that in speed trials of late September 1944, the ship could make good only 26.8 knots.

The maximum turbine speed of 5,904 rpm was much too fast for effective propeller thrust in the sea, so power from the turbines was transferred to the shafts through reduction gears, similar to a car's transmission system. NORTH CAROLINA's double reduction gears produced a maximum shaft speed of 199 rpm. Each shaft turned a four-bladed propeller.

Auxiliary machinery included generators, air compressors, evaporators, refrigerating machinery, pumps, steering engines, blowers and much more. Throughout the ship there were hundreds of electric motors and machines of various types that powered boat cranes, anchor windlasses, capstans, the aircraft crane and ammunition hoists. They trained and elevated the guns and directors, pumped fresh water for showers and salt water for fire fighting. They ran dough mixers in the bakery, meat grinders in the butcher shop, planers in the carpenter shop and presses in the print shop. Electric motors turned the radar antennas, ran motion picture projectors, blowers, fans and dentist's drills.

The ship carried 7,167 tons (approximately 1.8 million gallons) of black oil propulsion fuel, providing a range of over 16,000 nautical miles at 15 knots, or 6,000 nautical miles at 25 knots. (A nautical mile is 6,076 feet, compared to 5,280 feet for a statute mile.) The ship also carried 700 tons (200,000 gallons) of diesel fuel for her generators and small boats and 22 tons (7,500 gallons) of aviation gasoline for her float planes. The total electrical

generating capacity was 8,400 kilowatts, provided by four 1,250-kw turbo-generators, four 850-kw diesel generators and two 200-kw emergency diesel generators. The ship's fresh-water tanks held 600 tons (144,500 gallons), and she could carry 400 tons (96,400 gallons) of reserve feed water for her boilers. Four sets of evaporators ran almost constantly, converting salt water to distilled water for the boilers and to potable water for crew consumption (drinking, cooking, bathing, laundry, etc.). Evaporator capacity was 80,000 gallons per day under normal conditions.

MAIN BATTERY ARMAMENT

A major change in main battery armament was decided upon one month after the keel was laid when the General Board pressed the Secretary of the Navy to order the 14-inch guns replaced by 16-inch. This, the board argued, was necessary in order to "maintain parity" with other navies. Although the 1936 London Naval Treaty included a provision limiting main batteries to 14-inch guns, U.S. naval intelligence soon learned that German, French and Italian battleships then under construction were being fitted with 15-inch guns. Meanwhile, the Japanese had refused to sign the 1936 treaty as they were planning to provide 16-inch, or possibly even larger guns, for their new battleships. In fact, the Japanese were secretly arming two super battleships, YAMATO and MUSASHI, then under construction, with 460-mm (18.1-inch) guns.

Consequently, a decision was reached in November 1937 to change the main battery of NORTH CAROLINA and WASHINGTON to nine 16-inch guns in three 3-gun turrets. Fortunately, turrets required for the three heavier guns were almost the same size as those needed for the four 14-inch guns. The changes in guns, additional alterations and the late delivery of materials delayed construction for months. Despite the resulting frustration, hundreds of men worked eagerly to fashion this great ship. They took such pride in the task that 60 years later they still spoke lovingly of the care they had taken to build her.

NORTH CAROLINA was designed in an era when battleships were the principal combatants of the world's great navies, their role being to "slug it out" with big guns at ranges of up to 20 miles. Although

The big guns of Turrets I and II are shown here in their "at rest" position. Note the size of the huge barrels compared with the men in the foreground. When the guns were not in use the canvas muzzle covers shown here were kept in place to protect the bore from corrosion by salt spray. Should it become necessary to fire the guns on short notice, compressed air was forced through the barrels from inside the turret, instantly blowing the covers off.

"I was only 19 when I went to work at the New York Navy Yard as an apprentice machinist. Being associated with the construction of the USS NORTH CAROLINA beginning in 1939 was one of the most significant accomplishments of my career. The work force consisted of highly motivated and skilled craftsmen whose objectives were to build the most powerful battleship in the world, to build it properly, and to get the job done on schedule. I know we succeeded."

— Leonard Silvern, Machinist, New York Navy Yard

NORTH CAROLINA never engaged in such a clash, she was well equipped to hold her own with the guns finally selected as her main battery. Her nine 16-inch/ 45-caliber rifles have an internal barrel diameter of 16 inches, and a length of 45 times that diameter or 60 feet. Each rifle weighs 96 tons; the weight of an entire turret is over 1,400 tons.

The turrets rotated in a horizontal plane, called train, while the gun barrels were raised or depressed in a vertical plane, called elevation. Regardless of their great size and weight, the turrets were fairly responsive to aiming orders. They could be trained 180 degrees in 45 seconds. Each turret's guns could fire singly or together at the same target, but not at different targets. The three separate turrets were capable of firing upon three separate targets at the same time. Each firing of the guns was called a salvo, whether only one gun was fired or all nine at once. The time required to load, aim and fire one salvo was 30 seconds. The main battery was effective against ships and shore targets, but was too ponderous for use against aircraft. Two officers and 170 men served each one of NORTH CAROLINA's three turrets and its magazines.

Main battery projectiles were of two types: armor piercing (AP) and high capacity (HC). The AP shell, designed for use against enemy battleships, had an extremely hard, 2,700-pound steel body for piercing armor. Only a relatively small cavity was available for the 40.47 pounds of explosive charge. Nevertheless, during World War II AP projectiles were often fired with devastating effect against Japanese concrete gun emplacements, commonly called "pillboxes." The AP projectiles could penetrate more than 20 inches of the strongest hardened steel armor at ranges up to 15,000 yards and more than 10 inches at 35,000 yards. Muzzle velocity was 2,300 feet per second. Maximum range, achieved at a gun elevation angle of 45 degrees, was 36,900 yards or 21 statute miles. When fired at a range of 10,000 yards, the projectiles had a very flat trajectory and hit the target at an angle of only 6.8 degrees from the horizontal. At a range of 35,000 yards, following a maximum ordinate (highest in-flight altitude) of 22,490 feet, the projectiles crashed down on the target like bombs with an angle of fall of 45.16 degrees.

The 1,900-pound HC projectiles were designed for use against unarmored surface vessels such as destroyers, tankers and troopships; or against objectives ashore such as buildings, airstrips and enemy troops. The weight of the explosive charge was 153.58 pounds. Muzzle velocity was 2,635 feet per second. Maximum range, achieved at a gun elevation angle of 45 degrees, was 40,180 yards or 23 statute miles. In a shore bombardment one HC projectile could blow a hole in the ground 20 feet deep and 50 feet in diameter.

Protected magazines several decks below the main deck housed the projectiles and powder bags. Elevator-type electric hoists raised the projectiles and powder bags to the gun chambers. First to arrive there was the projectile, which came to rest on a hinged loading tray aligned with the gun barrel. Thereupon a hydraulic rammer shoved it into the breech. Next to arrive were six 90-pound bags of gunpowder, the charge normally used to fire a single round from one gun. The gun crew lined up the bags on the loading tray and very, very carefully used the rammer to seat them behind the projectile inside the barrel. The breech block (rear end plug) was then closed, readying the gun for firing. While gun elevation limits ranged from 45 degrees to minus two degrees, the guns were always loaded at an elevation angle of five degrees. In other words, no matter what elevation was required to hit the target, after each salvo the barrel was positioned at five degrees elevation for re-loading before being returned to firing elevation. This greatly simplified gun mount design.

A full nine-gun salvo, or "broadside," of AP projectiles weighed 24,300 pounds. When the guns fired they recoiled four feet. The reverse thrust, or "jolt," felt on board the ship upon firing such a salvo was so forceful that the entire ship appeared to move sideways through the water. In fact, such sideways motion, if any, was negligible. When ignited, the six 90-pound bags of gunpowder generated a gas bubble of incredible expanding force, accelerating the huge AP projectile to 2,300 feet per second in 60 feet. The gas bubble followed the projectile out the barrel, instantly expanding with such force that a person standing 20 feet away from the muzzle would be thrown violently to the deck. A steel toolbox at the same distance would implode. The effect of a full broadside of nine 16-inch guns was to flatten the waves the ship's full length for 200 feet in the firing direction.

Though the ship's main battery never fired upon another battleship, it was used in nine shore bombardments. In most of them the purpose was to soften defenses in preparation for troop landings as part of the island-hopping strategy in the Pacific Theater. The longest range at which NORTH CAROLINA ever fired in combat was 35,000 yards (19.88 statute miles) against the Hitachi Industrial Complex, Honshu, Japan, July 17, 1945. Records indicate that during World War II NORTH CAROLINA expended a total of 2,396 rounds of 16-inch ammunition in combat, plus many more in target practice.

Top Left Extreme care and the help of a winch were required to "parbuckle" (move in this manner) the heavy projectiles.

Top Right Six 90-pound powder bags about to be rammed home behind a projectile.

Middle Right View of a projectile flat and hoist.

Bottom Right The two forward turrets are trained out to the port beam ready to fire at short range, as evidenced by the low elevation angle of the gun barrels.

Bottom Left A projectile about to be rammed into the breech of a gun.

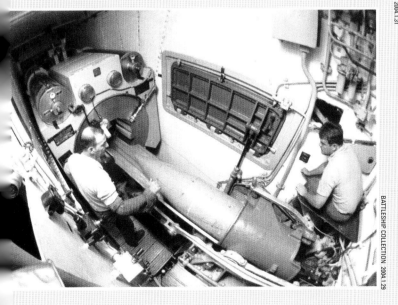

BATTLESHIP NORTH CAROLINA

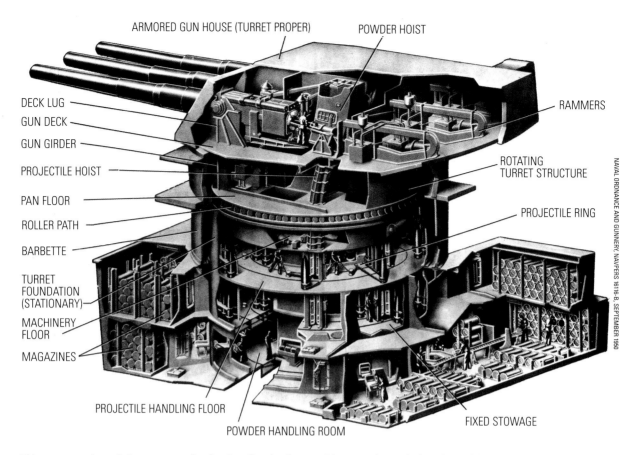

ARMORED GUN HOUSE (TURRET PROPER)　　POWDER HOIST

DECK LUG
GUN DECK
GUN GIRDER
PROJECTILE HOIST
PAN FLOOR
ROLLER PATH
BARBETTE
TURRET
FOUNDATION
(STATIONARY)
MACHINERY
FLOOR
MAGAZINES

RAMMERS

ROTATING
TURRET STRUCTURE

PROJECTILE RING

PROJECTILE HANDLING FLOOR

POWDER HANDLING ROOM

FIXED STOWAGE

NAVAL ORDNANCE AND GUNNERY, NAVPERS 16116-B, SEPTEMBER 1950

This cutaway of a main battery turret, its size dwarfing the figures of the men, shows the locations of the gun house, barbette, handling rooms, shell deck (projectile handling floor) and magazines, altogether five decks in height.

CONTROL OF MAIN BATTERY GUNFIRE

The finest guns are of little use without the means to direct their fire accurately at the target. For this purpose NORTH CAROLINA was originally equipped with the most sophisticated naval fire control measures known in her day. Subsequent acquisition of radar greatly enhanced the system's effectiveness for most purposes. Effective fire control required the means to accomplish the following:

■ Locate the target

■ Provide a steady stream of target positions, expressed in bearing (direction) and range (distance) from the ship

■ Establish the target's track, in order to determine its course (direction of movement) and speed

■ Determine a future target position at which the target and a projectile will intercept

■ Integrate this information with other variables, including own ship's motion

■ Aim the guns and optical sights to the future target position

■ Provide a means to make adjustments in the aiming point as changes require

The ship's main battery fire control system consisted of several similar groups of equipment located at various shipboard stations. These stations were linked electrically and functioned separately or together to control the firing of the guns, individually or in groups. This flexibility was critical. If one location was damaged or if multiple targets appeared, control of the aiming and firing could be shifted among locations as needed. Main physical components of the ship's original (pre-radar) main battery fire control system were as follows:

■ Two Mark 38 directors/optical range finders aloft, called "Spot 1" at the top of the tower foremast and "Spot 2" at an elevated location immediately abaft (behind) the mainmast (The word "Mark," followed by numerals, indicates the generation, or "vintage," of a given device.)

■ An extremely long-based optical range finder in each turret

■ A "Control" battle station in the upper (03) level of the conning tower, manned by the gunnery officer and equipped with a stereoscopic spotting glass and small computer

■ The main battery plotting room and its computers located amidships on the first platform deck

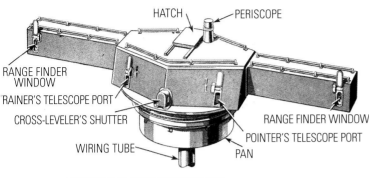

HATCH   PERISCOPE

RANGE FINDER
WINDOW
RAINER'S TELESCOPE PORT
CROSS-LEVELER'S SHUTTER

RANGE FINDER WINDOW
POINTER'S TELESCOPE PORT

WIRING TUBE   PAN

NAVAL ORDNANCE AND GUNNERY, NAVPERS 16116, MAY 1944

This drawing shows the principal external features of a Mark 38 main battery director such as those comprising Spot 1 and Spot 2. Radar antenna was mounted on top.

Each of the two Mark 38 directors contained an optical range finder and later radar, which could transmit a continuous stream of bearings and ranges to the controlling "rangekeepers" (computers) in the main battery plotting room. The director crews used sound-powered telephones (to be explained later) for voice communication with the plotting room.

The main battery plotting room, commonly called "Plot," was the nerve center of the entire system. To protect Plot's important equipment from damage as well as heat and humidity, the space was located inside the armored citadel and was air-conditioned. Within Plot were two computer systems, each consisting of a rangekeeper and a stable vertical.

The rangekeeper was an analog computer comprised of various mechanical devices such as cams, gears and component solvers. It converted the continuously inputted target bearing and range information into a calculation of the target's course (heading) and speed in order to predict its future bearing and range for firing. The rangekeeper also continuously received inputs correcting for own ship's motion and other variables. These inputs were entered into the rangekeeper either electronically, or manually through a specific knob and dial combination on the top of the rangekeeper.

Own ship's motion, including roll and pitch in a rough sea, complicated the gun aim problem to a degree not encountered by land-based artillery. To solve that problem, linked to each rangekeeper was a "stable vertical," a device containing a high-speed gyroscope which established and maintained true vertical, regardless of ship's motion. Among the many other variables inputted into the rangekeeper were own ship's course and speed, air temperature, air pressure, wind direction and velocity, weight of projectile, wear in the gun barrel, powder temperature, and direction and velocity of the ocean current (for shore bombardment). All of these factors combined to determine the trajectory (flight path) of the projectile. With most subject to constant change, fire control was a highly complex process requiring continuous measurements and corrections.

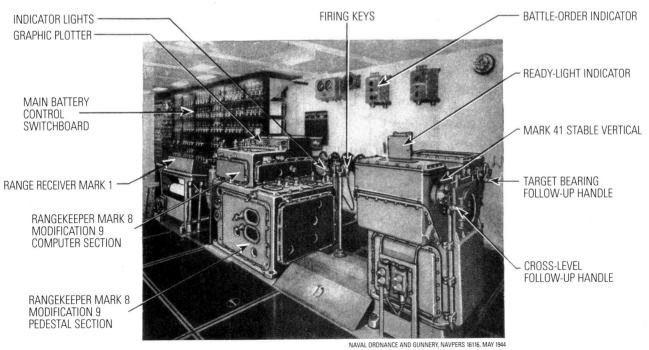

INDICATOR LIGHTS
GRAPHIC PLOTTER

FIRING KEYS

BATTLE-ORDER INDICATOR

READY-LIGHT INDICATOR

MAIN BATTERY
CONTROL
SWITCHBOARD

MARK 41 STABLE VERTICAL

RANGE RECEIVER MARK 1

TARGET BEARING
FOLLOW-UP HANDLE

RANGEKEEPER MARK 8
MODIFICATION 9
COMPUTER SECTION

CROSS-LEVEL
FOLLOW-UP HANDLE

RANGEKEEPER MARK 8
MODIFICATION 9
PEDESTAL SECTION

NAVAL ORDNANCE AND GUNNERY, NAVPERS 16116, MAY 1944

This illustration of the main battery plotting room components shows, left to right, the main battery electrical switchboard, a rangekeeper and a stable vertical.

Shown here at left, protruding from the sides of the two forward turrets, are the armored housings protecting the main lenses of the turrets' optical range finders. The large vertical rectangles containing the lenses are in the closed position.

Plot also contained electrical switchboards linking the various individual fire control components with each other and with the turret guns. The switchboards could link either of the fire control directors to a specific rangekeeper as well as to any one or more turrets. Because of this flexibility, the switchboards could respond quickly to changes in the tactical situation or battle damage.

Determining target bearing was relatively easy, but accurately determining target range was much more challenging. Optical range finders were located in each 16-inch turret and aloft in the two Mark 38 directors. Of these, the turrets' optical range finders were more accurate because of their extremely long base length of over 50 feet. One was positioned at the rear of each turret's gun house with its main lens assemblies enclosed in armored housings (called "ears") extending several feet out to each side of the turret. The Mark 38 directors' shorter 26.5-foot optical range finders, though less precise, were effective at much greater ranges because of their higher elevation, and therefore more distant horizon. Thus, the director range finders were most often used for tracking targets and were excellent for "spotting" as well. Spotting consisted of observing the fall of shot, or "splashes," and estimating corrections necessary to place the next salvo on target.

Whichever range finder (or radar, when incorporated into the system) was used for tracking the target, the observations were continuously entered into the controlling rangekeeper in Plot.

Once the rangekeeper generated a solution, which normally required only two or three minutes of continuous target bearing and range information, electrical signals were sent automatically to the tracking director and to the turrets, enabling all to remain "on target" automatically. The Mark 38 directors had electrical power drives which, when in automatic, enabled them to follow the rangekeeper's computed present target position. The director crew continued to observe and track the target, making overriding adjustments as necessary to correct the rangekeeper's computations. Within each turret, separate hydraulic drives trained the turret and elevated each gun barrel, automatically and continuously maintaining the correct aiming point to reach the rangekeeper's predicted future target position at the moment of projectile impact or "splash." To the viewer, the guns appeared to be staring at a fixed point in space, while the ship rolled and pitched beneath them like the proverbial dog being wagged by its tail.

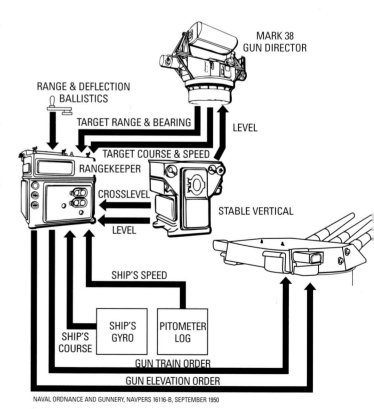

NAVAL ORDNANCE AND GUNNERY, NAVPERS 16116-B, SEPTEMBER 1950

This schematic shows the relationship among principal elements of the main battery fire control system.

Overall control of the main battery was the responsibility of the gunnery officer, but on board NORTH CAROLINA the main battery assistant normally exercised direct control from his battle station in Spot 1. If enemy action destroyed or disabled that station, direct control of the entire main battery could revert to Control, Spot 2, Turret II, or Plot. Likewise, in divided fire, with the turrets simultaneously engaging multiple targets, it was a simple matter to divide fire control among these stations or to place each turret in local control.

Located in each station able to control the battery was a set of three electric "firing keys," as shown in the photograph at right. Thus, the 16-inch guns could be fired from any one of several locations, including the two directors, Plot, the conning tower or the gun turrets themselves. When firing on a given target, the keys were on a single electrical circuit. When preparing to fire, the circuit had to be "complete," meaning that all of the keys had to be in the "closed" position, except for the one in the designated controlling station, where the controlling key was kept "open" until ready to fire. Closing the key(s) in the controlling station completed the circuit and the guns instantly fired. If a station's keys became damaged, the switchboard could remove the affected keys from the firing circuit. All told, the main battery fire control system was endowed with great strength and resiliency due to its armor protection, redundancy and flexibility.

FIRE CONTROL IN SHORE BOMBARDMENT

Shore bombardment involved aiming problems similar to those presented by ship targets, with a few important differences. While the task was somewhat simplified by the fact that the target was usually stationary, the gunners often found it much more difficult to identify and fix the position of a target located in a cluttered landscape ashore. Ship-to-ship combat presented a simpler problem because the target was usually silhouetted on a clean horizon. Not so ashore. Reduced visibility at night, rain, fog or reverse slope targets made shore bombardment more difficult, even after radar became available, because radar could not discriminate between most objects at ground level ashore.

NATIONAL ARCHIVES 181-A-BB-55-1-323, CLOSE-UP

Main battery firing keys like the three shown here are brass, pistol-grip "triggers" used to fire the guns. Those shown are mounted on a stable element in Secondary Battery Plot.

At short ranges, when the target could be observed clearly and the guns aimed optically, shore bombardment presented few problems and permitted highly accurate fire. For example, on the afternoon of D-Day at Iwo Jima, February 19, 1945, NORTH CAROLINA operated close to shore on the right flank of the landing beach and repeatedly fired 16-inch projectiles dead center at enemy bunkers and directly into the mouths of caves. However, as distance increased or visibility decreased, accurate determination of range became much more difficult without assistance from spotters in the air or ashore.

Most of NORTH CAROLINA's shore bombardments were controlled in the following manner. Both Main Battery Plot and the navigator on the bridge were equipped with an accurate navigational chart showing both sea approaches and the target area ashore. The portion of the chart showing the target area was overprinted with grid coordinates, a system of squares subdivided into smaller squares. Using a standard numbering system, the chart provided an accurate way to fix a target's position within a square. Prior to the bombardment, the positions of all pre-designated targets (usually identified by pre-landing aerial photography) were precisely fixed on these charts, with elevations above sea level noted. During the approach and firing phases, the ship was navigated with great care and her position continually maintained and compared between charts in Plot and on the bridge. The effects of "set" and "drift" (the movement of the ship caused by current and wind) were calculated in order to help plot the ship's future track. From this track, at regular intervals of one to two minutes, range and bearing to the target were measured on the chart and then entered immediately into the rangekeeper, just as though the target was being tracked in the normal manner by one of the fire control directors. Once a firing solution was obtained, the guns could be kept trained on the target automatically, ready to fire as ordered.

A slightly different procedure was used for "call fire." Call fire was the term used for gunfire requested by troop units ashore on the spur of the moment, usually against newly discovered targets barring their advance. For this type of fire the "spotter" ashore radioed the ship with exact target position using the same navigation chart with grid coordinates. Thereafter, fire control procedures were the same as those described above.

November 1941 photograph of foremast and forward superstructure, with important stations and equipment identified. Key to numbers:

1. CXAM air search "bedsprings" radar antenna atop foremast
2. Spot 1, forward main battery fire control director
3. Sky Control, air defense officer's battle station
4. "Batt Two," executive officer's battle station
5. Sky I, the forward 5-inch battery director
6. Sky III, the starboard 5-inch battery director
7. Charthouse
8. Pilothouse
9. Upper level, conning tower, gunnery officer's battle station
10. Flag radio for embarked admiral's staff; combat information center (CIC) after September 1944
11. Signal bridge
12. Lower level, conning tower, captain's battle station in event of a surface action
13. 5-inch gun mount

CROSS-SECTION AMIDSHIPS

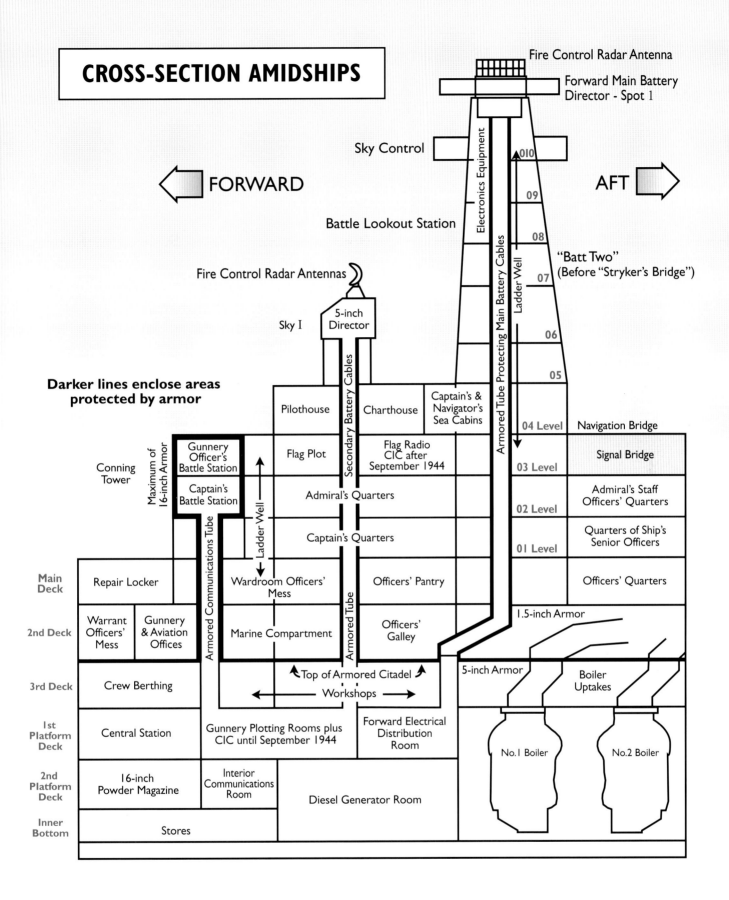

← FORWARD

AFT →

Fire Control Radar Antenna

Forward Main Battery Director - Spot 1

Sky Control

Battle Lookout Station

Electronics Equipment

Armored Tube Protecting Main Battery Cables

Ladder Well

010

09

08

07

06

05

04 Level

03 Level

02 Level

01 Level

Navigation Bridge

"Batt Two"
(Before "Stryker's Bridge")

Fire Control Radar Antennas

Sky I

5-inch Director

Darker lines enclose areas protected by armor

Secondary Battery Cables

Pilothouse

Charthouse

Captain's & Navigator's Sea Cabins

Conning Tower

Maximum of 16-inch Armor

Gunnery Officer's Battle Station

Flag Plot

Flag Radio CIC after September 1944

Signal Bridge

Captain's Battle Station

Admiral's Quarters

Admiral's Staff Officers' Quarters

Armored Communications Tube

Ladder Well

Captain's Quarters

Quarters of Ship's Senior Officers

Main Deck

Repair Locker

Wardroom Officers' Mess

Officers' Pantry

Officers' Quarters

2nd Deck

Warrant Officers' Mess

Gunnery & Aviation Offices

Marine Compartment

Armored Tube

Officers' Galley

1.5-inch Armor

3rd Deck

Crew Berthing

Top of Armored Citadel

Workshops

5-inch Armor

Boiler Uptakes

1st Platform Deck

Central Station

Gunnery Plotting Rooms plus CIC until September 1944

Forward Electrical Distribution Room

No.1 Boiler

No.2 Boiler

2nd Platform Deck

16-inch Powder Magazine

Interior Communications Room

Diesel Generator Room

Inner Bottom

Stores

Bombardment results, when the guns were not under optical control, depended largely on the accuracy of the chart and the skill of the navigation team. The task was made more difficult by the absence of the usual aids to navigation, such as charted buildings or lighthouses, on an unfamiliar and hostile shore. Also, radar was notoriously inaccurate in discriminating beween sea and shore when ranging on flat terrain, such as that of some Pacific island shorelines. Hence, initial salvos were often inaccurate, but spotting quickly corrected errors in aim.

SECONDARY BATTERY ARMAMENT

The secondary battery of NORTH CAROLINA consisted of twenty 5-inch/38-caliber guns in 10 twin mounts, five on each side of the ship. These dual-purpose semi-automatic guns were intended mainly for the ship's defense against enemy ships and aircraft. They are clustered around the superstructure, staggered between the main deck and the 01 level, in positions providing excellent fields of fire in wide arcs to each side as well as overhead, without blocking the main battery.

The 5-inch gun used semi-fixed ammunition, which means that the projectile and propellant powder charge were separate, the latter contained in a brass cartridge case. Median projectile weight was 55 pounds, the powder charge 15 pounds. Different types of projectiles were of slightly different weights, resulting in differences in the projectile's flight path if not corrected. Pre-calculated fire control tables made it possible to compensate for these variances by entering corrections into the computers in the secondary battery plotting room.

The different types of projectiles provided for these versatile guns included the following: antiaircraft common (AAC), common (COM), white phosphorus (WP) and illuminating (ILLUM). AAC was fired against aircraft; COM proved effective in shore bombardments against trucks, buildings and

Close-up view of a 5-inch mount with crew tidying up after a shoot. Man at top of stepladder is greasing the barrel's recoil slide.

exposed troops; WP produced smoke to assist in spotting; ILLUM projectiles, commonly called "star shells," provided a combination flare and parachute to make night targets visible. To be effective, a star shell had to burst beyond the target to silhouette it. Use of star shells was risky in that they could also disclose the firing ship's position.

In February 1945, following a full replenishment of ammunition prior to the bombardment of Iwo Jima, NORTH CAROLINA sailed with Task Force 58 from the fleet anchorage at Ulithi Atoll with a total of 12,800 five-inch shells: 10,200 AAC, 1,200 COM, 400 WP and 1,000 ILLUM. Of the 10,200 AAC, 7,200 were equipped with mechanically timed fuzes while 3,000 had "proximity" fuzes. There would have been more of the latter, but supply could not keep up with demand. (Important differences between these two types of fuzes will be discussed on pages 23-24.)

Designed rate of fire was 15 rounds per gun per minute, but NORTH CAROLINA's gun crews as well as those of some other ships, consistently achieved rates of up to 25 rounds per minute. Muzzle velocity of an antiaircraft common (AAC) projectile in a new gun barrel was 2,600 feet per second, giving a maximum horizontal range of 18,200 yards at a maximum altitude of 37,200 feet.

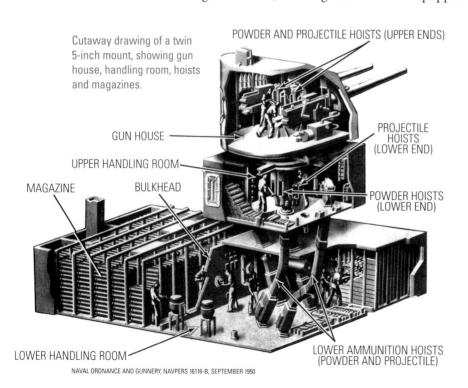

Cutaway drawing of a twin 5-inch mount, showing gun house, handling room, hoists and magazines.

POWDER AND PROJECTILE HOISTS (UPPER ENDS)

GUN HOUSE

UPPER HANDLING ROOM

MAGAZINE   BULKHEAD

PROJECTILE HOISTS (LOWER END)

POWDER HOISTS (LOWER END)

LOWER HANDLING ROOM

LOWER AMMUNITION HOISTS (POWDER AND PROJECTILE)

NAVAL ORDNANCE AND GUNNERY, NAVPERS 16116-B, SEPTEMBER 1950

When the crew was at battle stations, there were 13 men in each 5-inch mount, plus 24 more divided between the upper and lower handling rooms from which ammunition was fed upward to each mount. During the course of World War II NORTH CAROLINA fired nearly 12,000 five-inch rounds in combat: 7,736 in shore bombardments, 4,000 against aircraft and a small but unrecorded number against a Japanese cargo ship.

The 5-inch/38-caliber guns were highly effective by the standards of their day. Almost every ship in the Navy carried them during World War II, but no ship ever had enough. They fired a shell heavy enough to sink destroyers and cause extensive topside damage to battleships and cruisers. They were useful for illumination. They were excellent shore bombardment weapons against relatively "soft" targets. They were the only antiaircraft guns in the U.S. Navy effective at ranges over 5,000 yards, and the 5-inch shell was the only one heavy enough to make a sure kill on a Japanese suicide plane, better known as a "kamikaze" (to be explained later).

CONTROL OF SECONDARY BATTERY GUNFIRE

The secondary battery fire control system was similar to that described for the main battery, in that it was designed to cope with the same basic problem: tracking the target in order to generate accurate firing orders to the guns. However, there were two highly significant differences. First, the secondary system had to be geared to track much faster aircraft targets. Second, in addition to determining range and bearing, a third dimension — altitude — had to be taken into account. These factors greatly complicated the fire control problem.

Implicit in the overall design of the ship's fire control arrangements was an assumption that while the main battery was dedicated primarily to surface action against an enemy battleship, the secondary battery would likely be engaged at the same time in repelling attacks by enemy destroyers or aircraft. For these reasons, the main battery and secondary battery systems were designed to operate independently. Like the main battery system, the secondary was highly advanced for its day. Main components, or stations, of the original (pre-radar) secondary battery fire control system were as follows:

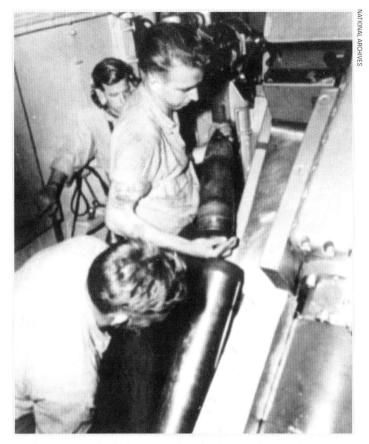

Loading practice. A 5-inch gun crew's projectileman, above, and powderman, below, prepare to load a projectile and its propellant powder charge into the breech of a gun. Projectile and powder will be rammed home together. Semi-fixed ammunition such as this permitted use of different projectile types with the same powder charge.

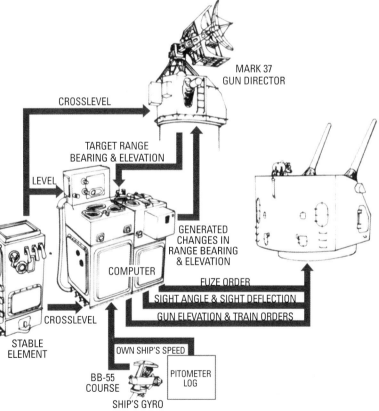

This seconday battery fire control system schematic shows the relationship among the controlling director, the plotting room and the guns. Not shown is the air defense officer in Sky Control who was in overall charge of this battery, but usually delegated control to the director best located to observe and track the target.

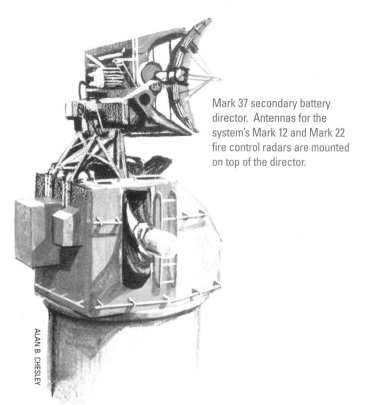

Mark 37 secondary battery director. Antennas for the system's Mark 12 and Mark 22 fire control radars are mounted on top of the director.

ALAN B. CHESLEY

■ "Sky Control," battle station of the air defense officer, located on the largest platform surrounding the upper portion of the foremast, one level below Spot One.

■ Four Mark 37 secondary battery directors, called "Sky I, II, III and IV," positioned atop prominent elevated trunks forward, aft and on each side of the superstructure. Each of these four directors incorporated a 15-foot optical stereoscopic range finder.

■ A secondary battery plotting room adjoining the main battery plotting room below decks in the citadel. Secondary Plot was equipped with four complete computer-stable element combinations, one for each director and each capable of producing solutions for air, surface or shore targets as well as star shell fire. The stable element, like the stable vertical for the main battery, corrected for ship's motion in roll and pitch.

■ Optical sighting scopes and local controls for train and elevation in each individual gun mount.

Sky Control normally exercised overall control of the secondary battery, whether engaged in air defense or surface firing. Actual control of the guns was assigned to the director(s) best positioned to see the target(s). The directors served as the eyes of the system, tracking the target and automatically providing a continuous flow of ranges, bearings and elevation angles to the plotting room. Plot integrated this information with all the other variables in the equation, sending continuous gun orders, including mechanical fuze settings for the AAC projectiles.

As a rule, within a few seconds after a director commenced tracking a target, Plot generated a fire control solution. The computers in Plot then sent signals which trained and elevated both the

Mark 37 director training mock-up with the seven-man crew at their stations. The large drum-like object in the foreground is the right end of the optical range finder.

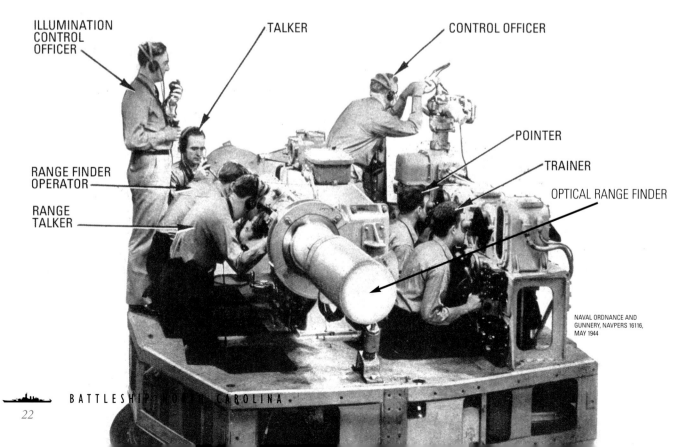

ILLUMINATION CONTROL OFFICER

TALKER

CONTROL OFFICER

RANGE FINDER OPERATOR

RANGE TALKER

POINTER

TRAINER

OPTICAL RANGE FINDER

NAVAL ORDNANCE AND GUNNERY, NAVPERS 16116, MAY 1944

Photograph shows the General Quarters crew of Secondary Plot. The battery's electrical switchboard can be seen in the background, while a Mark 1 fire control computer is manned in the foreground.

controlling director and the guns. The director automatically followed the calculated present target position. The director crew provided overriding corrections in range, bearing and elevation angle, as necessary. Meanwhile, the guns remained pointing in space, regardless of all ship motion, for the required trajectory to intercept the target. Although the 5-inch guns were normally controlled and fired from a director, they could be controlled locally at each mount or from Plot, as was the case for shore bombardment.

In the shore bombardments conducted by NORTH CAROLINA, the 5-inch battery usually fired many more rounds than did the main battery, provided suitable targets were within range of the 5-inch guns. The method for fire control was identical to that described earlier for the main battery, and the same navigational set-up was used for both batteries.

Prior to the introduction of radar and the proximity fuze, the secondary battery fire control system proved only marginally effective against aircraft. The primary problem was the inaccuracy of the AAC's mechanically timed fuze in common use at the start of World War II. This fuze was pre-set at the mount, theoretically to explode the shell an instant before it arrived at the predicted target position. Because the target was fast moving, the fuze setting calculation was critical, correct only for the briefest fraction of a second.

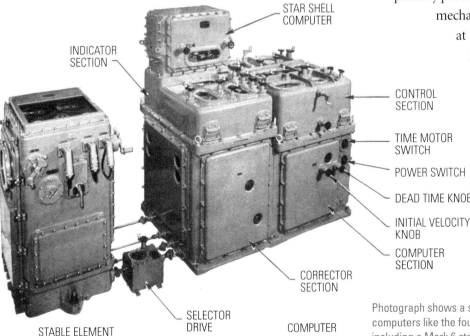

INDICATOR
SECTION

STAR SHELL
COMPUTER

CONTROL
SECTION

TIME MOTOR
SWITCH

POWER SWITCH

DEAD TIME KNOB

INITIAL VELOCITY
KNOB

COMPUTER
SECTION

CORRECTOR
SECTION

STABLE ELEMENT

SELECTOR
DRIVE

COMPUTER

NAVAL ORDNANCE AND GUNNERY, NAVPERS 16116, MAY 1944

Photograph shows a set of secondary battery computers like the four sets installed in BB-55, including a Mark 6 stable element at left and a Mark 1 analog computer at right.

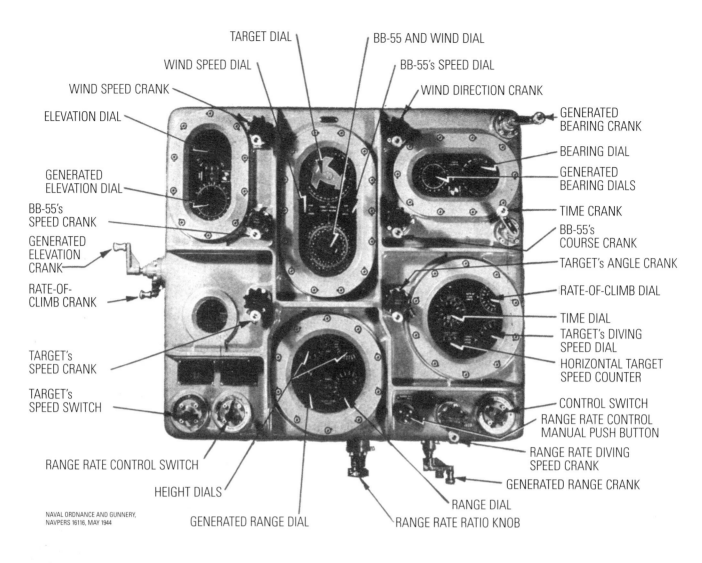

TARGET DIAL

BB-55 AND WIND DIAL

WIND SPEED DIAL

BB-55's SPEED DIAL

WIND SPEED CRANK

WIND DIRECTION CRANK

ELEVATION DIAL

GENERATED BEARING CRANK

BEARING DIAL

GENERATED ELEVATION DIAL

GENERATED BEARING DIALS

BB-55's SPEED CRANK

TIME CRANK

GENERATED ELEVATION CRANK

BB-55's COURSE CRANK

TARGET's ANGLE CRANK

RATE-OF-CLIMB CRANK

RATE-OF-CLIMB DIAL

TIME DIAL

TARGET's DIVING SPEED DIAL

TARGET's SPEED CRANK

HORIZONTAL TARGET SPEED COUNTER

TARGET's SPEED SWITCH

CONTROL SWITCH

RANGE RATE CONTROL MANUAL PUSH BUTTON

RANGE RATE CONTROL SWITCH

RANGE RATE DIVING SPEED CRANK

HEIGHT DIALS

GENERATED RANGE CRANK

NAVAL ORDNANCE AND GUNNERY, NAVPERS 16116, MAY 1944

GENERATED RANGE DIAL

RANGE DIAL

RANGE RATE RATIO KNOB

Top view of the controls and dials of a Mark 1 secondary battery computer. Note the multitude of factors, most subject to constant change, that needed to be entered into the computer to provide accurate firing orders.

That fuze setting, applied mechanically to the nose of each projectile immediately before loading, necessarily included not only the time of flight, but also the time taken by the gun crew to load and fire after setting the fuze. The latter interval was called "dead time." Correct fuze setting, which was necessarily the same for all guns firing at a given target, obviously demanded uniformity in timing by the different loading crews. This was difficult, if not impossible, to achieve. In fact, achieving such uniformity was the most challenging aspect of the antiaircraft fire control problem. Incessant daily drills on the 5-inch loading machine never quite solved the problem.

The "proximity" fuze, developed in tight secrecy for the Navy by American scientists early in World War II, neatly solved the fuzing problem, greatly improving the effectiveness of the 5-inch gun against aircraft. The secret was a very compact radio transceiver, a small device containing a combination radio transmitter and receiver. Carried in the nose of the projectile, the transmitter emitted a continuous signal after being fired. When an object was detected close ahead of the projectile, the object reflected the signal back to the transceiver which triggered the fuze. This instantly detonated the projectile's explosive charge, greeting the target with a shower of fragments. During World War II, the term "variable timed fuze" (VTF) was a deliberately ambiguous misnomer coined for the proximity fuze for security reasons.

As of 1943-44, before the appearance of Japanese suicide pilots, NORTH CAROLINA's gunners did not totally discard the mechanically timed fuze, but instead used a mix of both fuzes. According to 1943-44 Air Defense Officer Lieutenant Commander John E. Kirkpatrick, the mechanically timed fuze bursts ahead of the attacking planes discouraged some pilots, frustrating their attacks.

AUTOMATIC ANTIAIRCRAFT WEAPONS

When NORTH CAROLINA was placed in commission in April 1941, her automatic antiaircraft armament consisted of 12 obsolete, water-cooled .50-caliber machine guns, plus four 1.1-inch quadruple gun mounts totaling sixteen barrels. Combat experience in Europe prior to American entry into the war had already proven that such light armament was entirely inadequate to defend against the rapidly improving capabilities of military aircraft. Furthermore, as of 1941-1942, the 1.1-inch guns were unreliable, having a tendency to overheat and jam due to a faulty recoil and ejection system.

Accordingly, the Navy began procuring, testing and improving two superior antiaircraft weapons: the Swedish-designed Bofors 40-mm gun and the Swiss Oerlikon 20-mm antiaircraft cannon. Immediately after the Japanese attack on Pearl Harbor, December 7, 1941, NORTH CAROLINA's commanding officer, Captain Oscar C. Badger, demanded the installation of one hundred 20-mm Oerlikons, 40 of which were in place by April 1942. While the ship was at Pearl Harbor for repairs in November 1942, her .50-caliber and 1.1-inch guns were removed and ten 40-mm quadruple mounts installed, along with six additional 20-mm guns. As of late 1944 and all of 1945, the ship mounted fifteen 40-mm quad mounts and 48 single-barreled 20-mm guns, for a total of 108 automatic weapon barrels.

By then the ship was almost literally covered with these guns from bow to stern. If every automatic antiaircraft gun the ship carried were to open fire at once, and this came close to happening for brief periods on several occasions during heavy air attacks, it was theoretically possible for the ship to put out nearly 25,000 rounds per minute — impressive firepower by any standards.

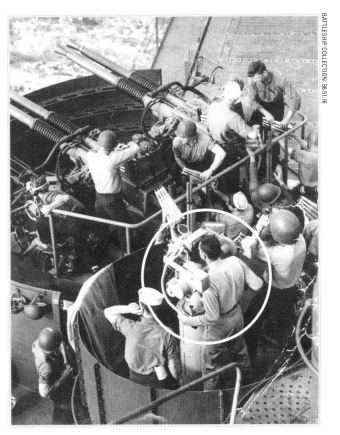

Loading drill for the crew of a 40-mm mount. Note officer manning Mark 51 director in foreground.

Twelve Browning .50-caliber machine guns like those shown at left, plus four of the quadruple 1.1-inch mounts at right, comprised the ship's entire automatic antiaircraft weaponry at the time of her commissioning.

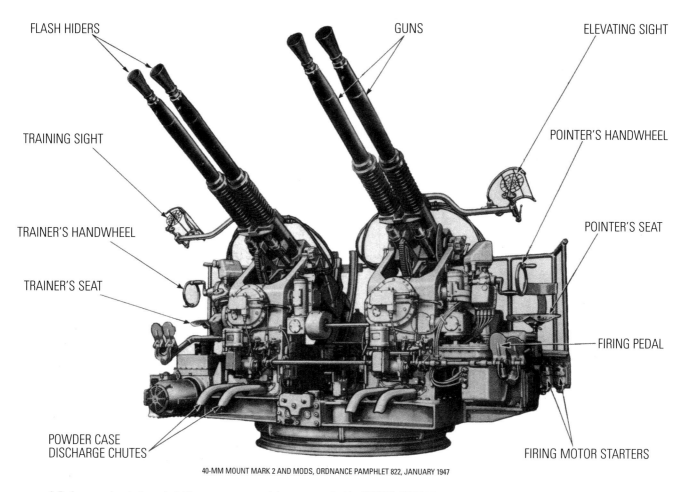

FLASH HIDERS

TRAINING SIGHT

TRAINER'S HANDWHEEL

TRAINER'S SEAT

POWDER CASE
DISCHARGE CHUTES

GUNS

ELEVATING SIGHT

POINTER'S HANDWHEEL

POINTER'S SEAT

FIRING PEDAL

FIRING MOTOR STARTERS

40-MM MOUNT MARK 2 AND MODS, ORDNANCE PAMPHLET 822, JANUARY 1947

A Bofors quadruple-barreled 40-mm gun mount of the type carried by NORTH CAROLINA after November 1942.

NORTH CAROLINA's gunners viewed the 40-mm guns as highly effective intermediate-range antiaircraft weapons. They were most lethal at ranges inside 4,000 yards. The firing rate was approximately 160 rounds per gun per minute. The gun crew fed ammunition by hand to each gun's loader in clips of four rounds. To help correct aim, each clip held one tracer round which produced a pyrotechnic streak to make its flight path visible, day or night. The projectiles exploded on impact. Guns were water-cooled, the gun mechanism entirely automatic in that it was operated by recoil. Although it was possible in an emergency to train and elevate the mounts manually through hand-cranked mechanical gear drives, they were normally operated by much faster electric-hydraulic power drives.

The crew of a quadruple-mount included 11 men: mount captain, pointer, trainer and eight loaders. In addition, there were seven or more "passers" handing ammunition up to the loaders. The men on the mount were only lightly protected by a thin

shield on the front of the gun mount and by open "gun tubs" surrounding the mounts. The unprotected passers stood on the exposed deck outside the tub.

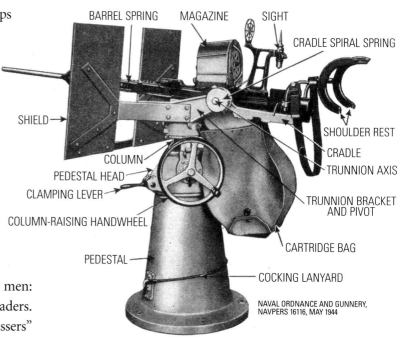

BARREL SPRING   MAGAZINE   SIGHT

CRADLE SPIRAL SPRING

SHIELD

SHOULDER REST

CRADLE

TRUNNION AXIS

COLUMN

PEDESTAL HEAD

CLAMPING LEVER

COLUMN-RAISING HANDWHEEL

TRUNNION BRACKET
AND PIVOT

CARTRIDGE BAG

PEDESTAL

COCKING LANYARD

NAVAL ORDNANCE AND GUNNERY,
NAVPERS 16116, MAY 1944

An Oerlikon single-barreled 20-mm gun of the type carried by NORTH CAROLINA.

Two of the Showboat's 20-mm gun crews on the alert for an air attack. Note hoses on deck providing pressurized air to cool these rapid-firing guns.

The rapid-fire 20-mm cannons were viewed as the last resort in an air attack since they were effective only within a 2,000-yard range. Mounted on a pedestal, the air-cooled gun was trained, elevated and fired manually by a gunner strapped snugly against the shoulder rests. A "trunnion operator" raised and lowered the pedestal (trunnion) on which the gun was mounted. The "spotter" observed gunfire and changed range settings on the Mark 14 gun sight accordingly. The "loader" fed heavy drum-shaped magazines onto the gun. Each magazine held 60 rounds, providing a theoretical maximum rate of fire of 450 rounds per minute. Like the 40-mm projectiles, the 20-mm exploded on impact.

CONTROL OF AUTOMATIC ANTIAIRCRAFT GUNFIRE

Although fire control systems for these guns were never as elaborate as those for the larger guns, fairly effective aiming devices were developed as World War II progressed. Under the air defense officer's direction, the "machine gun officer," as he was called, exercised overall control of the 40-mm and 20-mm batteries from Sky Control. As air attacks developed, he assigned control of groups of weapons in close proximity to one another to sector control officers located in the vicinity of the guns.

The main problem in firing at aircraft was their high speed. If a gunner aimed and fired at the target where he saw it, by the time the projectile arrived the target was long gone. So the gunner had to "lead the target" by pointing and firing at a future position, not an easy task. Computerized gun sights were developed for both the 40-mm and 20-mm guns to calculate future positions based on range, elevation, aircraft speed, line of sight, projectile velocity and line of fire. Each 20-mm gun had a ring sight, but was also equipped with a Mark 14 gyroscopic lead-computing sight for daylight use.

By late 1944 each 40-mm mount could be controlled by a nearby Mark 51 director. Built around the Sperry automatic lead-computing sight, the Mark 51 director became the primary daylight fire control instrument. As the director moved, it tracked the target and transmitted electrical signals to the gun mount, automatically training it and elevating the guns. Small Mark 29 radars with disc-shaped antennas were eventually incorporated into some of the directors, giving them a night-firing capability. Ring sights on the mounts served as backup in case all else failed.

Tracers were a key aid in the control of all automatic weapons fire, especially for the 20-mm guns. Likewise, the 40-mm guns relied on tracers and ring sights before directors became available. World War II motion picture films taken of NORTH CAROLINA firing her automatic weapons while under air attack on November 25, 1944, show a spectacular display of pyrotechnics caused by tracers. Since only one out of every four rounds was a tracer, the unseen total volume of fire was almost incredible.

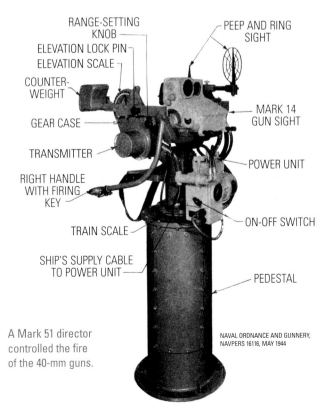

RANGE-SETTING KNOB
ELEVATION LOCK PIN
ELEVATION SCALE
COUNTER-WEIGHT
GEAR CASE
TRANSMITTER
RIGHT HANDLE WITH FIRING KEY
TRAIN SCALE
SHIP'S SUPPLY CABLE TO POWER UNIT
PEEP AND RING SIGHT
MARK 14 GUN SIGHT
POWER UNIT
ON-OFF SWITCH
PEDESTAL

A Mark 51 director controlled the fire of the 40-mm guns.

NAVAL ORDNANCE AND GUNNERY, NAVPERS 16116, MAY 1944

NORTH CAROLINA'S AIRCRAFT

Preparing to launch.

A post-war Seahawk airborne.

A Kingfisher in flight. Note radioman/gunner in rear cockpit manning .30-caliber machine gun.

Taxiing alongside after landing.

Under tow on the sled.

Being hoisted aboard.

The ship at anchor in Hampton Roads, Virginia, June 3, 1942. Note the three OS2U Kingfisher aircraft on the stern (below), two on the catapults, one on a dolly between. The ship was about to sail for the Panama Canal, thence to join the U.S. Pacific Fleet in the war against Japan.

AIRCRAFT

When NORTH CAROLINA was designed, radar was still in the future and the great navies of the world considered it essential for battleships to carry their own aircraft, primarily for "spotting," observing and correcting long-range gunfire. Other uses of the planes included antisubmarine patrol, air-sea rescue, message-drop, shore liaison, rudimentary aerial photography by hand-held camera, scouting and search. During the course of World War II, NORTH CAROLINA's aircraft were employed in virtually every one of these roles.

The ship was designed to carry three OS2U Vought-Sikorsky "Kingfisher" float planes, intended to be catapult-launched, landed in the sea alongside and hoisted aboard by the stern crane. The letter "O" stood for Observation, the "S" for Scouting, the "2" for second version, while the "U" identified the manufacturer, Vought-Sikorsky. The aircraft was a two-seated, low-winged monoplane with a central float and two wing floats. Engine specifications were as follows: 450-horsepower Pratt and Whitney nine-cylinder radial air-cooled engine; maximum speed 164 mph at 5,500 feet, 157 mph at sea level; normal cruising range 805 miles at 119 mph; service ceiling 13,000 feet; time to climb to 10,000 feet 29.1 minutes. Aircraft specifications: wing span 35 feet 10.8 inches; length 33 feet 10 inches; height 15 feet 1.5 inches; weight empty 4,123 pounds; loaded 5,600 pounds. In 1942 each plane cost $40,000.

To launch the planes, the ship carried two 68-foot catapults, one on each side of the fantail (main deck

at the stern). Preparatory to launching, a plane was positioned on a wheeled cradle mounted on the rear end of a catapult. Then, with the ship maneuvered so as to head the plane into the wind and with the plane's engine running at full throttle, a powder charge similar to that used in a 5-inch gun would be fired, sending the cradle and plane the length of the catapult. In that distance the plane would reach a speed of 65 to 70 mph and would be airborne.

The plane normally carried a two-man crew; the pilot in the front seat, a gunner/radioman in the rear. Since the ship had no flight deck, a plane could not be landed on board. Instead, upon return from a flight the pilot landed on the sea and the plane was then hoisted aboard. This maneuver sounds simple enough, but accomplishing it on the open sea could be quite dangerous, requiring great skill and team-work, not only on the part of the plane's crew but also by many individuals on board the ship. Moreover, the maneuver required the ship to slow for several minutes, making it more vulnerable to submarine attack. Hence, recovery had to be carried out as rapidly as possible.

First, the ship was placed on a course that put the wind 45 degrees on either side of the bow. Then, with the pilot ready to land, the ship would turn sharply through the wind, placing it 45 degrees on the opposite bow. This maneuver created a large, crescent-shaped "slick" on the water in the ship's lee (downwind). The plane landed on the slick and quickly taxied to a position alongside the ship's stern. There a hook on the underside of the plane's main pontoon would catch in a rope sled towed alongside the ship. The ship continued to maintain headway. With the plane now under tow, the pilot would cut the engine. Thereupon, the ship's stern crane would be swung out over the plane, where the radioman, standing erect on a wing, would place the crane's hook in the plane's wire hoisting sling. The crane would lift the plane and swing it aboard, to be placed on either a catapult or a dolly on deck between the two catapults.

These slow vulnerable planes were obviously no match for the higher performance aircraft of their day, and they were often troublesome. The planes themselves, together with the gasoline carried by the ship to fuel them, constituted serious fire hazards, especially in battle. The planes were so fragile that the blast and flame from the guns of Turret III, if fired with the planes on board, would have seriously damaged them or blown them over the side. They increased the ship's vulnerability to submarine attack since the ship's movement was restricted during launch or recovery. Nevertheless, they served well in their designed roles in situations where control of the air had been achieved by our carrier-based fighter planes. The most significant contribution of NORTH CAROLINA's aircraft occurred when they rescued downed aviators off Truk, April 30, 1944, and off northern Honshu, Japan, August 10, 1945.

Visitors to NORTH CAROLINA in Wilmington, North Carolina, see on the vessel's stern a Kingfisher identical to those which operated from the ship in

(Above) Volunteer retirees restoring OS2U Kingfisher.

the Pacific War. This particular plane crashed in Canada in 1942, but was salvaged in 1968. The Vought Aeronautical Company of Dallas, Texas, then offered to restore the plane. The wreckage was air-shipped to Dallas, where a group of retired aircraft workers painstakingly devoted an entire year to restoring it. In 1971 the wings and fuselage were trucked to Wilmington, and the plane was reassembled on board the ship.

Life aboard...

"During World War II shore bombardments, we [pilots] spent many more hours exposed to enemy fire over the target than did our counterparts flying attack missions from carriers. In the case of Iwo Jima, I spent nearly 40 hours over the island. We were asked to make low passes to try and locate enemy gun positions. The nature of spotting the ship's gunfire also meant that you had to fly 'low and slow' at altitudes of anywhere from 200 feet to 1,500 feet, at speeds of 80 to 120 knots. Such flying has been described as 'hours of sheer boredom broken with moments of stark terror.' On the other hand, we in OS2Us didn't have to attack enemy warships, which were the most dangerous targets of the war. After the war and until I retired in 1967, my flight operations were in fighter and attack carrier squadrons. I have made somewhere in the neighborhood of 400 day and 150 night carrier landings. In my judgment, OS2U recoveries were more demanding than carrier landings."

— Lieutenant (jg) Almon Oliver, Kingfisher pilot

Officers and crew of V Division pose in front of a Kingfisher.

Early June 1940, and the ship is ready to be launched. Note the platforms at lower left for participants in the ceremony, Navy officials and invited guests. Note also the portholes in the ship's hull and the huge anchor suspended temporarily amidships. All portholes below the main deck were eliminated prior to commissioning to provide greater watertight integrity.

LAUNCHING THE SHIP

While NORTH CAROLINA was under construction, World War II broke out in Europe with Nazi Germany invading Poland, Denmark, Norway, The Netherlands and France. Only four days before the ship was launched, Hitler's divisions occupied Paris. In the Far East, Japan had invaded China and was threatening aggression into Southeast Asia. Construction of NORTH CAROLINA drew increased national attention and the work was hastened, as it was clear that the ship would soon have important work to do.

Launching date was June 13, 1940. Speaking at the brilliantly impressive ceremony, North Carolina's Governor Clyde R. Hoey declared: "Its very power is fascinating. It commands our respect and will help us command the respect of the world. It speaks a language even a dictator can understand."

DEPARTMENT OF THE NAVY

The Commandant, Navy Yard, New York
requests the pleasure of your company
at the launching of the
United States Ship North Carolina
on Thursday, the thirteenth of June,
nineteen hundred and forty
at four o'clock p. m., Daylight Saving Time

Miss Isabel Hoey, Sponsor

R. S. V. P.

The governor's reference to a dictator was clearly aimed at Nazi Germany's dictator, Adolph Hitler, and fascist Italy's dictator, Benito Mussolini.

"I christen thee NORTH CAROLINA!" Miss Isabel Hoey, daughter of North Carolina's Governor Clyde R. Hoey, breaks the traditional bottle of champagne against the bow, and the ship is launched. Some of the spectators have turned away to avoid being splashed by the bubbly. Isabel Hoey shown, lower left.

With over 54,000 cheering spectators watching, Miss Isabel Hoey, the governor's daughter and ship's sponsor, smashed the traditional bottle of champagne against the bow with the words, "In the name of the United States I christen thee NORTH CAROLINA." A jammed block on the building ways caused a momentary delay before the hull slid down the greased ways into the East River, amid the strains of "Anchors Aweigh." Waiting tugs immediately surrounded the ship and nudged it alongside a nearby pier to commence "fitting out," a continuation of the building process which was to last another 10 months.

The cover of the launching program expressed both the spirit of the occasion and the widely held philosophy of former President Theodore Roosevelt, "Speak softly and carry a big stick."

LAUNCHING

The immense hull slides majestically down the ways and into the East River.

Pagoda-like scaffolding makes foremast look ironically Japanese.

Fitting out view of starboard bow.

FITTING OUT

"Fitting out" is the term used for completing a ship's construction after her launching. A warship is normally launched in a light condition, with the main hull structure complete but without thousands of tons of machinery, weapons and equipment. In the light condition the ship is much easier to launch because it does not put as much strain on the building ways and launching cradle. Also, since fitting out may take many months, builders are usually impatient to get a completed hull off the ways so a new keel can be laid.

A fitting out pier, such as that used for NORTH CAROLINA in the New York Navy Yard, was equipped with heavy cranes which could work alongside the ship from bow to stern. The turrets and guns were hoisted aboard and carefully lowered into position. Machinery was installed below decks, and unfinished decking was completed. The superstructure, some of which was pre-fabricated, was erected in place. Masts, stacks, fire control equipment, gun mounts, anchors and chains, boat skids, catapults, ladders and all other topside equipment were hoisted aboard or assembled in place. Below decks the piping, wiring and ventilation systems went in; bulkheads were insulated; compartments and passageways painted; furniture and other equipment installed.

The pre-commissioning detail reported on board and commenced work. This detail consisted of an initial increment of officers and enlisted men who were to serve as the nucleus of the ship's company. Eventually, a few at a time, the remainder of the crew reported. Fuel oil was pumped aboard and water tanks filled. Boilers, pumps, generators and turbines were given preliminary testing. Stores and food were loaded. All told, fitting out took much time and labor, extending over a period of 10 months for NORTH CAROLINA.

The cost to the U.S. government to construct, arm and equip NORTH CAROLINA totaled $76,885,750. For comparison purposes, the 1940 cost of a new pickup truck was around $450. Imagine the cost of building a similar battleship today.

Life aboard...

"In March, 1941, I walked through the Flushing Avenue gate of the Brooklyn Navy Yard to report for duty on board the NORTH CAROLINA. I looked down the street and there saw the first hundred feet of her bow, which was sort of peering out from behind some buildings that obscured the rest of the ship. The bow was red-leaded. [Red lead was a protective primer paint.] I walked on down the street, and found the ship in dry dock about a month from being commissioned. It was covered in red lead, scaffolding all over, but so help me God, she was the biggest damn thing I'd ever seen!"

— Lieutenant Julian Burke, Jr., 5-inch Director Officer

"When we arrived at the Navy Yard, we were marched down to the ship, and what a sight to see for the first time. It looked so big and so formidable as we went up the after gangway."

— William Taylor, Boatswain's Mate First Class

Part of a main battery turret is lifted aboard.

Note vintage 1930s truck with female driver, two sailors assisting.

A 16-inch gun barrel and breech is hoisted aboard. The barrel alone weighs 96 tons.

Fitting out view of port bow.

175 GROSS TONS

175 GROSS TONS

NAVY YARD N.Y. 4-17-41 U.S.S. NORTH CAROLINA

Captain Olaf M. Hustvedt, NORTH CAROLINA's first commanding officer, addresses the ship's company, invited guests and the press during the commissioning ceremony April 9, 1941. The event drew international as well as national attention, evidenced by the number of radio microphones and the reporter taking notes at far right.

COMMISSIONING

The Navy commissions a ship only when it considers that ship and its crew ready to begin tests and training operations at sea. Commissioning a ship signifies that the Navy is willing to accept responsibility for it as a member of the active fleet. The event is as important to a ship and her crew as a formal "coming out" party for a debutante. For NORTH CAROLINA, the big day came on April 9, 1941. The event received international news coverage because the vessel was already widely acclaimed as the most powerful warship in the world.

By the spring of 1941, Hitler's armies had consolidated Nazi control over most of continental Europe, and there were ominous signs that the United States might soon be drawn into war with Japan in the Pacific. It must have been with these thoughts in mind that Secretary of the Navy Frank Knox had this to say during the commissioning ceremony: "The NORTH CAROLINA is one of a new line of ships that will give the United States

unchallenged supremacy on the seas. America has no aggressive designs on any power on earth. The United States is still dedicated to peace. At long last we are convinced that peace and security can be had only by building a fleet with such strength that no one will want to challenge it."

Orders were read, the colors and commission pennant were raised, the watch set and the battleship was placed in commission. From that moment on she was legally an arm of the United States government, officially entitled to be called USS — United States Ship — NORTH CAROLINA. Under international law this meant that wherever she might sail, anywhere in the world, she spoke for the United States of America, her decks respected as United States soil, a sanctuary for American citizens in distress abroad. Almost five years had passed since the ship was authorized, but she was still not ready to serve her country, either in peace or war. After the commissioning of a warship the next step is an extensive "shakedown."

"We were in the New York Shipyard, getting the ship ready to go to war. The people in the shipyard had the same feeling that I had and that I still have about the wonderful ship NORTH CAROLINA. Every man of that crew in Brooklyn worked just as hard as he could to make it a going concern, because it was well known that the Japanese were building up their fleet. The commissioning ceremony in New York City was a really electric and satisfying event. The ovation that ended the celebration was a tribute to a bunch of hard-working people. Our sailors were ready to go out and do whatever had to be done to win that war. And they did it. They really did it."

— Commander Alfred Ward, Gunnery Officer

"The NORTH CAROLINA had something that no other ship I have ever been attached to had. There was an élan among the crew that was something special. Those of us in the original crew who were career officers went on and pursued careers in destroyers or submarines or aviation. Many of the crew went on to the nucleus of new construction battleships. But wherever we went, we were NORTH CAROLINA sailors. We always carried that with us. And I can tell you, this ship had a tremendous impact on the Navy — then and still today."

— Lieutenant Julian Burke, Jr., 5-inch Director Officer

The ship's company stands at attention, officers saluting, as the national anthem is played at the commissioning ceremony. Note the stands on both sides of the ship for the hundreds of invited guests.

Camera captures NORTH CAROLINA's 19-gun salvo, August 29, 1941.

NATIONAL ARCHIVES 80-GK-13501

BATTLESHIP COLLECTION 94.30.2

BATTLESHIP COLLECTION 92.8.4

Liberty party on the way to a big night on the town in Manhattan.

Liberty in Portland, Maine; fresh-faced innocence as yet untouched by war.

SHAKEDOWN

The foremost objective of shakedown was to weld all hands and the ship together to operate as a well-oiled machine. Hard work, inspired leadership and repetitive drilling were the keys. The shakedown involved every conceivable test of the ship and her entire array of weapons, machinery and equipment. An intensive schedule of drills for every member of the ship's company was carried out, day and night, over a period of many months. Every officer and enlisted man underwent continuous technical training in his specialty. At a gradually accelerating tempo, ship and crew together were repeatedly put through all of their paces in order to evaluate and improve readiness for combat and ability to cope with any emergency. As the months went by, constant drills at battle stations transformed the men into a team that could load, aim and fire the guns with record speed and accuracy. At the same time, the ship's company developed a superb *esprit*, which the coming war experience was to weld into a lifetime bond. As a result, NORTH CAROLINA was a fiercely proud ship throughout her active service.

NORTH CAROLINA's shakedown was unusually exhaustive, involving operations up and down the East Coast, south into the Caribbean and as far north as Casco Bay, Maine. There, in a test of the ship's structural strength conducted at night, August 29, 1941, all nine guns of the 16-inch battery, together with all 10 port side 5-inch guns, were fired simultaneously in one thunderous broadside. There was only minor superficial damage topside, and the only ill effects noted inside the ship were that a few electric light bulbs blinked out and a little dust settled from ventilation ducts.

On May 19, 1941, a foggy morning, the ship gets underway for sea for the first time, commencing shakedown. Stephen Hustvedt, proud teenage son of the ship's skipper, snapped this photograph from a Brooklyn hotel window.

BATTLESHIP COLLECTION 98.53.18

HOW THE SHIP WAS NICKNAMED "SHOWBOAT"

A ship undergoing shakedown returns repeatedly to her building yard for consultations, adjustments and modifications. These events brought NORTH CAROLINA back again and again to the New York Navy Yard. New Yorkers, including then popular radio commentator Walter Winchell, so often witnessed the spectacle of this shiny new "battlewagon" entering and departing the harbor that they began to call her the "Showboat," after the colorful river steamer in the popular Rogers and Hammerstein Broadway musical of the same name. In a spirit of friendly rivalry the crew of WASHINGTON picked up on this and began to taunt NORTH CAROLINA sailors with the not entirely flattering nickname. On one occasion, when WASHINGTON was at anchor in Hampton Roads, Virginia, and NORTH CAROLINA entered port to anchor nearby, WASHINGTON's band greeted her sister with the rollicking strains of "Here Comes the Showboat," a popular song from the musical. That did it. The proud crew affectionately called their favorite battleship by that name from then on. And so she is known to this day.

THE SHIP'S COMPANY

The expression "ship's company" includes all personnel permanently assigned to duty in, or on, a ship. (By custom, most American naval officers speak of serving *in* a ship, while enlisted men say they serve *on* it.) The word "crew" usually refers to all the people who operate a ship, boat, gun, etc., but in naval parlance crew more often refers only to the enlisted members of the ship's company.

A ship of war is only as effective as her officers and men, and this was strikingly true of NORTH CAROLINA. At the time of her commissioning, because she was the pride of the Navy, many of the personnel among the 1,500 officers and men then assigned were hand-picked. The result was an extraordinarily well-led and

The ship's company of the Showboat was a proud lot. This photograph, taken December 5, 1942, in the Fiji Islands shows Executive Officer Commander Lyman A. Thackrey leading Captains George H. Fort and Wilder D. Baker in an informal inspection of the crew. Baker relieved Fort as commanding officer that day, one of the rare occasions when the crew wore whites in the South Pacific.

"We had the best crew that any ship ever had, the finest young men from the high schools and colleges. The college graduates were coming in and being recruited, and they were smart boys. I was proud to be part of them. We in NORTH CAROLINA had the greatest number of people who were brilliant, who were loyal Americans. I have never seen spirit that exceeded this period in our life as a nation during those dark days when it was evident that the Japanese were going to come out and fight us."

— Commander Alfred Ward, Gunnery Officer

"I loved the USS NORTH CAROLINA. She was a great ship and had a great crew. We always had a great captain and executive officer. We were a finely tuned crew and took care of one another on board or ashore, regardless of what division you were in. She was the greatest ship that ever sailed."

— James Masie, Fire Controlman First Class

"There was nothing our crew couldn't do better and faster than any other ship in the fleet."

— Commander Joe Stryker, Executive Officer

"Being in New York City was just great at that [pre-war] time. We could ride the subway from Sand Street to Manhattan for about 10 cents. We could always get free tickets from the YMCA for the shows in New York City. We saw most of the big bands during that time — Glenn Miller, Tommy and Jimmy Dorsey, Benny Goodman and many others. At that time it was a great city to have fun in. Also, we had Coney Island, the amusement park. I have gone on a liberty in that city and had only 50 cents and still had a great time."

— Leo Bostwick, Machinist's Mate Second Class

"Over the next few weeks there were many working parties. Heard every day was 'Now here this: 10 men from each of the six deck divisions report to the quarter-deck to load stores.' I never knew a ship could hold so much stores, and when you thought it was full, it would start again. We had three-section liberty and I went home every night I was off duty, as I lived in the Bronx. It was an hour-and-a-half trip by streetcar, subway and bus. It cost me 12 cents each way. I went out the Sands Street gate. It was a notorious street with lots of bars and ladies of the night. They had names like Hungry Helen and Big Bertha and I was scared to linger long there. I was only 17."

— William Taylor, Boatswain's Mate First Class

well-organized crew, highly motivated from the start. Those assigned as of the commissioning were referred to in Navy parlance as "plankowners." They were proud of this distinction and strongly resented anyone claiming the honor without being entitled to it. The number of assigned personnel increased steadily after the ship joined the fleet, especially with the addition of ten 40-mm quadruple gun mounts in late 1942 and five more by late 1943. The ship's 1945 complement was approximately 144 commissioned officers and 2,195 enlisted men, including about 85 marines.

Along with the captain, executive officer (second in command) and department heads, the handpicked old-timers included warrant officers, chief petty officers and a few middle grade officers and petty officers. The rest of the crew consisted of hundreds of seamen and firemen — entry-level positions — who swabbed decks, broke out stores (food), passed ammunition, shined bright work (brass), served as "mess cooks" (crew waiters and dish-washers) and did anything else, and everything else, they were told to do. But these men, too, were more highly motivated than the average because a large proportion of them were among the early patri-ot volunteers of World War II, rather than draftees or men who had signed up merely to avoid being draft-ed into the Army.

The ship's company was organized into seven departments, headed in most cases by a comman-der or lieutenant commander. The department heads were charged with overall responsibility for the organization, training and performance of all assigned personnel. Next under the department heads were the division officers, mostly full lieu-tenants (two-stripers), with similar responsibilities over their men. In most divisions there were several more officer assistants in the ranks of lieutenant, lieutenant (junior grade) and ensign. They exercised general day-to-day supervision over assigned enlisted men, and were in training for more responsible positions. Next in seniority came the warrant officers, promoted from enlisted status, who had specialized in one of the technical fields, such as engineering, electricity, communications, electronics, gunnery, deck seamanship, etc. After the warrant officers, but no less important, came the chief petty officers, the ship's senior enlisted men. The chiefs, of long enlisted experience, normally

Lost in the mists of time is knowledge of the occasion on which this photograph was taken, probably during a change of command in the South Pacific. With the 5-inch guns elevated to the air defense position, the ship at sea and the crew in dungarees, it is obviously wartime; but probably not in the forward area where no such exposed gathering would have been prudent. Regardless, the shot provides a realistic glimpse of the ship's company as they normally looked during the war, the number particularly impressive.

exercised the most direct authority over the enlisted men in their divisions. Most were highly proficient technically in their specialties, thereby providing indispensable support to their officers, while serving as both leaders and role models for their men. Admiral William F. Halsey is quoted as having once said, "You see those battleships sitting there, and you think they float on the water. You are wrong. They are carried to sea on the backs of the chief petty officers."

Order of Navy rank/rate among NORTH CAROLINA's crew from the top down was captain, commander, lieutenant commander, lieutenant, lieutenant (junior grade), ensign, chief warrant officer, warrant officer, chief petty officer, petty officer first class, petty officer second class, petty officer third class, seaman first class, fireman first class, apprentice seaman. A captain in the Navy is the equivalent of a full colonel in the other services; a commander equates to a lieutenant colonel; a lieutenant commander to a major; a full lieutenant to a captain; a lieutenant junior grade to a first lieutenant; an ensign to a second lieutenant.

Life aboard...

A WHIMSICAL NORTH CAROLINA SONG

I

Tarheels we – in the New North C,
Will sweep the foemen from the sea,
We'll chase them down –
And watch them drown –
In every ocean where they're found;
We'll give them hell –
With every shell –
And drive them to perdition;
We'll make them sweat,
And all regret
The day we were commissioned.

II

The New North C will rule the sea,
From the River Platte to the old North Sea,
From Iceland's shore
To Singapore;
Throughout the world our guns will roar,
Our sixteen-inch,
In every pinch
Will so control conditions,
No ship may sail the seven seas,
Except with our permission.

— Lieutenant Commander John Zahm,
Assistant Damage Control Officer

Song printed in ship's paper, Tarheel, Vol. 1, No. XIX, August 16, 1941.

Life aboard...

"The depression of the early '30s was tough. It was especially hard for Negroes because jobs were so scarce and Negroes were not allowed to enlist in the armed forces. It was 1936 before the president opened up the Army and Navy to Negroes. The Secretary of the Navy said he would permit Negroes to come into the Navy at this time, but as mess attendants only.

"In May 1938, I finished high school. My chance of going to college was out because my dad died three years earlier and my mother could not afford to send me. I wanted to go into the Navy, but I first tried earning money for college — to no avail. So early April 1939 I went to the Navy recruiting office and signed up. In boot camp, we were in a segregated part of the base, of a segregated Navy, and in a segregated country.

"In mid-January 1941, I was transferred to the crew of the NORTH CAROLINA (not yet commissioned into the Navy). The mess attendants' duties aboard the NORTH CAROLINA were to clean officers' staterooms, make their bunks, put towels in their rooms; unpack, wash, and store dishes (for the officers' wardroom), clean silver (the ship had a 120-plus piece silver service, plus flatware and serving pieces); clean the wardroom, and anything else the officers asked us to do."

— Roosevelt Flenard, Mess Attendant First Class

"During World War II the Navy grew so rapidly in numbers of ships that many thousands of reservists were called to active duty to man them. In fact, as of January 1945, only 25 of the 125 commissioned officers attached to the NORTH CAROLINA were graduates of the Naval Academy at Annapolis. I was then a reservist. Relationships between the regulars and reserves were sometimes strained, due usually to the wide difference in our training. Most Academy graduates had undergone four intensive years of study in naval science, while the typical reservist's schooling consisted of a 30-day cruise on a World War I battleship, followed by three months of cramming in a reserve midshipman's school. As the saying goes, we knew just enough about seamanship, engineering and gunnery to be dangerous. Understandably, the regulars called us '90-day wonders.' We called them 'ring-knockers,' for the way a few of them pointedly reminded us of their superiority by tapping their USNA class rings on the nearest hard surface.

"As the war progressed and combat seasoned us, such pettiness gradually faded away. We reservists learned fast that we had to know our jobs to survive, so we needed all the help we could get from the regulars. They learned that they couldn't stand all the watches or man all the guns. They needed us as much as we needed them. So we put aside our differences and learned to serve together as a team. I will never forget the patience and consideration given to us reserves by the small cadre of regulars who showed us the ropes and kept us in line during those tough early days of the war."

— Author

The seven departments included Communications, Engineering, Gunnery, Hull, Medical, Navigation and Supply. They varied in numbers of personnel, with the Gunnery Department claiming over half the crew, while the Navigation Department had only 27 men. Within the Gunnery Department were 10 divisions: 1st, 2nd and 3rd were responsible for the three main battery gun turrets; 4th was assigned the automatic weapons; 5th and 6th had, respectively, the starboard and port 5-inch gun batteries; F Division was responsible for fire control; I Division manned the combat information center and provided lookouts; V Division (aviation detachment) operated and maintained the aircraft; and 7th Division (marines) manned two of the 5-inch twin mounts and several 20-mm guns.

The Engineering Department included four divisions: A Division was responsible for auxiliary machinery; B Division for boilers; M Division for the main engines; and E Division for the electrical systems. Under the Communications Department were three divisions: CR included radiomen; CS was signalmen; and CY was yeomen (clerks and typists), plus printers. Four departments contained only one division each. The Hull Department's R Division was responsible for the maintenance and repair of the hull and its fittings, together with damage control and the repair parties. The ship's band was also assigned to R Division. The Supply Department's S Division included cooks, bakers, butchers, disbursing clerks, storekeepers, officers' mess attendants, laundrymen, barbers, tailors and cobblers. The Navigation Department's N Division included the quartermasters (bridge personnel). The Medical Department's H Division consisted of medical and dental personnel.

Although the captain held overall command, it was the executive officer who organized the ship's daily affairs, oversaw the seven departments and was responsible for morale. His division, EX Division, handled personnel administration and issued the Plan of the Day, a daily schedule of the ship's activities (see Part Two). Under him two chaplains, with part-time help from two or three enlisted volunteers, administered to the spiritual and welfare needs of the crew, including management of the library. The "exec" was also in charge of the master-at-arms (MAA) force. Normally comprised of nine men drawn from the different divisions, this group functioned as the ship's police force.

Captain Oswald S. Colclough, left, and Chief Master at Arms Paul H. Minvielle, right, pose for a photograph in the captain's cabin, 1945.

COMMAND AND CONTROL IN BATTLE

Every man on board, including cooks, barbers and band members, had a battle station. A highly detailed "Battle Bill," its parts prepared separately by and for each division, listed the division's battle stations, naming which member of the division was designated to man each one. At the top of the command pyramid, of course, was the captain, who was in almost absolute authority over the entire ship, crew and armament. The command "Commence firing" was never given without his orders or by his delegated authority. The captain's battle station was normally on the bridge. In the event that the ship engaged enemy surface ships or shore batteries, the captain and a skeleton staff were expected to shift two decks below the bridge to the lower level of the heavily armored conning tower.

The battle station of the executive officer, called "Batt Two," was located halfway up the tower from the bridge. Batt Two was the first of several alternate conning (ship control) stations equipped with steering wheel, compass, engine order telegraph, etc. The exec had to be prepared at all times to relieve the captain of command in the event the "old man" was killed or disabled. The Showboat's captain sometimes

THE MARINE DETACHMENT

"The Marine Detachment performed many different functions. Marines stood lookout watches and in battle manned 20-mm guns and provided officers for two 40-mm mounts. They also manned two 5-inch mounts early in the ship's career. The marines furnished 24-hour orderly services to the captain and executive officer. In port they were responsible for the security of the ship. Marines helped provision the ship and load ammunition. Marine officers stood top gunnery watches, officer of the deck and junior officer of the deck watches. They regularly assisted in summary and general courts-martial, acting either as the prosecuting or defending officer. All marines were trained in ship-to-shore operations, so they were prepared to comprise a landing force when necessary. This became necessary near the end of the war when our detachment was transferred at sea to an attack transport and went into Yokosuka, Japan. This preceded the signing of the peace treaty by several days."

— First Lieutenant William Romm,
Marine Detachment Officer

A squad of marines from the ship's 85-man detachment prepares to honor dead shipmates in a burial service at sea.

gave the executive officer the "conn" (control of the ship's maneuvers) during air attacks because visibility from his loftier position was better than from the bridge. In fact, visibility at lower levels was often seriously impaired by the ship's own gun smoke. In Batt Two and on the bridge, the noise level from the guns often made spoken commands inaudible. Thus, the conning officer had to become adept at using hand signals for orders to the helmsman.

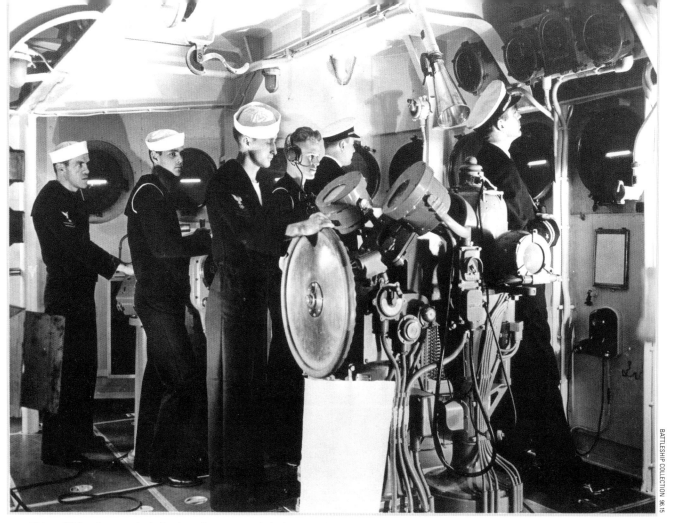

This publicity photograph, dating from the pre-war shakedown period, shows the normal steaming watch controlling the ship from the pilothouse. At right is the officer of the deck (OOD), responsible under the captain for the operation and maneuvering of the ship. To the OOD's left is his junior officer assistant (JOOD). Next, right to left, are a talker, the helmsman and two men manning the engine order telegraph and RPM indicator, through which orders were sent to the engineers. Not shown, but normally included in the bridge steaming watch, were a boatswain's mate, quartermaster, bugler and messenger. When the ship was at General Quarters two more phone talkers were added to the number present. Of course, the captain and navigator were nearly always at hand on the bridge. The white block in lower center was inserted by Navy censors to hide secret steering apparatus.

Life aboard...

"I served in NORTH CAROLINA under four of her nine commanding officers, Captains Thomas, Fahrion, Colclough and Hanlon. As the ship's combat intelligence officer, it was my job to brief the captain personally three or four times daily, often late at night. So I came to know them quite well, and I had great respect for every one of them. This is not to say that I was fond of them. Of course, they were gentlemen and experienced seamen, but they were the most demanding taskmasters I've ever known. In fairness, I must add that they were equally demanding of themselves. They had remarkable stamina, able to stay sharp and wary on the bridge, without sleep, longer than most younger officers. They were tough, stern and stubborn; rarely showing any sense of humor or tolerating any levity in their presence. So they were hard men to work for, but exactly the kind you'd want in command of a battleship in war."

— Author

Even Batt Two, as originally designed, did not afford adequate visibility during air attacks because the station was entirely enclosed within the foremast. Views around and above the ship were limited to what little could be seen through small portholes. Thus, while the ship was at Pearl Harbor from September 17 to November 10, 1943, maverick Commander Joe W. Stryker — navigator early in the war, later executive officer — ordered on his own authority that a tub-like structure similar to that of Sky Control be constructed around Batt Two (on page 45). This greatly improved visibility.

The gunnery officer's battle station was in "Control," located in the upper level of the conning tower. For improved visibility during air attacks and shore bombardments, the gunnery officer often took up a position in the open outside of, and occasionally on top of, the conning tower. The "gun boss," as he was called, coordinated the use of the entire armament and was responsible for its organization and effectiveness. He was nominally responsible for assigning targets to the main and secondary batteries, ordering divided fire as necessary to engage multiple targets, directing the batteries to shift targets, etc. In actual practice he normally delegated direct control of the batteries to his principal subordinates.

Under the gun boss, the main battery assistant normally controlled the turret guns from his battle station in the Mark 38 director, "Spot 1," at the top of the foremast. During shore bombardments, direct control of gunfire was delegated to the F division officer in Main Battery Plot. In the event of return fire occurring during a shore bombardment, or if enemy surface ships were to appear on the scene, authority could be shifted instantly to Control, Spot 1 or Spot 2, as necessary for better visibility.

The air defense officer in Sky Control normally controlled the 5-inch battery and, through an assistant in Sky Control, the automatic weapons. Although standard procedure required the permission of the captain to open fire, NORTH CAROLINA's air defense officer held delegated authority to open fire in the event of a sudden attack allowing no time to consult the captain.

In each fast carrier task group the officer in tactical command (OTC), normally a rear admiral embarked in an aircraft carrier, exercised control via VHF (very high frequency) voice radio over the operations of all his ships. VHF was used for most tactical communications at sea between both ships and aircraft because VHF range was normally limited to the horizon and could not be intercepted by a more distant enemy. The task group commander ordered all changes of formation, course and speed. He coordinated the use of the task group's armament and was empowered to order ships to "hold fire" when friendly aircraft were overhead. He usually followed this order with "guns free" when the friendly planes had departed or landed aboard the carriers. Under the "guns free" condition, which normally prevailed, individual ships were at liberty to open fire on any hostile threat at the discretion of their commanding officers. The task *group* commanders were subject to the orders of the task *force* commander, who exercised tactical command over the force as a whole, usually (after 1942) including up to five task groups.

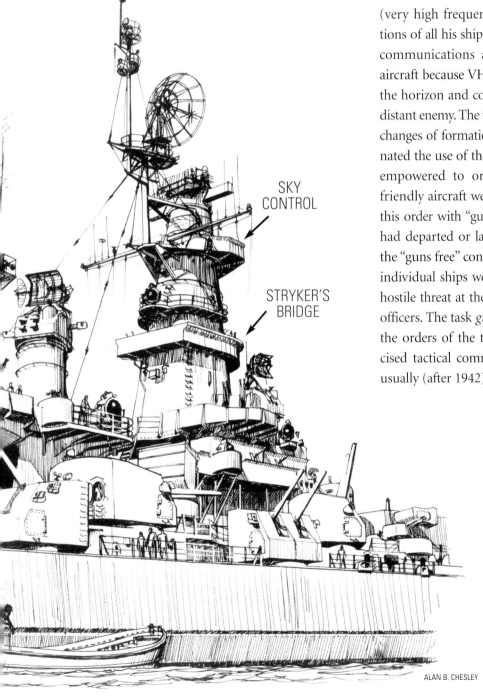

SKY CONTROL

STRYKER'S BRIDGE

ALAN B. CHESLEY

SHIPBOARD COMBAT COMMUNICATIONS

For immediate communications with the entire ship's company, the general announcing system, or public address (PA) system, was normally used. On board Navy ships this system was known as the 1MC. It was over this system that the boatswain's mate of the watch on the bridge would sound General Quarters when so ordered by the officer of the deck. Loud speakers throughout the ship boomed that alarm instantly to the entire crew. 1MC microphones were also positioned at other key locations, including Batt Two and the quarterdeck (main deck aft beside Turret III, where the officer of the deck stood watch when the ship was not underway). There were other smaller MC units that functioned like intercoms among stations such as the pilothouse, Batt Two, the combat information center (CIC), main radio and the signal bridge.

For instant voice communications among such key stations as the pilothouse, charthouse, the captain's sea cabin, the wings of the bridge and other maneuvering or control stations, voice tubes were available. Voice tubes were simply long hollow pipes through which individuals could converse. Pneumatic tubes for rapid delivery of written messages were provided among the main radio room, charthouse, CIC, flag plot and other key stations. This system was like that used in modern drive-in banks: written messages could be placed in special cartridges, called "bunnies," which were inserted at one station and sent to another using compressed air.

Lieutenants (jg) James M. Mason, left, and George E. Woodward, right, wearing sound-powered phone head sets in Secondary Plot.

SOUND-POWERED PHONES

When the crew was at battle stations or at stations for other emergencies, the principal means for rapid and reliable voice communication within the ship was the sound-powered phone. As the name implies, phones of this type were not dependent on any outside source of power, but were energized solely by the voice of the speaker. Almost every part of the ship was wired into one or more circuits of the sound-powered phone system. With the crew at battle stations, in most locations these phones were manned by "talkers," who relayed incoming and outgoing messages. With the system in good condition, a strong and clear voice generated sufficient vibrations to be heard at a number of different stations on the circuit, even in the most distant locations within the ship.

There were two types of sound-powered phones: the head set and hand set (see below). Both contained

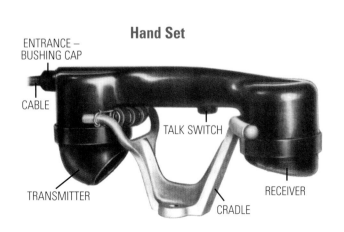

Hand Set

ENTRANCE – BUSHING CAP

CABLE

TALK SWITCH

TRANSMITTER

RECEIVER

CRADLE

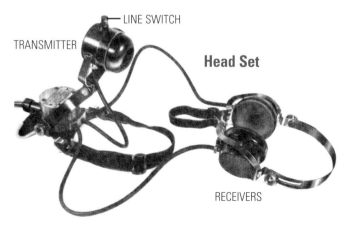

LINE SWITCH

TRANSMITTER

Head Set

RECEIVERS

U.S. NAVY SOUND POWERED TELEPHONES, I.C. INSTRUCTION BOOK NO.13P, RCA INSTRUCTIONS IB-38121

two crystal diaphragms: one in the mouthpiece for transmitting, the other in the ear piece for receiving. The speaker's voice vibrated the diaphragm and converted it into electrical impulses that were transmitted through the circuit wiring and then converted back to sound at the receiver diaphragm.

On board NORTH CAROLINA there were dozens of different sound-powered phone circuits. Two of the most important were designated the "JA" and "JV" circuits. The JA was the captain's primary battle circuit. It connected the captain's talker with Combat (CIC), Batt Two, Sky Control and Gunnery Control. The 1JV circuit was the primary maneuvering circuit. It connected the pilothouse with such stations as the main engine room, the steering engine room, the different mooring stations at the bow and stern, etc. Other circuits included those needed in exercising control of the different gun batteries, a circuit connecting the lookouts with CIC and the pilothouse, one connecting the damage control parties with each other and their controlling station, and circuits for communications among the various engineering stations.

Finally, for routine administrative use the ship was equipped with an electrically powered dial phone system such as commonly used ashore, known as the "ship's service" phone system.

Showboat cartoonist Mick Gorman created this work of art to spoof the tension generated in the combat information center when enemy planes approached. Note backwards plotter.

Air search radar operator at the SK-2 console in CIC. This man not only provided constant reports of air activity, but he also ascertained whether approaching planes were friendly or hostile by operating the radar's IFF feature.

THE COMBAT INFORMATION CENTER (CIC)

As its name implies, the combat information center served as the primary nerve center to collect, evaluate and disseminate tactical information needed by the captain and other senior officers to fight the ship effectively. Information gathered from radar, radio, search aircraft, intelligence, lookouts, and the ship's own topside personnel was continuously plotted, filtered, evaluated and disseminated to the captain, exec, gun boss, and a few others who needed to know. Usually such dissemination was done by sound-powered phones. The CIC was manned by 30 enlisted plotters and talkers, supervised by five commissioned officers headed by the "evaluator," an experienced lieutenant commander or lieutenant. "Combat," as the CIC was called, controlled the ship's search radars and was equipped with radios, plotting equipment and appropriate status boards for maintaining visual displays of important tactical information.

Three vitally important plots were maintained in the CIC: first a large vertical plot showing activity in the air within 100 miles of the task force; second a similar but smaller horizontal air plot; and third a horizontal plot of the surface situation out to a distance of about 25 nautical miles. The main air plot was maintained on a large, vertical sheet of transparent plastic on which concentric circles had

Layout of 1944-45 Combat Information Center
Showing principal items of equipment and battle stations of key personnel
1 inch = approximately 3 feet

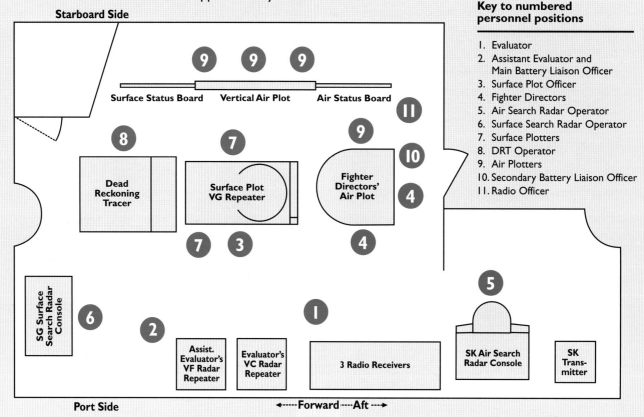

Starboard Side

Key to numbered personnel positions

1. Evaluator
2. Assistant Evaluator and Main Battery Liaison Officer
3. Surface Plot Officer
4. Fighter Directors
5. Air Search Radar Operator
6. Surface Search Radar Operator
7. Surface Plotters
8. DRT Operator
9. Air Plotters
10. Secondary Battery Liaison Officer
11. Radio Officer

Surface Status Board   Vertical Air Plot   Air Status Board

Dead Reckoning Tracer

Surface Plot VG Repeater

Fighter Directors' Air Plot

SG Surface Search Radar Console

Assist. Evaluator's VF Radar Repeater

Evaluator's VC Radar Repeater

3 Radio Receivers

SK Air Search Radar Console

SK Trans-mitter

Port Side   ◄----Forward----Aft----►

FROM DRAWING BY LT MAURICE CHARLES HOOD IV, USN, BATTLESHIP COLLECTION

been etched at 10-mile intervals, along with compass bearings at 10-degree intervals, from zero degrees (north) clockwise to 360 degrees. NORTH CAROLINA was assumed to be positioned at the center of this plot. Manning the plot were three enlisted men wearing sound-powered headphones connecting them with the air search radar operator. Unidentified aircraft, called "bogies," were plotted in red grease pencil and labeled as "Raid 1," "Raid 2," etc. When planes were identified as enemy they were called "bandits."

Friendly aircraft were identified as such by an ingenious electronic device called IFF (Identification, Friend or Foe), which was triggered by impulses riding the beam of the air search radar. The air search radar operator could electronically query any approaching plane and, in the absence of an IFF response, establish immediately that the intruder was probably hostile. On the air plot, friendly planes were lettered in blue and identified by flight numbers assigned by their parent aircraft carriers. Annotations beside the track of a plane indicated such details as the identity, time and altitude of each

plot. To avoid blocking view of their work, the air plotters stood behind the plot, lettering their work backwards.

Fighter director officers (FDOs), of whom NORTH CAROLINA had two, Lieutenants (jg) Ralph Sheffer and Robert W. Jewell, worked from the air plot, communicating via VHF radio with the combat air patrol (defensive fighter planes normally orbiting overhead). The Showboat's FDOs, when so ordered by the task group FDO, often performed the important task of controlling aircraft of the combat air patrol (CAP) by vectoring them out to intercept incoming enemy raids. The FDOs used the horizontal air plot mainly to calculate the maneuvers needed by the CAP to intercept bogies. Vectoring meant ordering the CAP to fly the correct course at the right altitude to intercept and shoot down enemy planes before they reached the ships of the task force. As soon as a CAP pilot visually sighted the enemy he would radio "Tally Ho!" Upon shooting down an enemy plane he would declare, for example, "Splash one 'Zeke.'" Zeke was the U.S. code name for the enemy's fast, highly maneuverable Mitsubishi "Zero" fighter plane.

The surface plot was maintained on a large, round horizontal plotting surface — actually a very large radar scope repeater in the shape of a table about 30 inches in diameter. The device was called a VG converter. The surface radar "picture" was displayed on the VG's transluscent plastic surface. Etched into the surface were concentric circles at 1,000-yard intervals out to 50,000 yards, plus bearings at 10-degree intervals from north clockwise to 360 degrees. As with the air plot, NORTH CAROLINA was assumed to be at the center of the plot, so that the approximate range and bearing from the Showboat of any "blip" could be determined at a glance. With the blips representing the units of NORTH CAROLINA's own task force constantly displayed on this plot, it was necessary only to keep each one properly labeled by blue grease pencil to display at all times the exact location of each ship. This was important in cases where a ship might report sighting a periscope or an attacking aircraft, making it vital to know immediately where that was happening. Had enemy ships appeared on the scene, they would have been plotted in red and identified as "Skunks." Adjacent to the surface plot was a Dead Reckoning Tracer (DRT), an electromechanical device which, with inputs of the ship's course and speed, recorded on a roll of paper a trace of the ship's maneuvers. The result was used mainly for record and reporting purposes.

In addition to the plots, two status boards, one on each side of the main air plot, were maintained to keep important data current. A surface status board displayed current tactical information about the task group's composition, formation, guide and station assignments. The fighter direction status board showed information on approaching enemy raids, voice call signs of friendly interceptors, and weather conditions important to pilots.

The evaluator, by standing in a position on the port side of the CIC from which he could see all three plots and both status boards, was able to maintain a grasp of the rapidly changing situation without having to waste time on questions and answers.

This post-war group photograph of CIC enlisted men gives an idea of how crowded the space was when fully manned. Note the evaluator's VC radar repeater at left, the VG surface plot at right.

EARLY TARGET ACQUISITION VITAL

"My principal duty in the CIC when we were at General Quarters was to help the radar operator in Spot 1 acquire a surface target. As mentioned before, this was necessary because fire control radar, with its very narrow beam, was no good in a search role unless its operator was told exactly where to search. I stood right behind the operator of our SG surface search radar, enabling me to see from his scopes the range and bearing of any suspicious surface target. At my left was an electronic device called a VF Repeater, by which I could select to view Spot 1's fire control radar picture. Wearing sound-powered headphones, I could also select to be in direct voice contact with the Spot 1 radar operator. Comparing the two radar pictures, I could give Spot 1 such orders as, right three degrees, up 200 yards, etc., until his radar acquired the target blip.

"Using distant large ships of our own task force as simulated targets, we drilled at this nearly every morning during the dawn alert. Our main purpose was to minimize the time taken to coach the main battery on target, ready to open fire. We became so proficient at it that at ranges of as much as 35,000 yards, day or night, we were confident of our ability to open fire and straddle the target [place all rounds on or around the target] *with our first salvo.* We were capable of doing this consistently within two or three minutes after initial radar contact. This capability probably would have given us a decisive advantage over any Japanese ship, including their YAMATO-class super battleships, because the Japanese were far behind the United States in the development and effective use of fire control radar."

— Author

Located close to the evaluator's position was a VC radar repeater, a device enabling him to select and view the radar picture of any one of the ship's radar equipments, including the fire control sets. The evaluator personally manned the JA phone circuit, through which he was in constant direct communication with an officer who stood at the elbow of the captain, as his talker on the bridge.

Another vitally important function of CIC was "target acquisition," which consisted of feeding search radar ranges and bearings to the fire control directors. This function was necessary because the fire control radars, though highly accurate with their very narrow beams, were relatively ineffective in a search capacity. Enabling the directors to quickly acquire a target, "lock on," and commence tracking

was critical because of the advantage gained over the enemy by being first to open fire. Combat's main battery and secondary battery liaison officers, who served in this capacity, did so over sound-powered phones, speaking directly to the fire control radar operators.

Until late 1944, the CIC was established within Main Battery Plot. This arrangement was devised before it became apparent that modern naval warfare, particularly with the invention of radar and the increasing volume of information to be processed, required a dedicated shipboard combat information center. Having the CIC combined with Plot in a relatively small space was very unsatisfactory due to crowding and mutual interference. During a shipyard overhaul in late 1944, a new CIC was created in Flag Radio, a much better location on the 03 level, directly below the navigation bridge.

RADAR

Radar was by far the most valuable tool at the disposal of the CIC. The word radar is an acronym for **RA**dio **D**etection **A**nd **R**anging. Radar made it possible to detect and track targets at distances greatly exceeding the capabilities of optical devices at night and in poor visibility. A British invention shared with the United States, this cutting-edge invention was the single most valuable technological breakthrough of World War II, and one that gave the U.S. a decisive advantage over the Japanese.

The principal components of radar were a transmitter, a receiver, an antenna and a console to display visual indications of bearing and range, and by which the operator could control the device. The transmitter sent out powerful short pulses of ultra high frequency (UHF) radio wave energy, concentrated by a directional antenna into focused beams of energy. When the waves hit an object, part of that energy was reflected back, like an echo, to the shipboard antenna, which passed the information to the receiver. The receiver amplified the weak signal, producing visual indications or "blips" of the echo on the console's range and bearing oscilloscopes (picture tubes). By focusing the antenna beam precisely on a target, accurate determinations of the target's bearing and altitude could be made. Target range was determined by measuring the time required for a burst of energy to travel to the target and return.

In August 1941, an early version of an air search radar was installed on NORTH CAROLINA. This device, called the CXAM, was popularly known as the "bedsprings" due to the appearance of its large rectangular antenna. Though far better than nothing, the CXAM was relatively unreliable, often broke down and was vulnerable to shock damage. Thanks to inspired work by British and American scientists, improvements in radar effectiveness and reliability were continuous throughout World War II, with superior equipment gradually replacing older models. The Showboat's ultimate suite of radar included four search radars and six fire control systems. Controlling consoles for the air search radar and one of the two surface search radars were conveniently located within CIC. As of 1945, the effective range of NORTH CAROLINA's SK-2 air search radar was in excess of 100 nautical miles; that of the two SG-2 surface search radars was 35,000-37,000 yards on major ship targets.

Shown at right is the "bedsprings" antenna for the CXAM air search radar installed on the ship in August 1941. The saucer-shaped antenna shown above is that of the SK-2 air search radar which replaced the CXAM in March 1943.

Her launching, fitting out, commissioning and shakedown completed with flying colors, the mighty Showboat sails forth to war. She transited the Panama Canal June 9-10, 1942, on her way to reinforce our hard-pressed Pacific Fleet fighting against Japan.

PART II — A TYPICAL WARTIME DAY AT SEA

THE PLAN OF THE DAY

The "Plan of the Day" was a schedule of events prepared each evening by the executive officer, with copies distributed throughout the ship. Its purpose was to inform all hands of the activities planned for the following day. **Shown in blue below are the main entries for a typical wartime Plan of the Day.** They are followed by explanations of what action each entry normally required. The plan is used here as a framework to explain how the ship's company spent a typical non-combat day at sea.

NAVY TIME

On Navy ships the hours of a day are divided not into two 12-hour periods but into one 24-hour period. The hours and minutes of one complete day are expressed with four numerals from 0001 (one minute after midnight) to 2400 (midnight). Any expression of time before noon is the same as ashore, except that with Navy time there is no colon between the hours and minutes. After noon the hour count goes from 1300 (1:00 p.m.) to 2400. To keep the crew aware of time, the ship's bell is sounded at half hour intervals, from one bell up to eight bells over each four-hour period. For example, one bell is sounded at 0430 in the morning, two at 0500, three at 0530, and so on. Two or more bells are sounded in pairs of strokes. For instance, the four bells for 0600 are sounded as "gong-gong, gong-gong." The five bells for 0630, as "gong-gong, gong-gong, gong." By 0800, the eight-bell cycle is complete and is then started over again with one gong at 0830. This cycle corresponds to the crew's watch schedule in which men on watch are normally relieved every four hours. However, the watch from 1600 to 2000 is usually split into two two-hour stints, called "dog watches." The shorter periods ensured those on watch had dinner.

Highline station personnel prepare to transfer a sailor from the battleship to another ship steaming alongside, just one of the many jobs the crew performed during a normal day at sea.

A boatswain's mate sounds his pipe preparatory to passing word over the 1MC. His announcements generally initiated events scheduled in the Plan of the Day.

0430 – Reveille. The soundest sleepers were rudely awakened by the peal of the boatswain's pipe over the 1MC, followed by the words, "Reveille, reveille for all hands." Next came the even less welcome word, "General Quarters (battle stations for the daily dawn alert) will be sounded in five minutes." With that, in the dim red light of night lighting, 2,300 yawning officers and men, all in their skivvies (Navy slang for underwear), rolled out of their "sacks," rubbed their eyes and began pulling on their clothes. (The red light in night lighting was the best color for preserving night vision.)

0435 – General Quarters. Set material condition "Zed" throughout the ship. As a matter of normal routine throughout World War II, all hands were ordered to battle stations twice every day for one hour before sunrise and one hour after sunset. These were the times when surprise attack was thought most likely. Again came the shrill peal of the boatswain's pipe, followed in rapid order by the

"When the boatswain's mate piped reveille you sprang from your rack and grabbed your socks. You'd rather sleep in? Only if you'd stood watch from midnight until 0400 could you sleep until 0700. If so, you tied a piece of toilet paper to your berth, which kept the master-at-arms from banging your berth with his billy club. You triced up your berth to create more room in the crowded compartment. This means you made up your bed, folded the blanket and placed it on the end. You spread a fireproof cover over the bedding. You tied it all down with two canvas straps. You lifted up the outside of the berth and moved the chain from the outer to the inner hook. Your berth was now at a steep angle and out of the way. You pulled on your clothes as fast as you could, went to the head (toilet) and took off for your battle station. Nobody ever got enough sleep."

— Paul Wieser, Boatswain's Mate First Class

"Below decks it was HOT, no air conditioning. Air was taken from topside and blown into the living compartments. At night when you slept in your bunk, you would sweat. Your mattress would get real damp. When you got up the first thing you did was cover up your mattress with a fireproof cover. This would be almost airtight, and after a few weeks your bunk became pretty ripe. At first chance the ship would air bedding. You would take your bedding topside and air it tied to the lifelines. I had a large air duct alongside my bunk. I cut a small hole in it and fitted a piece of a tin can to divert some air onto me. It helped."

— William Taylor, Boatswain's Mate First Class

"I hated the troughs that we were forced to sit over for relieving ourselves. Not only were we embarrassed sitting on the slats, elbow to elbow, but we also suffered from flaming newspaper floated down the stream by pranksters. Occasionally someone would open wide the valve flushing the trough and we would get a rear end wash."

— Paul Marko, Machinist's Mate Second Class

clang! clang! clang! of the general alarm bell and the spine-tingling words: "General Quarters! General Quarters! All hands, man your battle stations!" Then came the General Quarters bugle call. Running feet pounded on the decks throughout the ship, watertight doors and hatches were slammed shut, setting material condition Zed. Fumbling with life jackets and helmets, the men with exposed battle stations hurried topside. To avoid collisions, those going up or forward stayed on the starboard side, those going down or aft stayed to port. Electric motors whirred as gun crews tested the elevation and train of their weapons. Metal rattled against metal as clips and drums of 40-mm and 20-mm ammunition were thrust into place, ready for firing.

On the bridge, in the darkness of the crowded pilothouse, talkers wearing headphones beneath over-sized helmets reported to the officer of the deck: "Engineering Department manned and ready, sir." "Gunnery Department manned and ready, sir." "Combat manned and ready, sir," etc. Usually, within five minutes after the alarm sounded, the officer of the deck could report to the captain, "The ship is manned and ready for action, sir." "Very well," was the calm reply of the captain. The "Old Man," in helmet and life jacket like everyone else, was usually hunched in his leather-bound chair in the starboard forward corner of the pilothouse, peering warily into the darkness ahead.

 0435-0535 – General Quarters Drills. These drills varied at the discretion of department heads and division officers, but were intended to exercise the crew in their duties in battle. For instance, the main battery was exercised by tracking other ships in our task force, as though they were enemy battleships. The 5-inch battery was drilled by the tracking friendly ships or aircraft. The guns of both batteries were trained and elevated accordingly. One at a time, the 5-inch gun crews were sent to the practice-loading machine on the 01 level to hone their skill at rapid loading. Meanwhile, damage control personnel drilled at repairing battle damage, fire-fighting, counter-flooding to correct list, etc. Doctors and corpsmen practiced treating battle casualties.

NATIONAL ARCHIVES 80-G-12265

Is this a peaceful sunrise over the South Pacific, with the crew still sound asleep and the ship harmless? Hardly. This deceptively placid scene was repeated during the hour before sunrise most mornings throughout World War II. Photograph was taken during a routine dawn alert, with all hands at battle stations and every gun ready to open fire on a moment's notice.

 0535 – Sunrise. Secure from General Quarters. Set Readiness Condition Three and Material Condition "Yoke." Light ship. Light the smoking lamp. Readiness Condition Three meant that one-third of the guns were manned. Material Condition Yoke meant that most watertight doors and hatches above the third deck were opened, as was ventilation. Light ship meant that, whereas no external lights had been permitted during the night, that restriction was now lifted. Likewise, "Light the smoking lamp" meant that smoking in designated safe areas, which had been prohibited during the night, was now permitted.

Wide awake by now and hungry as lions, the men eagerly welcomed the opportunity to leave their battle stations, stow their helmets and life jackets, wash up and get ready for breakfast. Skeleton galley crews had been excused early from General Quarters in order to prepare the food.

 0600 – Breakfast for the crew. The enlisted men, other than chief petty officers, were fed cafeteria-style from the main galley. The menu typically varied between scrambled or fried eggs,

hash, or creamed dried beef on toast. Often as not the crew enjoyed ham, bacon or sausage with breakfast. Usually hotcakes, toast or biscuits were offered, along with fried potatoes or grits and cereals. The crew sat on folding benches at folding tables, stowed in overhead brackets when not in use. The chiefs had similar menus, but with meals served to them in their own private quarters, with tables, chairs and china.

During periods of combat with the crew at battle stations at meal time, all hands, including the officers, were fed nothing but dry luncheon meat sandwiches and coffee at their stations during lulls in the fighting.

 0700 – Breakfast for officers in the wardroom. The wardroom breakfast menu most often included eggs to order with the usual side dishes of bacon, ham, grits or hash browns. Of course, in all messes coffee was abundant, as were various canned fruit juices. Unlike the enlisted men, the officers paid for their food with a mess bill that might average around $1.00 per day, no great bargain in that era. The money thus credited to the supply officer's accounts enabled the officers to enjoy a few extras. Meanwhile, the captain was served breakfast by his personal steward's mate who brought it to the

"When someone did something that deserved punishment but was not considered serious enough to warrant a court-martial, there were numerous ways to see that military justice was served. The division first class petty officer [appointed administrative leader] could sentence you to extra duty or hold your liberty card [so you couldn't go ashore]. Next up the ladder would be the division officer who could sentence you likewise, but the extra duty might be more severe, and it was he who decided whether you needed to go up to exec's mast. If the offense was this serious, the executive officer was likely to take you up for captain's mast. The captain had a variety of punishments to choose from, including the following: withholding of liberty, leave and/or pay; extra duty; reduction in rating; confinement in the brig or in the brig with bread and water; or even discharge from the Navy. The captain was the ultimate law and [in those days] there was no appeal. His decision was final."

— Paul Wieser, Boatswain's Mate First Class

0800 – Muster on station. Turn to, ships work. Sick Call. "Muster on station" meant that each division petty officer carried out an on-the-job roll call to make sure all assigned men were present in order to ascertain whether anyone was missing overboard or shirking duty. "Ship's work" meant whatever routine work was then in progress within each division, such as cleaning, painting, repairing equipment or machinery, swabbing decks, cleaning gun barrels, lubricating machinery, schooling those eligible for promotion, etc. For "Sick Call" the ship's medical officers and corpsmen were in the sick bay (hospital spaces), standing by to render appropriate care.

bridge on a tray. Likewise, the navigator was served breakfast on the bridge by a wardroom steward's mate. These two officers never left the bridge when the ship was at sea in the combat area, as they were duty-bound to be at their posts in order to respond promptly to any emergency. Both slept in their small sea cabins located toward the rear of the bridge.

The captain lived a lonely life, with rare breaks in the monotony of reading in his sea cabin or sitting in his leather-upholstered chair in the pilothouse, while sternly overseeing the performance of the officer of the deck. The latter normally conned (maneuvered) the ship, subject of course to any orders of the captain. There was no banter, no levity, in the captain's presence. His rare personal contact with enlisted men other than those on watch on the bridge took place about once a week when he held mast (court) over men who had been placed on report for misbehavior. In disciplining these cases, often sentencing men to fines, reduction in rating or confinement in the brig, the captain's word was law. Hence, to most of the crew he was about as distant and omnipotent as God.

"We had 'sick call' every morning. The bugler sounded sick call and the word was passed over the 1MC. If you needed to go, you notified your division petty officer and then you reported to sick bay. A pharmacist's mate wrote up your complaint and either took care of you or referred you to one of the ship's four doctors. One time my gums were infected. After I was treated, I went for a follow-up exam and the doctor asked me about my tonsils. I said they seemed fine. The doctor asked me if I got colds and when I said sometimes, the doctor said, 'Let's take out your tonsils.' So he did, using a local anesthetic. I remember hearing the scissors cut them out."

— Paul Wieser, Boatswain's Mate First Class

"We received shots constantly. Every time we moved into a new area we had to get injected! There were always long lines. Lots of guys would faint. There was this one pharmacist's mate [corpsman] who would stand several feet away from the person and throw the needle like a dart. One after another, each guy would be instructed to lie face down on the table and he would toss it at their bottoms. He was really good. He never missed."

— Dante Renta, Seaman First Class

While the main wartime role of the captain was to be on the bridge at all times ready for any emergency, the executive officer, second in command, actually ran the ship in almost every other way. In addition to directing the daily routine through the Plan of the Day, he assigned duties to all officers other than specialists (doctors, dentists, chaplains, etc.). He moderated any disputes among the different departments. He previewed disciplinary cases before bringing them to the attention of the captain. He supervised the preparation of official correspondence, sparing the captain from as much minor detail as possible. He was the person most actively responsible for morale. He kept the captain posted on all important developments affecting the ship's combat readiness. From his battle station in Batt Two, he was ready to assume command of the ship should the captain be disabled. Of course the captain, who bore ultimate responsibility for everything that went right or wrong on the ship, could countermand any order of the exec.

 0830 – The six deck divisions each send a 10-man working party to the galley to break out stores. This was a frequent occurrence, to provide enough food for such a large crew of young men who were always hungry. The stores to be brought up from refrigerators and storerooms far down in the bowels of the ship routinely included frozen meats, eggs, butter, flour, potatoes, rice, canned goods or (when available) fresh fruits and vegetables. (See typical provisions inventory, p. 63.)

Life aboard...

"Drill, drill, drill until you are blue in the face; in the daylight; in the dark. You know, General Quarters in the middle of the night. Darken ship. You knew where all the steps were on the ladders. You knew where all the instructions were. In fact, you could tell how old the people were aboard ship because if they had beat up heads and scraped shins, they hadn't been here too long."

— John Van Sambeek, Boatswain's Mate Third Class

 0900 – Set Condition One (battle stations) in the antiaircraft battery for AA firing practice. This was a live firing exercise, the targets being unmanned drone aircraft, cloth sleeves (similar to windsocks) towed by manned aircraft, or merely shell bursts at surprise locations in the sky.

 1100 – Secure from (terminate) AA firing practice. Pipe sweepers. For the latter event, the word passed by the boatswain's mate was "Sweepers man your brooms; clean sweep down fore and aft, all decks and ladders." This was normal daily routine, but was particularly necessary after a live firing to dispose of the scattered residue of burnt gunpowder and cork wadding (used as cushions between 5-inch projectiles and powder charges).

Life aboard...

"'Mail call' was probably the favorite of any sailor aboard any ship in the United States Navy during World War II or any other war. When you heard that call you also heard a roar go up, and everyone would run to his division berthing space while each mail call petty officer would run down and get the mail and start calling out everybody's name. I don't think there was anything that beat this! I especially remember Christmas of 1944, when one of my boxes that cookies came in was so burnt that we couldn't eat the cookies. We figured that one of the ships carrying the mail was bombed or torpedoed and they managed to save some of the things."

— Robert Palomaris, Gunner's Mate First Class

 1130 – Dinner for the crew. The crew was usually offered a substantial meal at mid-day, hence the following are a few of the typical menu items: fried or roasted chicken, turkey, baked ham, wieners and sauerkraut, spaghetti and meat balls, corned beef and cabbage, beef and vegetable stew, etc. Pie, cake or fruit (most often canned) were the usual desserts.

Life aboard...

"The first person served from the crew's mess was the officer of the deck, or when we were at sea, the junior OOD. He had to come down and look at the chow and eat it, as a test. If it was suitable to him, then the chow line started. We ate very well on here. We had fresh baked goods all the time; pies and cakes and jelly doughnuts. We had ice cream all the time. We ate better than at home. This ship fed very well considering the number of crew we had and how rarely we were in port for supplies. We were feeding 2,000 or more men three meals a day. The chow line would take about two hours altogether to feed, and that's including the early watch, the regular crew and the watch coming off duty."

— Herbert Sisco, Ship's Cook Second Class

 1200 – Lunch for officers in the wardroom. The officers, most of whom were a few years older than the average enlisted man, generally preferred a lighter meal at lunch. This was especially true when the ship was in the tropics, as was the case for most of World War II. Thus, typical lunch items in the wardroom might include soup and sandwiches, cold cuts of meat with potato salad or chicken salad; when available fresh fruit salad with assorted cheeses; pudding or cobbler for dessert. Iced tea was always available, along with the Navy's ubiquitous coffee.

 1300 (1:00 p.m.) – Turn to, ship's work. The summary court-martial in the case of Sailor, John Q., BM3, will convene in the warrant officers' mess. This mess was a private and convenient place for a court to hold forth and was often used for that purpose. Naval justice in those days provided four levels of formal jurisprudence. In order of severity and levels of punishment, they were captain's mast, deck court, summary court-martial, and general court-martial. At mast, the captain would either award minor punishment for minor offenses, or he could refer more serious cases to one of the higher courts.

 1330 – Rig to fuel destroyers alongside, port and starboard. This was a common occurrence, since destroyers carried far less fuel than battleships and "topping off" their tanks was necessary every three or four days. When a destroyer was alongside with the Showboat's hoses delivering the oil, her band was usually on deck serenading with popular "Big Band" music. As a further bonus for a smaller ship which did not have the means to produce ice cream, the battleship sent over to the destroyer by highline (similar to a breeches buoy) enough gallons of ice cream (made in a special machine from powdered milk) to treat the destroyer's entire crew of over 300 men. Needless to say, this added up to a festive, foot-tapping occasion for men otherwise usually bored stiff. Better yet was mail from home, usually delivered by a refueling destroyer.

BATTLESHIP COLLECTION 98.1.55

BATTLESHIP COLLECTION 98.2.34

Fueling while underway occurred frequently throughout the war. When the battleship's fuel ran low, a tanker was always available to fill her up again. Every three or four days NORTH CAROLINA, herself, served as a source of fuel for short-legged destroyers.

"We made out good in the laundry. We had a system for all of the money that came out of the clothes that were being washed. We would put all the money in one place, and at the end of the week, we'd divide it – kind of like a tip. We also had hot baths in the laundry. We would put water in the washer and take a bath. Some guy would play a trick on you and push the button – you might go round and round a couple of times before they would let you out. We did a good job with the butchers' and the bakers' clothes. We put creases in their dungarees and shirts. They looked better than the rest of the crew. In return, they brought us meat, pies and cakes."

— William Jenkins, Seaman Second Class, Laundryman

"They had a machine down there that would tear the buttons off your shirts and shoot them through your socks."

— Lieutenant (jg) Ralph Sheffer, Fighter Director Officer

 1500 – All officers not on watch assemble in the wardroom to censor mail. This was required at least once a week throughout the war. The purpose, of course, was to eliminate any violations of wartime security, such as mention of the ship's whereabouts, future movements, battle casualties, etc. The ship's mail clerks would bring to the wardroom several huge bags of unsealed letters, which they piled on the tables before the seated officers. Scissors, together with black ink and small brushes to blot out forbidden references, were provided at each table. The task was necessary, but hated by every officer as well as by every crewmember whose letters to wives or sweethearts (occasionally both) were sometimes left almost meaningless.

 1600 – Secure from ship's work. Pipe sweepers.

 1630 – Supper for the crew. Again the menu for the crew was substantial, but not exactly gourmet cuisine. Meat and potatoes were staples; desserts might include pie, cake or fruit. As a rule, the only extended period of relaxation for the crew was during the period after their supper meal and before the daily alert at sunset. Most of the men used this time to shower and shave, with strict orders to use a minimum of precious fresh water. With dozens of men waiting in line at the washrooms, the rules were "wet down, turn it off, soap up, rinse off, and get out." In good weather during this period, if the band had not already played it was often put to work topside, its relaxing rhythms greatly enjoyed by everyone on board. Writing letters home also occupied many of the men after supper, as did card games, bull sessions, hobbies, mending clothing and studying for advancement in rating.

"Modesty? I don't recall any modesty. There was no modesty on a ship with 2,300 sailors... certainly not in the communal shower rooms where sailors must hang out to get clean. Every sailor knows the scene — naked guys with towels draped around their necks, drooped over arms or tied around the waist, clad only in clodhoppers, carrying a toiletry bag. Often there was no hot water."

— Gordon Knapp, Yeoman First Class

"Sometimes the evaporators would go haywire, and 'salt water showers only' would be announced. You could either choose to take a cold salt-water shower or wait. At the worst, it could be two days before there was fresh water, but most likely the problem was fixed within 24 hours. Regular soap did not work on salt water showers. There were huge bricks of soap especially made for salt water. This was the same soap used for washing hammocks out on the main deck. We perfumed ourselves up like we were going somewhere, but we were really 5,000 miles from nowhere."

— Charles Paty, Jr., Radioman Second Class

"My recollection of all my ships, you know I served on a lot of ships...but the NORTH CAROLINA, honestly, was the happiest ship I ever served on. I think it was because of the officers, because everything starts at the top. We had a taut, happy ship."

— Douglas Blancheri, Chief Yeoman

1730 – Sunset. General Quarters for the routine dusk alert. Darken ship. As was done before sunrise, the ship's company was summoned to battle stations for a period of one hour following sunset, in order to be prepared for a surprise attack. "Darken ship" meant that all portholes, doors and hatches leading topside were to be closed so that no lights were left visible on the exterior of the ship.

 1830 – Secure from General Quarters. Muster the lifeboat crew. Dinner in the wardroom. A lifeboat crew was always on standby, ready to be launched in a hurry should there be a man overboard.

Dinner for the officers was announced by a wardroom steward's mate sounding the tune of the bugle call, "Mess Gear," on a small xylophone over the 1MC. As with the crew, this meal usually offered a filling, meat-and-potatoes menu. Another favorite, popular in wardrooms throughout the Navy, was curried chicken, lamb, beef or shrimp, accompanied by the many spicy condiments usually served in Southeast Asia. This type of food reflected the experience of many U.S. naval officers who had served in the pre-war Asiatic Fleet.

Dinner was the only meal at which there was formality in the wardroom. On ordinary evenings when there was nothing in particular to celebrate, the formality simply required that all officers be standing at their places on time, awaiting the arrival of the president of the mess, the executive officer. Upon his arrival, he nodded to the chaplain, who said grace, following which all took their seats. At the conclusion of the meal no one smoked until senior officers at the head table had lighted up, and no one left his place until the executive officer did so.

On special occasions, such as Christmas, New Year's Day, Independence Day, Navy Day, Thanksgiving, etc., provided that enemy action was not deemed likely, the wardroom took on a modestly festive atmosphere. A combo from the ship's band played light airs in one corner of the room, while small lamps on the tables created a semblance of candlelight. These amenities, coupled with the starched white tablecloths, napkins and jackets of the steward's mates, gave the wardroom the feel of an upscale stateside restaurant or night club. The crew's mess also celebrated such occasions with a sumptuous feast, such as roast turkey with all the trimmings. These events were greatly enjoyed by all hands.

A few middle grade and senior officers await dinner in the wardroom, left to right: Lieutenant David G. Barkin, Air Defense Officer; Lieutenant Theodore T. Frankenberg, Assistant Engineer Officer; Commander Kemp Tolley, Navigator; Commander Thomas H. Morton, Gunnery Officer; Lieutenant Arthur Moore, Jr., Assistant Damage Control Officer; Lieutenant Commander John N. Gerber, Assistant Engineer Officer; Commander Robert C. Boyden, Medical Officer. Photograph dates from January 1945.

Dining in the wardroom on this special occasion are, left to right, Commander Kemp Tolley, Navigator; newly arrived Captain Oswald S. Colclough; departing Captain Frank G. Fahrion; Commander Harold S. Harnly, Executive Officer; Commander Emil F. Redman, Chaplain; and Lieutenant Commander Widmer C. Hansen, Assistant Gunnery Officer. The two captains were guests of the wardroom January 26, 1945, coincident with the change of command. The captain dined in the wardroom only when invited.

BATTLESHIP COLLECTION 80.12.26

Life aboard...

"Holiday chow aboard one of these ships was unbelievable. There is nothing nearer and dearer to a sailor's heart than plenty to eat. Good food: pumpkin pie, roast turkey, ham, steaks, mashed potatoes and gravy. Everybody complained about the food, but it was fairly good. They ate plenty of it. Anyway, here comes our big Thanksgiving chow. About 5:00, they started serving. At 5:15, we got contact on the radar, 'Hostile planes approaching.' Sounded air defense. Everybody jumped up and left their beautiful chow sitting in front of them to go to battle stations. The cooks have to secure their area.

All the food went in the garbage. A half hour later we secured from General Quarters. The plane didn't come in. They got ready to serve chow again. More enemy planes coming in. They threw it out the second time. We stayed at General Quarters until just short of 10:00 that night. Finally, we opened enough doors so that the mess cooks could get through to the galley and prepare battle rations. Battle rations were buckets with a piece of bread, lunchmeat, bread. Bread, lunchmeat, bread. Bread, lunchmeat, bread."

— Donald Wickham, Musician Second Class

1900 – Movies for the crew. With only one print usually available, the film was shown one reel at a time, first in a starboard mess hall, then in a port mess hall, spaces into which only a small percent of the crew could be crammed. Despite the heat and stale air, the movie always played to a full house and was viewed by most crewmembers as a welcome escape from the realities of war.

 1955 – Eight O'Clock Reports. Department heads lined up outside the executive officer's quarters, where he heard each officer affirm that all was secure for the night in his department. Movies in the wardroom followed. On the bridge, where the captain had usually retired to his sea cabin, his marine orderly knocked at his door before carrying out the following time-honored ritual: "Sir, the officer of the deck reports eight o'clock, galley fires are out, chronometers have been wound, request permission to strike eight bells." "Make it so" was the Old Man's response. Thereupon, the boatswain's mate of the watch struck eight bells. This ritual, dating back 150 years in the U.S. Navy, was designed partly to remind the crew of the captain's omnipotence, even to confirming the time of day.

 2200 – Taps. Just before taps, the chaplain's voice came over the 1MC with a short prayer for the safety and well-being of the ship, its officers and men and their loved ones at home. The following words were then passed over the 1MC by the boatswain's mate of the watch: "Lights out. The smoking lamp is out. All hands maintain silence about the decks." Taps was then sounded by the bugler over the 1 MC.

Life aboard...

"Routine [for the signal gang] was to bring your mattress up from the bunk down below because nobody wanted to get caught below if we got torpedoed. We slept up on the signal bridge. Every once in a while you'd wake up in a puddle. It would rain in on you."

— Jackson Belford, Signalman Third Class

"When I came off watch at midnight, I'd get a blanket and a pillow and go up by the forward 16-inch guns and sleep on the deck until it was time to go on watch again. That's the only way you could stay cool."

— Ortho Farrar, Machinist's Mate First Class

"The trick was to take a shower and get quietly in your bunk. Even though the temperature in the ship might be 100 degrees, you'd go to bed before you started sweating again, to get at least a half hour sleep before you'd wake up again from the sweat."

— Leo Neumann, Machinist's Mate First Class

"A lot of times you'd be very tired and you'd get very little sleep. You'd lie down as soon as you could get a break. I'd hang my arms over the gun's shield and just doze off. I could go to sleep standing up."

— Ollie Goad, Seaman First Class

Life aboard...

"When you went to battle stations, you had to have shoes, socks, trousers, your dungaree shirt on especially. You must remember that at Pearl Harbor most of the men died from flash burns from explosions. You would have to have your shirts long-sleeved to give you protection from flashing guns or explosions, to keep you from being burned. We dyed our white hats blue so they wouldn't be quite so easy to see from the air. The wood deck was painted blue also. What you would do if you weren't completely naked is grab your clothes and get up there and dress at your battle station as best you could. We took pride in the fact that we used to man the signal bridge so damn quick."

— Jackson Belford, Signalman Third Class

"The average time it took us to set General Quarters was five minutes. I don't know whether you appreciate how fast that is. If General Quarters sounds at 4:30 a.m., the entire ship except the people on watch are in their sacks. You have to get out of bed with men everywhere, put on your clothes, travel probably a city block, up and down a ladder or two, through hatches and then to your battle station. Make sure about all the hatches, the ready boxes, and the gun crew — everything that you have to do to make the ship ready to fight. Fully ready to fight in five minutes is extremely fast."

— Donald Wickham, Musician Second Class

UNIFORM OF THE DAY

Throughout World War II in the Pacific, the uniforms usually prescribed for officers and enlisted men serving on ships in the combat area were as follows: officers and chief petty officers wore washable cotton khaki trousers with matching long-sleeved khaki shirts. They were allowed to wear dungarees and blue chambray shirts when working or standing watch in engineering spaces, or otherwise engaged in work that could stain clothing. They could choose between visored caps or foldable cotton "fore and aft" caps. Enlisted men other than chief petty officers wore dungaree trousers and long-sleeved blue chambray shirts, with the usual sailor's white hat. Toward the end of the war enlisted men's white hats were dyed blue to make them less visible at night.

A TYPICAL INVENTORY OF PROVISIONS

In order to provide an idea of the vast amount of food normally stocked by the ship in its storerooms and reefers (refrigerators), the following list includes selected items from a typical inventory of provisions dated June 20, 1943: 6,954 pounds of fresh apples, 4,459 pounds of bacon, 30,723 pounds of frozen beef, 4,800 pounds of butter, 901 pounds of catsup, 1,000 pounds of cheddar cheese, 3,876 pounds of frozen chicken, 7,699 pounds of canned corn, 15,500 pounds of coffee, 7,620 dozen eggs, 85,612 pounds of wheat flour, 3,591 pounds of canned grapefruit juice, 3,520 pounds of canned orange juice, 7,600 pounds of canned ham, 8,876 pounds of canned luncheon meat, 17,390 pounds of evaporated milk, 2,400 pounds of fresh onions, 8,550 pounds of fresh oranges, 30,000 pounds of Irish potatoes, 5,400 pounds of rice, 5,000 pounds of table salt, 44,200 pounds of granulated sugar, 5,340 pounds of frozen turkey, and the list went on.

WARTIME LIFE AT SEA

Wartime photographs on this and following pages give examples of the many different activities that took place on board the ship on a typical day at sea. Cartoons, the work of Mick Gorman, 4th Division, were taken from the ship's cruise book, *The Showboat*, published at the end of the war.

Abandon ship drill.

The Deck Force

Rigging to fuel a destroyer.

Transfer by highline. Scary!

Scrubba, scrubba, scrubba.

Repairing a cargo net.

*Stowing forecastle gear
after getting underway.*

Loading onions.

Combat Information & Intelligence

Here they come!

Lookout in harness.

Secret intelligence reports.

Shore bombardment plot.

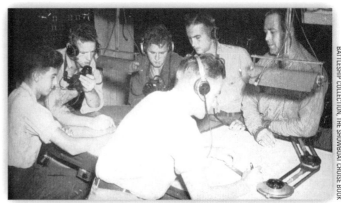

The Gunners

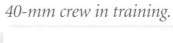

40-mm crew in training.

Gunnery office.

5-inch loading practice.

Firing keys for 16-inch guns.

Inside a 16-inch turret.

Shipboard Recreation

Fish for dinner.

Captain Fahrion with medicine ball and three junior officers.

A quiet Sunday afternoon.

Check!

The brig. Forced R and R.

"Big shots" at the movies.

Bridge Watch

Flashing light.

Roger.

Stand by your bag (flag bag).

Take a bearing.

Engineers & Repairmen

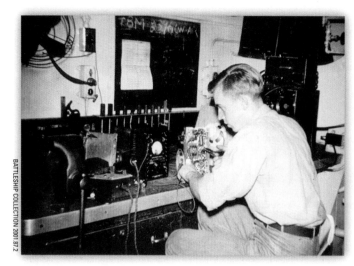

Fixing a radio.

Forward electrical distribution.

Main engine control.

Metalsmiths.

Machine shop.

Chow

Dinner in the wardroom.

Chopping the meat.

Chow line.

Loading stores.

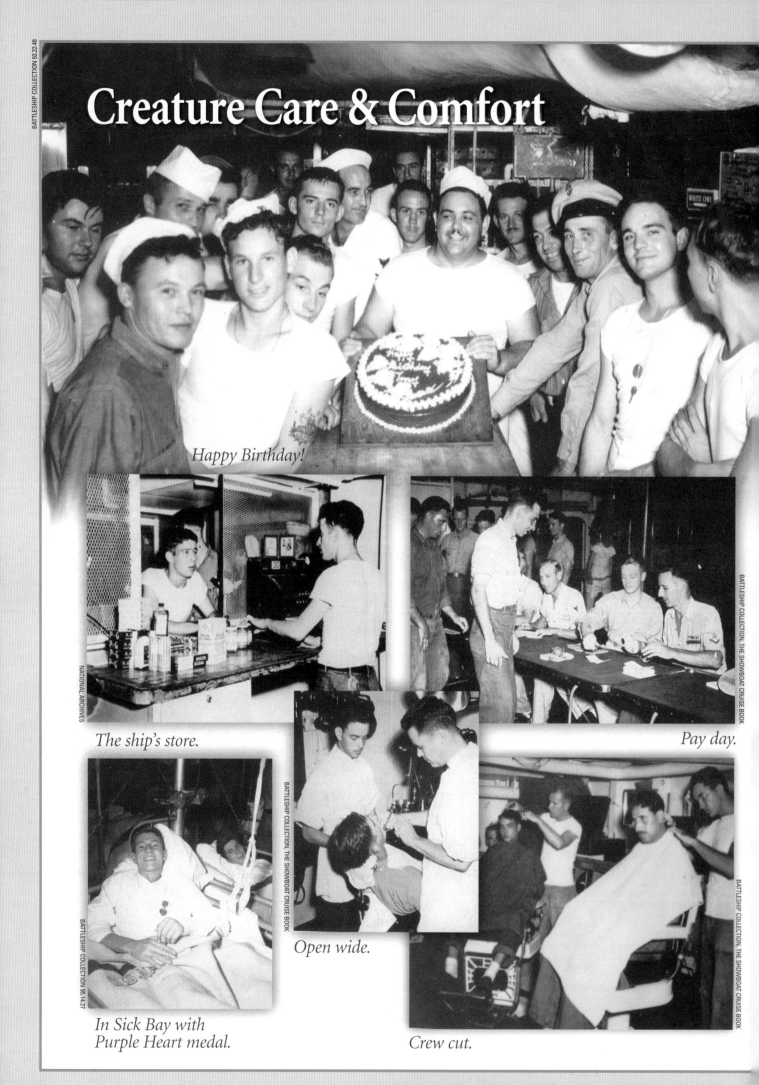

Creature Care & Comfort

Happy Birthday!

The ship's store.

Pay day.

Open wide.

In Sick Bay with Purple Heart medal.

Crew cut.

Entertainment, Mostly Home Grown

Mostly teenagers, the crew tried hard not to reveal their fears and their longing for home. They yearned to laugh, have fun and help each other forget the war, if only for a few carefree minutes.

Sexy strippers.

A "smoker" with boxing matches.

Comedian Joe E. Brown entertains.

BB-55 band entertains ashore.

Talented trippers.

Curtain call.

Foldout map of

Pacific Ocean

NORTH CAROLINA'S OPERATIONS DURING WWII

PRELUDE TO COMBAT
December 1941-July 1942

The epic story of USS NORTH CAROLINA in the Pacific Theater of World War II — a story filled with the flames and smoke of battle — reads almost like the history of the war itself. From her arrival in the Pacific Theater of war in July 1942 until the very end of the conflict, the Showboat fought in every major campaign: from Guadalcanal in the Solomon Islands, through the Gilberts, Marshalls, Carolines, New Guinea, the Marianas, the Philippines, Iwo Jima and Okinawa, to the shores of Japan and finally to victory in Tokyo Bay.

The Japanese sneak attack on Pearl Harbor, Sunday, December 7, 1941, found NORTH CAROLINA and her crew in port for the weekend at the New York Navy Yard, shakedown training not yet completed. Within minutes after initial word of the attack came crackling over the radio, the Showboat's duty officers began recalling all hands from liberty and shore leave to ready the ship for war. For the few senior officers who could be told the awful truth — that eight U.S. Pacific Fleet battleships had been sunk or severely damaged in Pearl Harbor — came as a profound shock. For NORTH CAROLINA in particular, the full implications of this blow to our battle line strength were staggering. What odds would the Showboat now face when sent out to defend America against the Imperial Japanese Navy?

One of the first reactions of NORTH CAROLINA's pugnacious skipper, now Captain Oscar C. Badger, was to pound on the desk of the Navy yard commander and demand that 100 new 20-mm automatic antiaircraft guns be installed on his ship at once. Forty of the rapid-fire Oerlikons were promptly mounted on the Showboat, with additional men ordered on board to man them. Gunnery drills and target practice became almost full-time preoccupations for most of the crew as the ship hurried through final tests of her engineering plant and readied herself for battle.

Life aboard...

"We were in the Brooklyn Navy Yard. I was boatswain's mate of the watch and had the duty of passing the word that we were at war. We soon got the word, bogies [unidentified aircraft] approaching, and we went to General Quarters. We had ammunition in the 5-inch mounts. We got the word to 'Stand by.' We'd heard that many times before in our drills. Our next order would have been 'Commence firing!' Just then, we got the word to rest easy; the plane was a 'friendly.'"

— Paul Wieser, Boatswain's Mate First Class

"December 7, 1941, I was at home in Jersey City and planned to take my mother to a New York City movie. The radio had a bulletin about Pearl Harbor. Details were sketchy and we proceeded to take the bus to New York. As we exited the movie, it was dark and people came up to me and said, 'You better get back to your ship, sailor.' I took my mother to the bus depot and then returned to the Brooklyn Navy Yard. I remember distinctly my surprise when two guards with rifles accosted me as I walked to the ship. Things had changed."

— Larry Resen, Fire Controlman First Class

"December 7, 1941. I had the duty this weekend and was asleep in my top bunk when the word came. 'This is not a drill. The Japanese have bombed Pearl Harbor. We are in a state of war.' We went to General Quarters and started setting up guard posts throughout the ship. I was given a .45-caliber automatic pistol and duty belt and stood watch outside a lower 5-inch handling room. Some of our crew patrolled the opening to the Navy yard in our launches, watching for anything suspicious. I had no idea where Pearl Harbor was, and knew little about the Japanese. I soon learned.

"Before Pearl Harbor, the public didn't have too good an opinion of a sailor. Even my girlfriend's mother didn't trust me after I joined. But Monday when I headed home, I couldn't put a nickel in the fare box. I was being treated like a hero. What a difference a war made. My family didn't expect me and they were all gathered as if they wouldn't see me again till the war was over. When I walked in you would have thought I'd been gone for years. 'Home the Hero.'"

— William Taylor, Boatswain's Mate First Class

Meanwhile, in the Pacific the remnants of our fleet were engaged in a desperate struggle for survival. After Pearl Harbor, the odds between the two opposing sea forces were overwhelmingly in favor of the Imperial Japanese Navy (IJN), a tough, well-trained and fiercely aggressive opponent. Unfortunately, before the war most American Navy men did not believe this. Even after the Pearl Harbor attack, many stereotyped the Japanese as myopic, buck-toothed copiers of Western technology with neither the originality nor the technical know-how to fight their ships effectively. This, the author has suspected, was due in part to deliberate deception — to the pre-war tendency of IJN naval officers to feign inferiority when in contact with Americans, such as when mingling with each other in foreign ports. They wanted us to be overconfident. The truth was that the pre-war IJN trained and exercised much more aggressively than did the USN, taking chances at dangerously high speeds as normal routine in night battle practice. Even if the odds had not been altered by the Pearl Harbor attack, their fleet was in every important branch, including the air arm and all ship types — in gunnery, navigation, ship handling, strategy, tactics and fighting spirit — a world-class adversary. But that wasn't all.

The IJN began the war with 10 aircraft carriers and 12 battleships, while the U.S. Pacific Fleet, until reinforced later, included only three carriers and, thanks to the Pearl Harbor disaster, only one operational battleship too slow to keep up with the carriers, USS COLORADO (BB-45), which happened to be undergoing overhaul at Bremerton, Washington, when the Japanese attacked. The three aircraft carriers in our Pacific Fleet as of December 1941 were LEXINGTON (CV-2), SARATOGA (CV-3) and ENTERPRISE (CV-6). ("CV" stood for aircraft carrier; the numbers following meant the second, third and sixth carriers ever built by the U.S. Navy.) By the end of January 1942, YORKTOWN (CV-5) plus three old and slow battleships, NEW MEXICO (BB-40), MISSISSIPPI (BB-41) and IDAHO (BB-42), had been transferred to the Pacific from the Atlantic; but the IJN still retained a strong numerical advantage.

As an inevitable consequence of these odds, the relentless advance across a vast Pacific domain by Japanese invasion forces defined the first six months of the war. They seized Wake Island, Guam, the Philippines, Indo-China, Borneo, Singapore, Malaya, the Dutch East Indies, the Gilbert Islands, Nauru and Rabaul (see foldout map). In the face of this onslaught, our thin line of ships could offer little more than hit-and-run tactics and delaying actions. It was tough going. Small, hastily improvised task groups, usually composed of a single aircraft carrier screened by a handful of rusty old cruisers and destroyers, were kept at sea sometimes for more than a hundred days at a time, without rest for the men or upkeep for the ships. There were occasions when they returned from sea without a morsel of food left on board, having rationed their dwindling supplies of rice, dehydrated eggs, potatoes and wormy flour until the last meager meal before entering port. The gaunt men waited anxiously — desperately — for help to arrive from the States, but America had been caught unprepared for war, and reinforcements were many months in coming.

DEMANDS OF THE ATLANTIC THEATER OF WAR VS. THE PACIFIC

The gravity of the situation in the Pacific was fully understood in Washington, but the demands of war against Germany in the Atlantic were considered more urgent. Early in 1942 the Navy Department had prepared orders which would have sent NORTH CAROLINA at full speed to the Pacific. However, the move was held up and the ship kept in the Atlantic for several more months so she would be on hand to fight the new German battleship, TIRPITZ, should that powerful ship be sent out to prey on convoys from America to Britain. Meanwhile, sister ship WASHINGTON, whose commissioning and shakedown had followed closely behind those of NORTH CAROLINA, was actually sent across the Atlantic to operate with the British Home Fleet protecting Allied convoys on the dangerous run to Murmansk on the Arctic coast of the Soviet Union.

Then in May came better news from the Pacific when Navy fliers from our carriers LEXINGTON and YORKTOWN halted a Japanese advance into the

USS NORTH CAROLINA entering Pearl Harbor November 18, 1942, after two days at sea to test 40-mm guns, installed following repairs to her torpedo damage.

region of the Coral Sea, dangerously close to our ally, Australia. One month later, thanks in large measure to the deciphering of secret Japanese naval communications codes by U.S. Navy cryptologists, a brilliant victory was achieved over a numerically superior Japanese invasion force attempting to seize Midway Island, at the northwestern end of the Hawaiian Islands. In this action, Navy pilots from carriers ENTERPRISE, YORKTOWN and HORNET (CV-8) — the latter newly arrived from the Atlantic — stopped the enemy cold, sinking four of their aircraft carriers. Another Japanese carrier had been sunk at Coral Sea, while we lost carriers LEXINGTON at Coral Sea and YORKTOWN at Midway. These two clashes gave the enemy a bloody nose and took some of the momentum out of his offensive, but the odds were still stacked heavily against the United States, and the outlook was grim.

ARRIVAL OF BATTLESHIP NORTH CAROLINA AT PEARL HARBOR
July 11, 1942

Late on the afternoon of July 11, 1942, the crews of the few old battle-scarred ships present in Pearl Harbor witnessed one of the most stirring sights of their lives. From the signal tower high above the harbor, sailors on watch sighted an unfamiliar giant of a ship with a tower foremast approaching the harbor entrance. Signal lights flashed and semaphore flags snapped in the wind, passing the news to all ships present. As the word was shouted down the hatches, hundreds of men surged topside, crowding the upper decks of every ship for a better view. What those men saw gliding majestically into the ravaged harbor, around Ford Island, past the charred wreckage of battleship ARIZONA, to her berth in the navy yard, was to them the most beautiful battleship in the world — evidence that America, the sleeping giant, had at last awakened. Morale of the fleet soared.

THE SHOWBOAT'S ARRIVAL AS SEEN FROM A TUGBOAT AND A CRUISER

"July 11, 1942, I was stationed aboard a fleet tug when NORTH CAROLINA arrived at the entrance to the channel of Pearl Harbor. We were to meet her, along with four other tugs. I was 19 years old and this was the first major man-of-war we had seen. After the devastation of Pearl Harbor and our losses at Coral Sea and Midway, NORTH CAROLINA was a godsend. As I stood there on that small tug with 16 other members watching NORTH CAROLINA come down the channel, this beautiful ship and the hundreds of men aboard her brought a ray of hope that we were going to come back. As NORTH CAROLINA sailors and officers on the bridge looked down at us and around the harbor they saw devastation they had never expected. Pictures had been very limited in the news as to what had happened in Pearl. But as we looked up at them, we saw hope."

— Kenneth Dews, Former Chairman,
USS NORTH CAROLINA Battleship Commission

Life aboard...

"The thing I remember most distinctly was the day we arrived at Pearl Harbor. Even with all the movies and pictures you saw, you couldn't appreciate the devastation that had taken place there. As we arrived and I looked at the oil-covered harbor and the broken rows of ships, I choked up. There were all the sailors who had seen nothing but the damage that the Japanese caused here, who had gotten a very sharp kick in the teeth at Pearl Harbor and who had, in the months that followed, lost other ships in battle. And these crews, they cheered and cheered us. I couldn't help saying to myself, 'They're cheering us for nothing.' We hadn't done anything. We had not fired a shot yet. But to them, we were the symbol of help finally arriving in force. It broke me up. I admit to being a misty-eyed 18-year-old."

— Larry Resen, Fire Controlman First Class

"I was then a lieutenant (jg) in the heavy cruiser PENSACOLA (CA-24), moored in Pearl Harbor alongside the cruiser NORTHAMPTON (CA-26). We had recently come in from the Battle of Midway, and though we'd won that battle, the enemy still outnumbered us, and morale was low. Late that afternoon somebody yelled down the hatch to get topside right away because a really big ship was entering port. I rushed up to the signal bridge, where I found most of our crew clustered like birds in a tree, staring eagerly out toward the harbor entrance. All we could see at first above the aircraft hangars on Ford Island was a huge tower foremast. We watched it move slowly around the island until the whole gorgeous thing finally came into full view, and boy what a sight! A great new battleship flying the Stars and Stripes, bristling with guns, her new paintwork and brass glistening in the sunlight, signal flags flapping at her yardarms, her proud crew in whites at quarters. She turned toward us, and as she passed by close astern, a grizzled old chief on board NORTHAMPTON mounted a turret and led his shipmates in a cheer; 'Hip, hip hurrah! Hip, hip hurrah!' We joined in, and the cheering quickly spread to every ship in the harbor. Ashore, workmen in the navy yard poured out of the shops, while doctors, nurses and even wounded men in wheelchairs streamed from the naval hospital. The cheering became a roar that didn't stop until the ship was tied up at Pier 12."

— Author

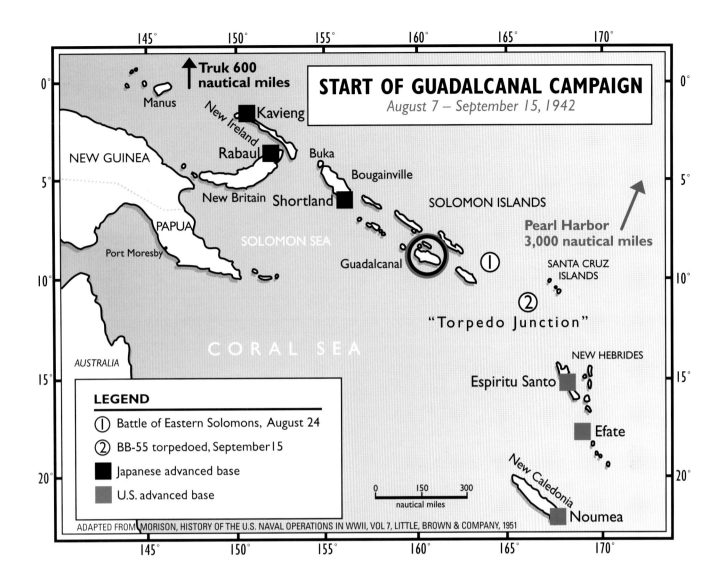

START OF GUADALCANAL CAMPAIGN
August 7 – September 15, 1942

Truk 600 nautical miles

Manus
Kavieng
New Ireland
NEW GUINEA
Rabaul
New Britain
Buka
Bougainville
Shortland
SOLOMON ISLANDS
PAPUA
SOLOMON SEA
Port Moresby
Guadalcanal
Pearl Harbor 3,000 nautical miles
SANTA CRUZ ISLANDS
①
②
"Torpedo Junction"
CORAL SEA
AUSTRALIA
NEW HEBRIDES
Espiritu Santo
Efate
New Caledonia
Noumea

LEGEND
① Battle of Eastern Solomons, August 24
② BB-55 torpedoed, September 15
■ Japanese advanced base
■ U.S. advanced base

0 150 300
nautical miles

ADAPTED FROM MORISON, HISTORY OF THE U.S. NAVAL OPERATIONS IN WWII, VOL 7, LITTLE, BROWN & COMPANY, 1951

START OF THE GUADALCANAL CAMPAIGN
August 7-9, 1942

After the Battles of Coral Sea and Midway, the next move on the part of the United States was to dislodge the enemy from the Solomon Islands in order to eliminate that threat to our sea communications with Australia, and begin the rollback of the Japanese tide. The first step was taken August 7-9 when some 19,000 leathernecks of the 1st Marine Division were landed by the Navy on the previously unheard-of islands of Guadalcanal and Tulagi, located in the southern Solomons (see chart page 82). For this operation NORTH CAROLINA, because of her state of the art antiaircraft battery, was assigned the important task of escorting and protecting our aircraft carriers ENTERPRISE, SARATOGA and WASP (CV-7), the latter recently arrived from the Atlantic.

The landings went off successfully with relatively minor opposition — at first. Cruisers and destroyers supported the marines with gunfire while the carriers provided air support from a distance. The initial absence of any strong enemy reaction was dangerously misleading. The Solomons campaign soon erupted into a fierce and bloody series of battles, both ashore and afloat, in which the U.S. Navy and Marine Corps would experience more fighting than they had seen in all their previous history.

The first of these sea battles was the Battle of Savo Island, a disaster for the United States Navy and its allies. In the early hours of August 9, a column of Japanese cruisers and destroyers raced into what soon became known as "Ironbottom Sound," off the northeast coast of Guadalcanal, sinking five cruisers (four American and one Australian) without losing a single ship of their own. This battle shocked the U.S. Navy almost as much as had the Pearl Harbor attack. Americans had grossly underestimated the fighting ability of the Japanese Navy.

Photograph taken from Sky Control of NORTH CAROLINA shows barrage of 5-inch shell bursts over ENTERPRISE during the Battle of the Eastern Solomons.

BATTLE OF THE EASTERN SOLOMONS
August 24, 1942

For the first two weeks after the landing on Guadalcanal, NORTH CAROLINA missed out on most of the action. Her guns were needed to protect the aircraft carriers, ENTERPRISE and SARATOGA, located southeast of the objective area to minimize unnecessary exposure to the high level of enemy air activity. But such exposure soon became imperative when the Japanese gathered powerful forces for a showdown clash at sea east of the Solomons, coincident with a reinforcement of their troops on Guadalcanal. Three Japanese carriers and three battleships, screened by assorted cruisers and destroyers, made up the force that churned south to destroy the Americans. Two of our own "flattops" (slang for carriers), ENTERPRISE and SARATOGA, escorted by NORTH CAROLINA, cruisers and destroyers, advanced to meet them.

On the afternoon of August 24, 1942, the Showboat was guarding ENTERPRISE when 36 dive-bombers, escorted by many Mitsubishi "Zero" fighters, flashed out of the sun in a fiercely determined attack on our

ships. The volume of the battleship's gunfire was spectacular. During the initial dive-bombing attack on ENTERPRISE, the Showboat's 5-inch guns put up a protective barrage over the carrier which filled the sky above her with bursting shells. Meanwhile, NORTH CAROLINA herself became the target of a rapid series of follow-on attacks by other enemy planes. At one point six dive-bombers were opposed only by 20-mm guns, all other guns on both sides of the ship already engaged. At the height of the battle, with NORTH CAROLINA enveloped in smoke and solid sheets of flame from her own guns, Commander Task Force 16, Rear Admiral Thomas C. Kincaid, embarked in ENTERPRISE, signaled her in alarm, "Are you afire?" Turning and twisting to dodge the bombs, the mighty battlewagon narrowly escaped seven near misses. Credit for this success was due largely to the skillful direction of the ship's antiaircraft gunfire by Air Defense Officer John Kirkpatrick, and to expert ship handling by Navigator Joe W. Stryker, who deftly maneuvered the ship out from under several bombs.

In that first battle of her life, NORTH CAROLINA proved her worth by shooting down seven planes,

"The engagement lasted only seven minutes. It seemed like hours at the time. I remember talking later with the men in my division in the starboard battery. The seamen were manning these machine guns, .50 calibers and 20-mm, and they were the most excited and proud people. They talked like they had knocked down every plane in the sky. We were all claiming to have shot down about 350 aircraft, and really there were only about 75 [sic]. The Japanese suffered a terrible loss that afternoon. But we became men. The maturity of our seamen and our officers after that — the change in maturity and attitude and the way we approached problems — was entirely different. We had grown up in seven minutes."

— Lieutenant Julian Burke, 5-inch Director Officer

"All of a sudden all hell broke loose. You could see these dive-bombers coming down on the ENTERPRISE. It was hit. All of a sudden, the planes were coming our way and attacking us. I think it was just a matter of minutes, a total of about eight minutes of action. It's the old story about it seeming like an eternity. One thing stands out to me very clearly; a Japanese plane that roared by close beside us. This was the first new battleship they had seen out there. He was just staring at it. I could see his face, and I could see his eyes; and he was just trying to get a fix. I think what he wanted to do was hope he would get away and report exactly what the ship looked like. And all of a sudden, he got hit. I think one of our 20-mm got him."

— Larry Resen, Fire Controlman First Class

assisting in shooting down at least seven more, and frustrating the attacks by many others. One sailor was killed by strafing, but the ship was undamaged. This performance is more remarkable when one considers that the Showboat had none of the new 40-mm guns at that time, and the proximity fuze, which would have made her 5-inch battery much more effective, had not yet become available to the fleet. This remarkable fuze (see page 24) was first used in combat when employed with extraordinary success by battleship SOUTH DAKOTA (BB-57) and other ships in the Battle of the Santa Cruz Islands, October 26, 1942.

ENTERPRISE received moderate damage from three bomb hits, but survived to fight on to the end of the war as the most gallant and famous of our carriers. NORTH CAROLINA had unquestionably helped save ENTERPRISE, thus establishing the primary role of all U.S. fast battleships throughout World War II as protectors of aircraft carriers. What's more, our pilots in that battle sank an enemy carrier, the Japanese fleet was turned back, and their intended troop reinforcements did not make it to Guadalcanal.

Photograph taken immediately after the Battle of the Eastern Solomons is of Air Defense Officer Lieutenant Commander John Kirkpatrick, right, and his principal assistant, Fire Controlman First Class Larry Resen. In that battle Kirkpatrick controlled the port antiaircraft batteries, Resen the starboard.

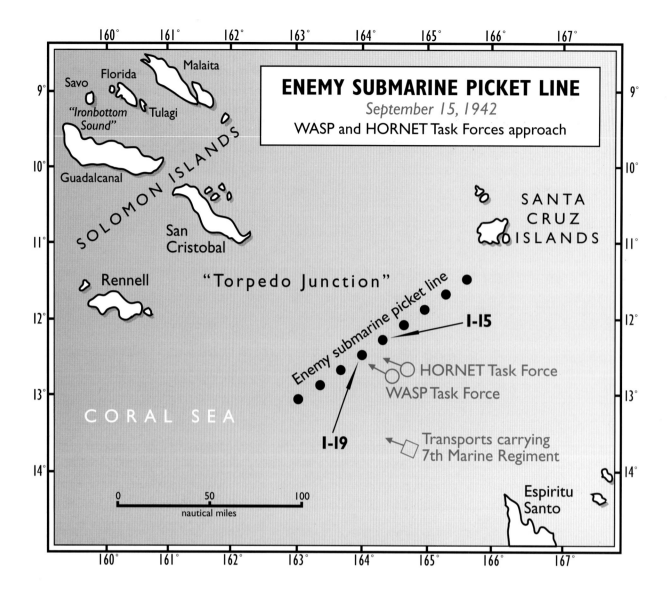

ENEMY SUBMARINE PICKET LINE
September 15, 1942
WASP and HORNET Task Forces approach

Malaita

Florida

Savo

"Ironbottom Sound"

Tulagi

SOLOMON ISLANDS

Guadalcanal

San Cristobal

SANTA CRUZ ISLANDS

Rennell

"Torpedo Junction"

Enemy submarine picket line

I-15

HORNET Task Force

WASP Task Force

I-19

CORAL SEA

Transports carrying 7th Marine Regiment

Espiritu Santo

0   50   100
nautical miles

WASP, NORTH CAROLINA AND O'BRIEN TORPEDOED
September 15, 1942

Following the Battle of the Eastern Solomons, ENTERPRISE was rushed to Pearl Harbor for repairs. NORTH CAROLINA, together with carriers SARATOGA, WASP and escorts, remained in the waters to the south and east of Guadalcanal while covering a continuous movement of transports and cargo ships reinforcing and supplying the marines ashore. American carrier strength on the scene was soon restored to three with the arrival of HORNET (CV-8), but the number was promptly knocked back down to two when a Japanese submarine put a "fish" into "SARA" August 31, placing her out of action for three months. That incident, together with a marked increase in underwater sound contacts and periscope sightings, gave ample warning of more trouble ahead. What the Americans did not know was that nine Japanese submarines were on station in a picket line astride the southeastern approaches to Guadalcanal.

Trouble came in triple measure on the afternoon of September 15, another black day in the history of the U.S. Navy. WASP and HORNET were escorting six transports carrying the 7th Marine Regiment to reinforce marines desperately needing help on Guadalcanal. With the transports on a parallel course over the horizon to the south, the carriers steamed within sight of each other through an area of open sea about 250 miles southeast of "The Canal." Each carrier formed the nucleus of a task force, the two task forces normally separated by seven to 10 nautical miles, as measured between the carriers (see diagram on adjacent page). NORTH CAROLINA was with the HORNET force, northeast of the WASP force. The sky was clear; a 20-knot trade wind blew from the southeast, covering the surface of the sea with whitecaps. Such weather provided good hunting conditions for submarines and dangerous for their prey, since whitecaps cover the wakes created by submarines' periscopes and torpedos.

On board the Showboat, first warning that something was wrong came at 1445 (2:45 p.m.). WASP had just completed a launch and recovery of aircraft during which all ships of both task forces had steamed temporarily on a southeasterly course, into the wind. With flight operations over, all ships commenced a right turn together to resume base course 280 degrees, on their roundabout advance toward Guadalcanal. At the start of this turn, the officer of the deck of NORTH CAROLINA, Lieutenant (jg) Robert J. Celustka, noticed smoke rising from WASP. Peering curiously at the carrier through his binoculars from a distance of about 12,000 yards (six nautical miles), Celustka could see that one of WASP's planes had somehow dropped overboard and was floating nose-down past her stern. This fact, coupled with the absence of any radioed alarm or other emergency signal, led to the false conclusion that an aircraft accident on WASP's flight deck had started a fire, and a burning plane had been pushed over the side to prevent the fire from spreading. Such occurrences were not unusual during wartime flight operations and were no cause for particular apprehension on board other ships.

Two or three minutes passed and still there was no explanation. More and more smoke was now boiling upward from WASP, which was slowing and had stopped her right turn. Violent explosions erupted from the carrier's flight and hangar decks, indicating that fire had probably reached armed aircraft. Although a serious emergency obviously existed, it remained unknown to the hundreds of officers and men anxiously watching from ships of the HORNET force that WASP had been struck on her starboard side (her far side, as viewed from the HORNET force) by three torpedoes, apparently launched from a submarine. The result was severe below-decks damage and raging fires fed by gasoline. All attention remained riveted on the stricken carrier, as the HORNET force, at 18 knots, continued its right turn toward base course, 280 degrees.

Suddenly the tense silence on all ships' bridges was broken by a burst of static from the tactical radio speakers, followed by an incomplete and partly unintelligible message, ". . . torpedo headed for formation, course zero eight zero!" This alarm, it was soon learned, had come from destroyer

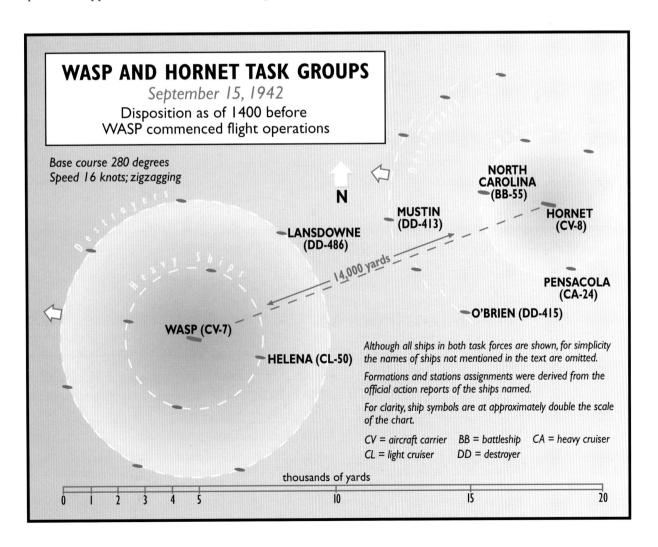

WASP AND HORNET TASK GROUPS
September 15, 1942
Disposition as of 1400 before
WASP commenced flight operations

Base course 280 degrees
Speed 16 knots; zigzagging

N

NORTH
CAROLINA
(BB-55)

MUSTIN
(DD-413)

HORNET
(CV-8)

LANSDOWNE
(DD-486)

14,000 yards

PENSACOLA
(CA-24)

O'BRIEN (DD-415)

WASP (CV-7)

HELENA (CL-50)

Although all ships in both task forces are shown, for simplicity the names of ships not mentioned in the text are omitted.

Formations and stations assignments were derived from the official action reports of the ships named.

For clarity, ship symbols are at approximately double the scale of the chart.

CV = aircraft carrier   BB = battleship   CA = heavy cruiser
CL = light cruiser   DD = destroyer

thousands of yards

0   1   2   3   4   5   10   15   20

Destroyer O'BRIEN is struck by a torpedo while WASP burns in the distance.

LANSDOWNE (DD-486) in WASP's screen. Because of LANSDOWNE's position between the carriers, it could only mean that a torpedo was headed toward the HORNET force. But voice radio was unreliable in those days, and on at least some of the ships, LANSDOWNE's warning was not understood.

Then, at about the time the HORNET force reached and steadied on course 280 degrees, another warning blared from the speakers; but it, too, was tantalizingly incomplete: "...torpedo just passed astern of me, headed for you!" That was all. No identification was heard. Several excited voices speaking at once over the radio made all unintelligible. Emergency signal flags flying at the yardarm of destroyer MUSTIN (DD-413), in HORNET's screen, warned of a torpedo; but just what ship had been meant by "you" remained undetermined. All eyes scanned the white-capped sea for torpedo wakes, but none could be seen until it was too late. Meanwhile, HORNET, whose movements were required to be followed by her escorts, was seen to be turning sharply right, distancing herself from WASP.

"Right full rudder! Emergency flank speed!" shouted Captain George H. Fort, skipper of the Showboat. Engine room blowers quickly whined louder as they speeded up, while vibrations from the propellers shook the ship as they churned faster in the sea. Topside and below decks, the battleship's crew sensed at once that something was wrong, and many began running for their battle stations before the alarm sounded.

To those on the bridge of the ponderous ship, time seemed to stand still as the seconds ticked slowly by on the pilothouse clock. NORTH CAROLINA was just beginning to lean into her turn when a loud explosion boomed from off her port quarter. There a great plume of white spray leaped skyward to completely engulf destroyer O'BRIEN (DD-415), whose bow had just been shattered by a torpedo.

Then at 1452, while NORTH CAROLINA was passing course 295 degrees and beginning to pick up speed, there was an explosion like a thunderclap as a torpedo slammed into her port bow abreast of Turret I. The entire ship suddenly lurched like a bucking bronco. A tower of oil and water shot into the air as high as the stacks, and an immense churning cloud of spray and smoke enveloped the ship's upper works. Tons of water cascaded down over the superstructure and tumbled aft along the decks, washing one man to his death over the side. Below decks, men of the repair parties rushed through acrid yellowish smoke to the scene of damage. There, as was later learned, a hole as big as a large truck had been blasted clear through the side protection below the armor belt. Nearly a thousand tons of water had flooded into the ship.

A CLOSE CALL

Far more serious than flooding was the presence of burning oil from ruptured fuel tanks on the deck of the Turret II projectile room. This posed the horrendous possibility of a magazine explosion which would have destroyed the ship in an instant and killed most if not all of the crew. Fortunately, quick-thinking members of the turret crew turned on the magazine sprinkling system in time to put out the fire.

The task force commander, Rear Admiral George D. Murray in HORNET, led his ships through two consecutive emergency turns to the right and increased speed to 25 knots to clear the area. Men watching NORTH CAROLINA from other ships were astonished to see her take these maneuvers in stride, maintaining her station in the formation as though nothing had happened. Although the ship had taken a list of five and one-half degrees to port immediately after the hit, in about five minutes the list was corrected by counter-flooding. Four men in a third deck washroom lost their lives; another was lost overboard, while 23 were wounded. Of course, repairs in a drydock were now imperative, but the Showboat's quick and effective reaction to such serious damage was an impressive performance by a tough ship and a well-trained crew.

Temporary repairs quickly effected after the torpedo hit included installation of heavy timbers to "shore up" (brace) weakened watertight doors and bulkheads to prevent their collapse from sea water pressure in the flooded spaces.

A LESSON IN DAMAGE CONTROL
September 15, 1942
Flooding and counter-flooding following torpedo hit

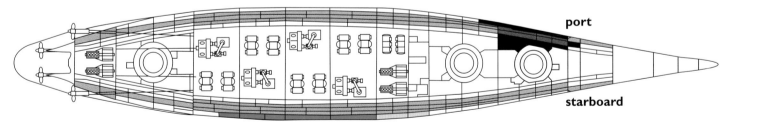

port

starboard

Flooding – Nearly 1,000 tons of sea water caused the ship to list 5 degrees to port.

Counter-flooding – Prompt action by damage control team corrected list in less than five minutes.

ADAPTED FROM LOTT AND SUMRALL, SHIP'S DATA 1, 1982.

COLOR CODE

Approximate liquid loading (fuel oil and ballast) before torpedo hit

Area flooded by torpedo hit

Void tanks counter-flooded immediately after torpedo hit

Void tanks counter-flooded and pumped out within one hour

OH-OH!

"ALL HANDS MAN YOUR BATTLE STATIONS TOOT-TOOT-TOOT!"

BATTLESHIP COLLECTION 93.6.315

"I was knocked ass over teakettle, but was able to make it to my battle station. The torpedo punctured some fuel tanks and started a fire which got into the lower handling room of Turret II. The fuel was actually burning on the floor of the projectile room. The sprinklers were activated and the turret crew came streaming out the hatch with the smoke in swift pursuit. The word was passed 'Stand by to abandon ship' because if Turret II went, the whole ship would explode like a Chinese firecracker, right down the middle where all the 5-inch magazines were. It so happened that we were one life jacket short, for some reason, so I didn't have one. My phone talker, assessing the situation, said, 'Here Mr. Gallagher, take my life jacket, I'm a good swimmer.' Fortunately, the situation improved so abandoning the ship wasn't necessary, but I'll always remember that young sailor's gallant offer."

— Lieutenant Edward Gallagher, 4th Division Officer

"I was down taking a shower, didn't have a stitch of clothes on, had just gotten out of the shower and had the towel drying my back. There was a big explosion. I couldn't hear anything, and the next thing I knew I was in the water and oil, and there were two other guys pretty close to me, but I somehow got out. But I'll never forget it, the sight that I saw. I saw the prettiest roses you ever laid your eyes on. I saw my name. At the time I was from Lynchburg, Virginia. And I saw my name in the Lynchburg paper, 'Walter T. Babcock,' and I'm going to tell you like it was; 'Walter T. Babcock, killed in action.' And I don't remember getting from down on the third deck up to topside. The only thing I know, and I'm telling the truth, I saw my mother and father. One caught one hand and one caught the other and I actually talked to them."

— Walter Babcock, Ship's Cook Third Class

"We had never thought about an order to abandon ship. We were resigned to stay at our battle stations. The secured compartments were designed to prevent the spread of fire and flooding. We were a fighting warship that was prepared to meet the enemy and fight to the finish. We were the NORTH CAROLINA."

— Charles Foster, Patternmaker First Class

"I knew that the WASP was torpedoed so I went to my battle station right away and I was sitting up on top of Sky Two before we got hit. One of the fire controlmen was the hairiest guy we ever saw. He was in the shower at the time. He was all soaped up and when we got hit, he took off from the shower and was running forward on the port side of the ship and I am looking down at him as he runs by on the main deck and all I can see is hair and soapsuds. No clothes on. He went into Turret I. That was his battle station. There was a fire in the magazines so they flooded the magazine and they abandoned Turret I. Here he comes, still with no clothes on, but soapsuds, running back down again. I was telling him about it afterwards. He said, 'Well, it wasn't funny.' I said, 'You weren't sitting where I was.' "

— Harold Smith, Fire Controlman First Class

"The crew at battle stations topside had life jackets. The men at battle stations below the main deck did not have life jackets. When you realize the condition the ship would have to be in before it would be abandoned and you are dogged [locked in for watertight integrity] three or more decks down in powder rooms, engine rooms, radio rooms, etc., life jackets are not of much use. I always accepted the fact that from that area, with the ship sinking, and a half dozen or more dogged down hatches to go through to get topside to the life jackets, I would be going down with the ship."

— Richard McCullough, Radioman First Class

"As officer of the deck of cruiser PENSACOLA, steaming astern of NORTH CAROLINA, I watched this disaster unfold. I was devastated, not only by what was happening to WASP, but also to see our champion, mighty Showboat, so badly damaged when we needed her so desperately. Then, watching her correct her list and charge forward to 25 knots, keeping up with the rest of us regardless of her torpedo damage, was a thrill I'll never forget. She proved that day that she could take it as well as dish it out."

— Author

Pre-war photograph of Japanese scouting submarine I-19, which claimed to have destroyed WASP. Both this submarine and her sister ship, I-15, carried a reconnaissance float plane in a watertight hangar shown here extending forward from the conning tower. Farther forward, the launching catapult can be seen sloping upward to the bow. Photograph courtesy of Shichiro Tange, I-19 World War II crew.

The fate of WASP during the remainder of that disastrous day was to continue to burn out of control, explosions rocking her from bow to stern. Damage was so severe, its cause so apparent to everyone on board and her crew so preoccupied, it is understandable that no explanation or warning was passed to other ships. Despite heroic efforts to save her, at 1520 WASP was ordered abandoned. Her casualties were 193 killed and 367 wounded. That night our task force commander, Rear Admiral George D. Murray, who had shifted his flag to PENSACOLA, ordered WASP sunk to keep her from falling prey to a powerful force of enemy surface ships, believed approaching from the north. At 2100 WASP was given the *coup de grace* by torpedoes from LANSDOWNE.

That night Japanese submarine I-19, in a radio message to its headquarters at Truk, claimed to have torpedoed WASP. The Japanese suffered no losses or casualties whatever in this encounter.

With WASP's demise, HORNET became for the next five weeks the only American carrier in the combat area of the Pacific. NORTH CAROLINA's sister ship, WASHINGTON, which had just arrived in the Pacific, now replaced the Showboat as the only battleship in the area. New battleship SOUTH DAKOTA, which had arrived only a few weeks earlier, was unavailable, having damaged her bottom August 21 on a coral head. This accident made it necessary for her to be withdrawn to Pearl Harbor several weeks for drydock repairs. And so, in just seven devastating minutes, Japanese submarine torpedoes had wreaked havoc with the U.S. Navy's South Pacific force, already stretched almost to the breaking point.

WHODUNNIT? EARLY SPECULATION AS TO HOW IT HAPPENED

How could such a lopsided disaster have occurred? With three ships torpedoed in widely separated locations, and with torpedo wakes sighted in three other locations, it appeared that several enemy submarines had attacked together. Had the Japanese adopted the German U-Boat tactic of coordinated attack by "wolf packs?" If so, how many subs took part? Where were they positioned? Which torpedoes were launched from which submarines? How could their attacks have been so successfully coordinated? How did they manage to avoid detection by WASP's and HORNET's destroyer screens? The fog of war was never thicker.

For 40 years these questions added up to one of the most baffling mysteries of World War II — baffling because no Japanese submarine ever claimed to have torpedoed O'BRIEN and NORTH CAROLINA. One possible explanation is that whichever sub or subs may have been responsible simply did not live to tell the tale. The facts do not support this conclusion. Instead, they point to a whole series of improbable coincidences and a stroke of luck so incredible as to defy the imagination.

The efforts of all who have sought to solve this mystery have been thwarted by the lack of official evidence from Japanese sources. I-15 was sunk with all hands near Guadalcanal November 2, 1942. I-19 failed to return from a patrol during the American operation to recover the Gilbert Islands in November 1943. Another handicap to research was that official records maintained by the Japanese Navy in Tokyo were almost totally destroyed by bombing and fire in 1945. In the immediate post-war years, concerted efforts were made to have former Japanese Navy command and staff officers reconstruct important records from memory. Results were valuable, but far from complete.

Several American historians, including Rear Admiral Samuel Eliot Morison, author of the authoritative 14-volume *History of United States Naval Operations in World War II*, have credited I-15 with the hits on the destroyer and battleship. This conclusion was evidently based on the mere fact of that submarine's presence at the scene of action six hours after the torpedoing. By a footnote, Morison mentions the possibility that I-19 was responsible for scoring on all three ships, but he discards this explanation with the comment that "her torpedoes would have had a mighty long run."

Other historians, including the respected German authority on submarine warfare, Jurgen Rohwer, have suggested that I-19 unknowingly accomplished all five hits. They claim that I-19 fired a spread of six torpedoes at her target, WASP. Three hit WASP and three continued racing across the several miles separating the two task forces and struck the other two ships by pure chance. (A spread is a launch of several torpedoes in quick succession, to run toward the target fan-like, in order to increase the probability that some will score.)

Although eyewitnesses on WASP's bridge actually saw only four torpedo wakes (three hits and one miss across the carrier's bow), it was normal Japanese practice to fire six torpedoes in a spread aimed at an important target. Thus, it appears that three of the spread missed WASP and kept going in the direction of the HORNET formation. The fact that I-19 did not claim hits on the battleship and destroyer does not by itself rule out that possibility. I-19's skipper could hardly have been expected to stick around to learn of such luck while fighting for his life against the angry pack of destroyers in WASP's screen.

As for the distance traveled, the torpedoes that missed WASP would have had to travel several hundred yards to reach WASP and then an additional 9,000 to 11,000 yards to reach O'BRIEN and NORTH CAROLINA. In the U.S. Navy at that time

it was not believed that Japanese submarine-launched torpedoes could be any better than our own Mk XIV, which could travel 4,500 yards at a top speed of 45 knots. Hence, the theory that I-19 torpedoed all three ships was deemed out of the question. Opinion in U.S. Navy circles was almost unanimous that at least one other submarine must have taken part, perhaps not surviving the rain of American depth charges that followed the torpedoing.

Post-war testimony of former IJN officers reveals that a picket line of nine submarines, including both I-15 and I-19, lay in wait for our ships en route to Guadalcanal (see chart on page 82). However, the same testimony shows that all nine of these boats survived that patrol and were undergoing maintenance at Truk in late September, when only the I-19 claimed a role in the action, and only against WASP. The absence of any reconstructed record or claim that any sub other than I-19 torpedoed the battleship and destroyer clearly leads to the conclusion that none did. And yet, if I-19 unknowingly did it all, how can the remarkable 12,000-yard run of her torpedoes be explained? How can the nearly miraculous chance hits on two untargetted ships in a vast ocean area be explained?

The answer to the first question is that during the decade preceding World War II Japan had secretly developed the most advanced torpedoes in the world. Best known and most potent of these was the surface-launched Type 92 "Long Lance," powered by kerosene and pure oxygen and capable of running 22,000 yards at 49 knots. Too large to be carried in Japanese submarines, but employed by Japanese destroyers and cruisers in surface actions around Guadalcanal, this torpedo sank or seriously damaged nearly a score of American cruisers and destroyers. A smaller, newer version of the Long Lance, developed for use in the tighter confines of submarines, was the Type 95, capable of running 13,000 yards at 45 knots. Thus, if I-19 was armed with this torpedo, the seemingly impossible was possible; but the Americans knew nothing about the Type 95 until well after the war. Even then, among most U.S. naval officers, the idea that a single submarine firing a single spread of torpedoes could achieve such amazing success was deemed impossible. As an eyewitness to the action, I suspected otherwise. In 1982, searching for evidence to ascertain the truth, I turned to the official action

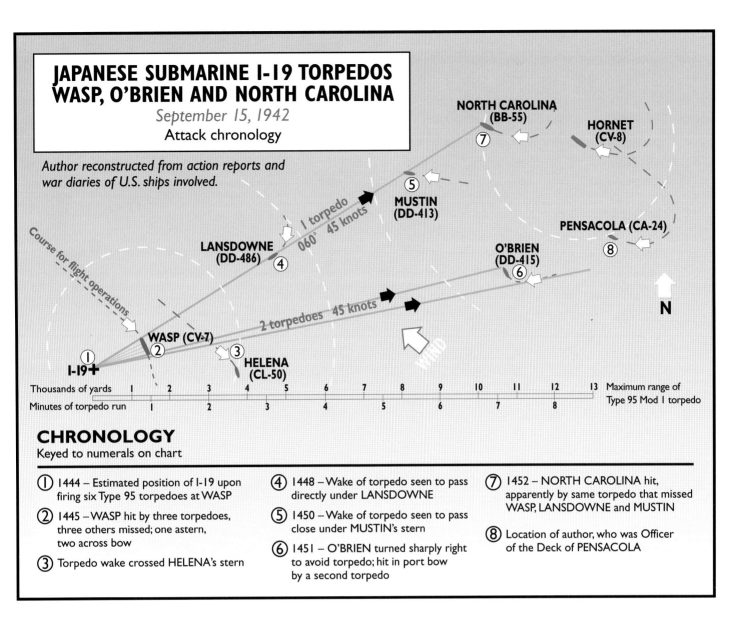

JAPANESE SUBMARINE I-19 TORPEDOS WASP, O'BRIEN AND NORTH CAROLINA

September 15, 1942
Attack chronology

Author reconstructed from action reports and war diaries of U.S. ships involved.

NORTH CAROLINA (BB-55) ⑦

HORNET (CV-8)

⑤ MUSTIN (DD-413)

PENSACOLA (CA-24) ⑧

LANSDOWNE (DD-486) ④

1 torpedo 060° 45 knots

O'BRIEN (DD-415) ⑥

2 torpedoes 45 knots

WIND

N

Course for flight operations

WASP (CV-7) ②

③ HELENA (CL-50)

I-19 ①

| Thousands of yards | 1 | 2 | 3 | 4 | 5 | 6 | 7 | 8 | 9 | 10 | 11 | 12 | 13 | Maximum range of Type 95 Mod 1 torpedo |
| Minutes of torpedo run | 1 | | 2 | | 3 | | 4 | | 5 | | 6 | | 7 | 8 | |

CHRONOLOGY
Keyed to numerals on chart

① 1444 – Estimated position of I-19 upon firing six Type 95 torpedoes at WASP

② 1445 – WASP hit by three torpedoes, three others missed; one astern, two across bow

③ Torpedo wake crossed HELENA's stern

④ 1448 – Wake of torpedo seen to pass directly under LANSDOWNE

⑤ 1450 – Wake of torpedo seen to pass close under MUSTIN's stern

⑥ 1451 – O'BRIEN turned sharply right to avoid torpedo; hit in port bow by a second torpedo

⑦ 1452 – NORTH CAROLINA hit, apparently by same torpedo that missed WASP, LANSDOWNE and MUSTIN

⑧ Location of author, who was Officer of the Deck of PENSACOLA

reports of the U.S. Navy participants, where I found more than enough circumstantial evidence to reach a responsible verdict. A summary of that evidence is presented in graphic form in the diagram above.

The one-submarine (I-19) theory conforms almost precisely to the established facts of the tactical situation that applied to all six U.S. ships from which torpedo wakes were sighted. The series of near misses is, by itself, extraordinarily coincidental. That NORTH CAROLINA and O'BRIEN were struck by stray torpedoes reveals, when this diagram is examined, that the two ships — entirely by chance — ran into the torpedoes, rather than the other way around. Adding to the unprecedented luck enjoyed by I-19 is the fact that the torpedo which struck NORTH CAROLINA was within seconds of running out of fuel. And yet, such an improbable series of coincidences left many diehards in the U.S. Navy unconvinced.

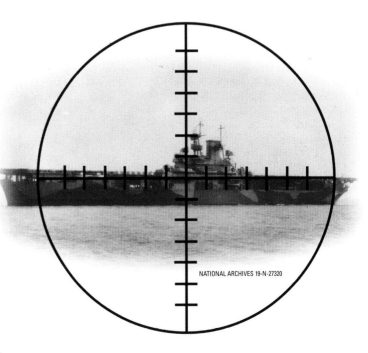

NATIONAL ARCHIVES 19-N-27320

How WASP must have looked through I-19's periscope as torpedoes were launched.

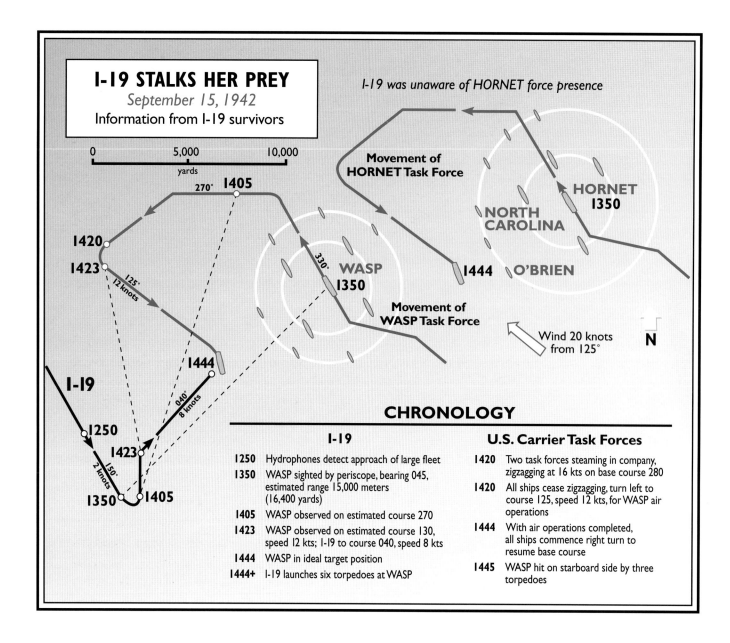

I-19 STALKS HER PREY
September 15, 1942
Information from I-19 survivors

I-19 was unaware of HORNET force presence

Movement of HORNET Task Force

0   5,000   10,000
yards

270° 1405

1420

1423

125°
12 knots

I-19

1250

1423

1350

1405

1444

040°
8 knots

150°
2 knots

330°

WASP
1350

Movement of WASP Task Force

NORTH CAROLINA

HORNET
1350

1444   O'BRIEN

Wind 20 knots from 125°

N

CHRONOLOGY

I-19

1250	Hydrophones detect approach of large fleet
1350	WASP sighted by periscope, bearing 045, estimated range 15,000 meters (16,400 yards)
1405	WASP observed on estimated course 270
1423	WASP observed on estimated course 130, speed 12 kts; I-19 to course 040, speed 8 kts
1444	WASP in ideal target position
1444+	I-19 launches six torpedoes at WASP

U.S. Carrier Task Forces

1420	Two task forces steaming in company, zigzagging at 16 kts on base course 280
1420	All ships cease zigzagging, turn left to course 125, speed 12 kts, for WASP air operations
1444	With air operations completed, all ships commence right turn to resume base course
1445	WASP hit on starboard side by three torpedoes

THE BREAKTHROUGH THAT PROVED WHODUNNIT

As of 1982, while researching this mystery for the first edition of this book, I mistakenly took it for granted that there were no surviving Japanese participants. I believed this because, as mentioned previously, both the I-15 and I-19 were lost with all hands later in the war. Thus, I was surprised to learn in 1983 from a Japanese friend, Masaru Yotsuzuka, that at least 15 members of I-19's 1942 crew were alive in Japan. These men lived through the war because some were on sick leave, while others had been detached from I-19 when she sailed on her final war patrol. Yotsuzuka was a bilingual WWII naval warfare buff who frequently visited the Showboat while in Wilmington on business for his chemical company, Takeda, which operated a factory there. He put me in touch with the I-19 survivors and served as liaison in a lengthy exchange of correspondence.

Of particular value was a written account of I-19's role in the action, as recorded immediately after the event by Lieutenant Ikuo Shibuya, the submarine's engineer officer. According to Shibuya's narrative, the maneuvers of I-19 as she detected and stalked her prey were as shown in the diagram above. This new information filled in most of the gaps in the foregoing explanation of what happened under the sea that fateful day in 1942.

My relationship with the I-19 crewmembers culminated in a three-day joint reunion on board the battleship at Wilmington, North Carolina, June 24-26, 1986, with four of I-19's 1942 crew in attendance. They included Lieutenant Juichiro Miyazawa, the sub's surgeon; Torpedomen Tadataka Ohtani and Shichiro Tange, who actually launched the torpedo spread at WASP; and Quartermaster Rishichi Sugiyama, who was in the conning tower at the elbow of the sub's captain, Commander Takaichi Kinashi,

Receiving line of Showboat crewmembers greets crewmembers of I-19 at start of 1986 joint reunion. Photograph by Richard R. Sartore.

During the joint reunion, Torpedoman Tadataka Ohtani of I-19 explains the Japanese role in the action. Author is at left. Second from right is Masaru Yotsuzuka, the helpful Japanese catalyst and interpreter who made the get-together possible. Photograph by Richard R. Sartore.

throughout the action. The Showboat was represented by eight "designated hosts," all members of the USS NORTH CAROLINA Battleship Association (former crewmembers). Highlight of the get-together was a lengthy review of the torpedoing, with participants on both sides spelling out their recollections of how it happened. Both the working sessions and the attendant social events were marked by honest rapport, mutual respect and warm cordiality between former enemies, now friends.

The most significant fact revealed by the Japanese was that the six torpedoes launched by I-19 at WASP were in fact Type 95 Mod 1, capable of running 13,000 yards at 45 knots. This established beyond doubt that it was physically possible for torpedoes that missed WASP to reach NORTH CAROLINA and O'BRIEN. Another surprise was that the warhead in the nose of this torpedo contained an explosive charge weighing 891 pounds, over five times the charge carried in the battleship's 16-inch HC projectiles. As of 1942, the warhead of the standard U.S. Navy Mark XIV submarine-launched torpedo contained a charge of only 504 pounds of trinitrotoluene (TNT). Another significant revelation was that shortly after the torpedoing, when all nine of the picket line submarines were together at Truk exchanging news of their exploits at sea, no crewmembers other than those of the I-19 claimed any role in the torpedoing of September 15, 1942. This surely confirms that none did.

The Japanese participants in the joint reunion were deeply impressed by the magnanimity and cordiality extended to them by the Americans. The following remarks of Torpedoman Tange are typical:

"It gave me the most exalted experience of my life to participate in the solemn joint memorial service. I humbly take off my cap before the broad-mindedness and tolerance of the American spirit. An old Japanese proverb says, 'You have to meet people in person to understand them.' I never felt we were with former enemies. Rather I felt we were among comrades with whom we had risked our lives in common on the battlefield. My heart was filled with fond feeling that I was able to meet these comrades after 40 years. If only all the people of the world can proceed hand in hand with courage and determination to maintain peace in the world after the pattern set by this reunion! We have a solemn obligation to convey this feeling to our descendants."

FRAGMENT OF A STRAY TORPEDO

Fired by I-19, retrieved by BB-55, Sept. 15, 1942.

Returned to I-19 June 24, 1986, with apologies for damage done to it when we hit it.

USS North Carolina Battleship Association

☆ ☆ ☆ ☆ ☆ ☆ ☆ ☆ ☆ ☆ ☆ ☆ ☆ ☆ ☆

As a memento of the 1986 joint reunion, the Americans presented the Japanese with a framed fist-size fragment of I-19's torpedo, recovered from inside the battleship while undergoing drydock repairs. A brass label on the polished mahogany presentation box was engraved as above. The 15 stars across the bottom of the label were intended as a not very subtle reminder of the Showboat's survival of the torpedoing, to earn 15 World War II battle stars. This trophy is now on permanent display at the Japanese Naval Academy, Etajima, Japan.

Drydock view of the hole made by the torpedo in the ship's side. It measured 32 feet long by 18 feet high. Drydock repairs at the Pearl Harbor Navy Yard were completed in 21 days, an amazing achievement.

TORPEDO DAMAGE — DETAILS AND ASSESSMENT

Although NORTH CAROLINA's torpedo damage was not serious enough to threaten her survival or completely eliminate her fighting capacity, it was sufficient to make withdrawal for repairs mandatory. After dark on September 15, with two destroyers as escort, the ship headed for a safe haven at Tongatabu in the Friendly Islands, 250 miles southeast of Fiji. There the bodies of four men killed were removed from flooded compartments and taken ashore for burial. The traditional Navy service was conducted by the chaplain, Captain Frances L. Albert, and attended by a detachment of the ship's company. Meanwhile, divers from a repair ship cut off shards of torn metal projecting from the ship's hull. With the Showboat trimmed down aft, several flooded spaces forward were pumped out and shored more thoroughly in preparation for the trip to Pearl Harbor. The ship arrived there safely September 30, 1942. Repairs were delayed, however, because the only drydock big enough to hold a battleship was occupied by SOUTH DAKOTA.

Upon entering the drydock October 10, the full extent of the ship's underwater damage was exposed and a more detailed assessment could be made. The torpedo struck the hull at a point 20 feet below the waterline, well below the bottom of the side armor abreast of Turret I, at frames 45-46. The "fish" exploded on impact, tearing a hole in the ship's side 32 feet long and 18 feet high.

Three sections of the armor belt were cracked and remain so to this day, as it was not considered necessary to replace them. The second and third decks were buckled and ruptured, a roller plate support for Turret I was damaged and several adjacent bulkheads (walls) failed. Although Turret I itself was not damaged, the structural damage immediately below it meant that until permanent repairs could be made, the guns of that turret could be fired only in extreme necessity. In addition to the hull and structural damage below decks, the CXAM search radar antenna at the top of the foremast was disabled because its supports were fractured and its high frequency transmission line ruptured, evidence of the whiplash effect of the torpedo explosion.

Clearly, the torpedo defeated the ship's underwater protection, but it should be noted that chance, which played such an incredibly persistent role in this entire incident, placed the hit at the most vulnerable part of the ship's torpedo defense system. At any point that far forward in most ships, the narrowing of the hull as it approaches the bow appreciably decreases its volume and, in the case of NORTH CAROLINA, allowed for only four protective compartments as opposed to the five provided elsewhere. Also significant was the fact that, although the ship's built-in defenses against torpedoes were designed to cope with an explosive charge of up to 700 pounds of TNT, the warhead of the Type 95 torpedo carried a charge of 891 pounds, consisting of 60 percent TNT and 40 percent hexanitrodiphenylamine (hexyl), a mix with more explosive power than 100 percent TNT. From lessons learned in this experience, the Navy incorporated radical improvements in the underwater protection of the IOWA-class battleships, then under construction.

Finally, mention must be made of the speed with which the Pearl Harbor Navy Yard, aided by the ship's force, completed repairs of such extensive damage. The ship was in and out of drydock in 21 days. This was a remarkable accomplishment, hastening the Showboat's return to the combat area at a time when she was sorely needed.

GUADALCANAL OPERATIONS
October – November 1942

At this crucial stage in the campaign for control of the South Pacific, with the opposing forces engaged in a life-or-death struggle for Guadalcanal, America's stake in the war still depended on a naval force of pitifully few ships and men. Fortunately, some help was on the way. By mid-October, new battleship SOUTH DAKOTA was back on the scene and ENTERPRISE, hastily patched up at Pearl Harbor, was returning at full speed.

Then on October 26, with the Showboat still undergoing repairs at Pearl Harbor, the fourth and last of the great carrier battles of 1942, the Battle of the Santa Cruz Islands, was fought east of Guadalcanal. In that battle the Japanese lost another carrier, and we lost HORNET. With that, battered ENTERPRISE

LUCK RUNS OUT FOR THE SKIPPER OF I-19

I-19's commanding officer as of September 15, 1942, was 40-year-old Commander Takaichi Kinashi, a 1926 graduate of the Japanese Naval Academy. Kinashi had previously served in seven different submarines, commanding three. He was credited with having torpedoed at least six Allied merchant ships in the Indian Ocean during the early months of the war. A brilliant tactician, he was known as a daring and aggressive fighter who remained cool in tight situations. The spectacular results Kinashi achieved September 15, 1942, even though due largely to extraordinary luck, entitle him and the I-19 to be credited with the most destructive torpedo spread ever launched in the history of submarine warfare.

Kinashi had another remarkable assignment during World War II. After taking command of another submarine, I-29, he was chosen for a highly secret undersea voyage halfway around the world to Nazi Germany. There, in March 1944, he met personally with Admiral Karl Donitz, Commander in Chief of the German Navy, who decorated Kinashi for destroying WASP. Of much greater significance, Donitz sent Kinashi home with a hoard of design documents and blueprints for new German weaponry. Included were details needed for Japan to duplicate and mass produce the V-1 flying bomb and V-2 rocket, soon to be used by Germany with terrifying effect on the civilian populations of Belgium and Britain. What use a desperate Japan might have made of those indiscriminate but extremely destructive weapons during the closing months of the war the world will never know, for the submarine bearing Kinashi and his papers home to Japan never made it. When U.S. naval intelligence decrypted I-29's radioed routing orders for the final leg of its voyage from Singapore to Japan, three American submarines were sent to ambush it in the Bashi Channel between Formosa and Luzon. There, on July 26, 1944, USS SAWFISH (SS-276) slammed three torpedoes into I-29, sending Kinashi and his blueprints to join WASP on the bottom of the sea.

became the only operational flattop left in the combat area on the American side. Understandably, both sides now became more hesitant than before to risk their carriers in battle, except under the most favorable circumstances. The emphasis shifted to more night surface action in and around "Ironbottom Sound." Ironbottom Sound was the sardonic name given by American sailors to the waters between Guadalcanal and Savo Island, where the sea bottom was becoming a watery graveyard for sunken warships, mostly American.

In those waters during the early hours of November 15, WASHINGTON and SOUTH DAKOTA with four destroyers, under command of Rear Admiral Willis A. Lee, engaged a Japanese force consisting of one battleship, three cruisers and nine destroyers. Although damage was heavy on both sides, the Japanese force was routed, primarily by the guns of WASHINGTON. The 16-inch and 5-inch shells of the Showboat's sister ship damaged the enemy battleship KIRISHIMA so severely that her crew had to scuttle her. WASHINGTON emerged unscathed. Unfortunately, SOUTH DAKOTA, which lost electrical power early in the action, was badly damaged and spent the next nine months in the Philadelphia Navy Yard undergoing repairs. Regardless, the effectiveness of WASHINGTON's radar-controlled gunfire in this battle proved, as nothing else could, that the gunnery of America's new battleships was superior to that of the Japanese. This was a lesson the Japanese appeared to take seriously, because the usual adversaries thereafter were cruisers and destroyers, which clashed in a series of savage battles north of Guadalcanal.

Japanese strategy at this time was to hold their carriers in readiness for a decisive daylight engagement with the few remaining major units of the U.S. Pacific Fleet. American strategy, in view of the continuing Japanese advantage in numbers, was to avoid such a lopsided fight, if possible, because an enemy victory at sea would have virtually doomed the marines on Guadalcanal, not to mention its long-term negative impact on America's stake in the war.

BACKING UP THE SOLOMONS CAMPAIGN
December 1942 – September 1943

NORTH CAROLINA remained at Pearl Harbor from September 30 until November 17, 1942, in drydock for repairs of her torpedo damage, then in the shipyard for installation of new 40-mm antiaircraft guns, replacing the unreliable 1.1-inch guns and .50-caliber machine guns. This work was completed as rapidly as possible and after two days of target practice off Oahu, the ship sailed at full speed for the South Pacific. She arrived in the combat area December 9, ready for action.

By this time Vice Admiral William F. Halsey, one of the U.S. Navy's most aggressive fighters, had been given command of all our forces in the Solomons area. "Bull" Halsey, as the press began calling him, had already become a hero in the eyes of most U.S. Navy men for his outspoken enmity against the Japanese and his boldness as a combat leader. Earlier in the war he had commanded carrier task forces in daring raids against Japanese bases in the central Pacific and even one that delivered a surprise attack on Tokyo by B-25 medium bombers of the U.S. Army Air Corps. Under Halsey's spirited leadership, the men of the Showboat eagerly anticipated giving the enemy a taste of 16-inch gunfire. Things didn't turn out that way. For the next 10 months the role of NORTH CAROLINA is best described as a passive one. She and the two or three other newly arrived fast battleships in the area served as heavy-weight backups for the cruisers and destroyers doing most of the fighting afloat. The fast battleships continued to operate mainly as carrier protectors, but during 1943 there were no great carrier battles and no surface engagements in which either side committed battleships.

The crew of the Showboat learned during those 10 months that their war, like most others, included prolonged periods of unrelieved nervous tension plus a lot of waiting and boredom. NORTH CAROLINA was not air-conditioned, except for a very few key spaces (Sick Bay, Plot, Main Radio, CIC and Flag Plot), so the tropical heat and humidity within the sun-kissed oven of her hull made life almost unbearable much of the time. Compounding the discomfort were three chronic health problems: heat rash, ear fungus and athlete's foot, which affected practically every member of the ship's company off and on for weeks at a time. Despite intensive medical care provided by the ship's doctors and corpsmen, these ailments were almost inescapable, due to the heat and humidity. Some cases became almost totally disabling.

In those days, when nearly every sailor was a smoker, a particular annoyance was soggy tobacco that refused to burn properly and tasted sour. On the other hand, the food by this stage of the war was normally plentiful, wholesome and well enough prepared to keep the men satisfied. The usual gripes were heard, of course, but meals provided almost the only enjoyment in the crew's daily existence. Movies came next after "chow" and mail from home.

The men were always tired enough to sleep almost anywhere, but in that heat sleep was a sweating, feverish torpor, which did little to refresh weary minds and bodies. Many sought relief by sleeping on deck topside, but as often as not a tropical rain squall put a sudden miserable end to that escape. Heat lightning, a nightly occurrence in those latitudes, added anxiety to the discomfort because sometimes it looked and sounded exactly like naval gunfire on the horizon, making one wonder whether a surprise enemy salvo was on the way.

In early 1943 Admiral Halsey, ever mindful of the morale of his men, arranged for canned beer to be carried by our ships; not for consumption on board, but for issue ashore to organized recreation parties, two cans per man. When the message bearing this news reached the Showboat there was rejoicing among the crew, but the executive officer suddenly discovered himself in a quandary. With over 2,000 sailors on board, many as crafty and resourceful as they were thirsty, where could several hundred cases of beer be securely stored? Commander Joe Stryker, now promoted to executive officer, summoned his two trustiest chief petty officers, Thomas W. Dillingham and Paul H. Minvielle, and put the question to them. They were sea dogs of long practical experience, and as usual when they wanted a problem solved, they had a solution: stow the beer in the brig. Lock the brig. Put an armed guard at the door. Warn the crew that the first time any sailor commits an offense that lands him in the brig, all the beer will be thrown overboard. "You see, Commander," explained one of the chiefs,

"that way we can kill two birds with one stone; protect the beer and resolve a lot of disciplinary problems."

Well, the plan worked. At least, it seemed to work because with its adoption the dozen or so offenders who had been brought every week to captain's mast suddenly dropped to almost none. From his lofty perch on the bridge the skipper, now Captain Wilder D. Baker, was probably unaware of some of the changes in disciplinary procedure that were occurring on board. "Minor offenses," it was said, "were being dealt with less formally and more expeditiously at lower levels." Anyway, the morale of the crew received a boost from the beer's evidence that the powers above cared. Thereafter, during occasional brief visits to isolated anchorages such as at Noumea, New Caledonia, or Efate in the New Hebrides, there was free beer along with the baseball and swimming. These small pleasures were always enjoyed, but no Showboat sailor was ever heard to say that he preferred them to the delights of New York or San Francisco.

Showboat sailors enjoy a rare break and a couple of warm beers on a remote island in the South Pacific.

Artie Shaw and his band, after being delivered to the South Pacific by the Showboat, entertain the crews of two destroyers moored side-by-side.

Life aboard...

"They made me first loader on a 5-inch. We were firing illumination star shells, and I was asleep in the mount. Of course, we were in automatic and this was practice. There were only two of us in the mount. The rest of the crew was outside the mount. Well, out of this cold sleep, the mount captain grabs me in the shirt and starts screaming at me to load. He had the headphones on, you see, so he got the order to load. Since the rest of the crew was outside, he takes the powder can and throws it in. I jump up and grab the shell and load it and ram it. Wham! I never heard as much confusion in my life. We had fired into the USS KIDD, one of our own ships. These two little hands are the ones that loaded it; but I was only a seaman, so it wasn't my responsibility. This was the officers' and director's fault, I suppose. Anyway, there were no casualties on the KIDD."

— Michael Horton, Seaman First Class

In mid-March of 1943, vibrations of the battleship's number two propeller shaft began to occur, requiring a return to Pearl Harbor for drydocking and repairs. The crew eagerly welcomed the trip to a cooler clime and some good liberty in Hawaii, but a more important bonus was the installation of new search and fire control radars. On the way back to the South Pacific, the ship carried as passengers Artie Shaw and his band, one of the most popular swing bands of that era. Daily serenades on deck, featuring such foot-tapping tunes as "Begin the Beguine" delighted the Showboat's crew. They also provided entertainment for hundreds of men on destroyers which came alongside every few days for fueling. With the ship's return to the combat area in May, the vacation was over and the deadly dangerous business of patrolling on the flanks of the Solomons resumed.

To keep the ship's gunners as sharp as possible, frequent drills and exercises were carried out, day and night. In one such drill during a dawn alert, NORTH CAROLINA accidentally fired into a friendly destroyer, USS KIDD (DD-661). Steaming parallel to the Showboat at a range of 10,000 yards, KIDD was acting as a simulated target for the battleship's guns. Two star shells were fired from one of the 5-inch mounts, but an aiming error sent them in a flat trajectory straight at KIDD, instead of being aimed to burst high above her. Both shells crashed into the destroyer with bull's-eye accuracy, one making

a shambles of the chiefs' quarters, the other breaking every dish and stick of furniture in the officers' mess. Fortunately, the crew of KIDD was also at battle stations, so no one was hurt. Three days later, when the wounded destroyer came alongside NORTH CAROLINA to fuel, a highline rigged between the two ships was used to send over a cake decorated with a purple heart. Fifty gallons of precious ice cream were also passed across, while NORTH CAROLINA's band played appropriate "shippin' over music." The destroyer skipper sportingly congratulated the Showboat's captain on his ship's excellent marksmanship, and all was more or less forgiven.

The cake decorated with a purple heart for the crew of the KIDD.

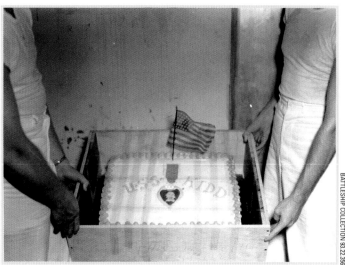

Battleship NORTH CAROLINA escorting aircraft carrier ENTERPRISE, comrades in arms for many months during 1942 and 1943 in the South Pacific. Dating from the Battle of the Eastern Solomons when the Showboat's guns helped save the carrier, the crews of these two ships were brothers, both at sea and ashore.

STEAMING, PATROLLING, WAITING

The days dragged on into weeks, which blurred into endless months of steaming, patrolling and waiting — waiting for something to happen. With only two aircraft carriers, ENTERPRISE and SARATOGA, available for most of this period, these priceless ships were always afforded battleship protection and were moved across the chessboard of the South Pacific with great care, often in a manner calculated to deceive the enemy. One tactic was for a carrier task force commander to permit his ships to be sighted by a Japanese search plane near dusk in one location. After dark he would reverse course and steam overnight at high speed to another enemy search area, where he would position his ships in a different formation, change course, and hope to be sighted again. This ruse may have dazzled the Japanese admirals, but as our amphibious ships and troops leap-frogged from island to island up the chain of the Solomons, strong enemy forces made several threatening advances toward them. These moves often prompted high-speed runs by the Showboat and other battleships toward a scene of possible action, but the Japanese would then withdraw, evidently declining to accept the challenge of American battleships' radar-controlled gunnery.

After April 1943, there were normally four new U.S. battleships on station in the South Pacific: WASHINGTON, INDIANA, MASSACHUSETTS and NORTH CAROLINA. SOUTH DAKOTA was still absent undergoing repairs of battle damage suffered in the previously mentioned night surface engagement off Guadalcanal, November 15, 1942. "SoDak" did not return to the combat area until August 1943. The other four great battleships comprised a force to be reckoned with, and the temporary silence of their guns during most of 1943 was no measure of their value to our Solomons Campaign. Merely by their presence, they did much to hold off a numerically superior Japanese fleet that might otherwise have halted the American offensive and decimated the troops fighting ashore in the Solomons.

By November 1943, the whole chain of the Solomons, from Guadalcanal northwest to Bougainville, was in American hands. Although there was still more fighting to be done in that region, the time had come to put added pressure on Japan by kicking off a whole new offensive across the central Pacific. This new offensive was to be under the overall direction of Fleet Admiral Chester W. Nimitz, with headquarters ashore at Pearl Harbor. The first step was the recovery of Tarawa and Makin Atolls in the Gilbert Islands, which Japan had seized from Britain early in the war.

Fleet Admiral Chester W. Nimitz, Commander in Chief Pacific and U.S. Pacific Fleet during most of World War II.

"We played cards, watched boxing and wrestling, wrote letters and read books from the library. Some guys had hobbies like making knife handles or rings. Some guys made gifts for girlfriends and wives, like aprons out of their neckerchiefs; or created purses and belts by making knots from rope; or made beautifully decorated leather belts from leather they managed to get from the bosun's locker. 'Smokers' took place on the fantail. Smokers meant musical groups, comedians, skits, singers, dancers, tug of war contests between divisions, boxing matches and similar stuff. Sports like division softball tournaments, baseball and basketball between ships had to take place on South Pacific recreational islands, such as Noumea and Efate...."

— Paul Wieser, Boatswain's Mate First Class

"That movie with Marlene Dietrich and Jimmy Stewart, *Destry Rides Again*, must have ridden all over the South Pacific. They would show *Destry Rides Again* tonight, tomorrow night and the next night, down in the mess hall. That is where you got hot. You would sit there and sweat and it didn't matter how many times they would show the movie, you would always go back and see it again."

— Donald Rogers, Boatswain's Mate Second Class

"Most fun of all was FIELD DAY. Local talent — dancers, singers, joke tellers — came forth both with quality and quantity. Then we had all sorts of games — trap shooting, knot tying, first aid, boatswains' piping, pistol and rifle shooting, small arms assembly, answering of questions relative to the ship, line heaving, rope climbing, boxing and wrestling. Best of all was a tug of war between 100 men of the Gunnery Department and 100 of the engineering gang, with the accompaniment of the ship's band. We started a lecture program over the battle circuits. We would give lectures on the weather or some incident at sea or something to build up added interest. During each watch we would read something of interest over the phones in an effort to keep the men awake and alert."

— Lieutenant Commander John Kirkpatrick, Air Defense Officer

"Religious service was usually held in the mess compartment aft on the starboard side. It was held on Sundays and special occasions. The attendance at the service was dependent on what we were headed for. If action was imminent, the attendance would go up. If not, only those who attended service regularly would be there. The chaplains were always there to help you. It was a tense time in our lives. They would comfort us and tell us everything would be all right and to just trust in God, which we did."

— Jim Masie, Fire Controlman First Class

RECOVERY OF THE GILBERT ISLANDS
November – December 1943

The operation to recover the Gilberts began in November 1943. By then the U.S. Pacific Fleet had been strongly reinforced by the addition of eight new fast carriers, including ESSEX (CV-9), a new LEXINGTON (CV-16), BUNKER HILL (CV-17), INDEPENDENCE (CVL-22), PRINCETON (CVL-23), BELLEAU WOOD (CVL-24), COWPENS (CVL-25) and MONTEREY (CVL-26). (CVL stood for light carrier; cruiser hulls with flight decks.) Veteran carriers SARATOGA and ENTERPRISE also took part in this operation. Several older battleships were now available, including PENNSYLVANIA (BB-38), NEW MEXICO (BB-40), MISSISSIPPI (BB-41), IDAHO (BB-42) and TENNESSEE (BB-43). Of these, the first and last named were restored victims of the Japanese attack on Pearl Harbor, December 7, 1941. New battleships participating included NORTH CAROLINA, WASHINGTON, SOUTH DAKOTA, INDIANA and MASSACHUSETTS. Although the new battleships carried out most pre-landing bombardments, the trusty older veterans were to serve as the primary, long-term gunfire support ships for this and most subsequent island campaigns in the Western Pacific.

In the Gilberts, Makin Atoll was to be taken by 6,000 troops of the Army's 27th Infantry Division, while Tarawa was the objective of the 18,000-man 2nd Marine Division. D-Day for the landings was November 20, with Vice Admiral Raymond A. Spruance, victor at the Battle of Midway, in overall command of the invasion forces. Following the pattern set in the Solomons, NORTH CAROLINA and other fast battleships were assigned to escort the fast carriers which supported and covered the operation.

At this time the main fighting strength of the Japanese Navy was based at Truk in the Caroline Islands, only 1,200 miles west of the Gilberts. Included among IJN ships based at Truk were the two super battleships, YAMATO and MUSASHI, armed with 18.1-inch guns, as opposed to the American maximum of 16-inch guns. Thus, our own fast battleships had to be kept positioned and ready for surface action, as well as for air defense of the carriers.

At Tarawa the enemy put up an especially strong defense and Marine Corps casualties were heavy. At the same time, the Japanese reacted with a series of aggressive air attacks against our ships, launched from airfields in the nearby Marshalls and Nauru Island. The attacks damaged several ships, and an enemy submarine sank one small carrier, LISCOME BAY (CVE-56). In turn, the Japanese lost two submarines, including I-19, which had torpedoed WASP, NORTH CAROLINA and O'BRIEN the previous year.

On the nights of November 25 and 26 the Showboat's task force was subjected to spectacular air attacks by large numbers of Japanese torpedo bombers. Brilliant flares and blinking float lights — red, white and green — lit up the night as the enemy planes closed in. Night fighters from our carriers, operating for the first time in that role, disrupted the attacks, while radar-controlled gunfire from our ships shot down several of the attacking planes. Two were claimed by NORTH CAROLINA. Although there was no damage to any of our ships, these attacks were long remembered by the Showboat's crew as hair-raising events. To be so brightly and nakedly illuminated in the night, exposed to attack by an unseen enemy, was one of the most unnerving experiences of the war for many of the crew.

The night of November 26 is also memorable for the loss of the U.S. Navy's first ace fighter pilot of World War II, Lieutenant Commander Edward H. "Butch" O'Hare, after whom Chicago's O'Hare International Airport is named. O'Hare was one of the night fighter pilots launched against the intruding enemy torpedo planes. He was under radar control of the Showboat's fighter director officer, Lieutenant (jg) Ralph Sheffer. While being vectored into an attack position, O'Hare found himself amidst a melee that suddenly developed among the Japanese planes in which they began shooting at each other. O'Hare's plane suddenly disappeared from the radar scope. He was not heard from again, and his loss was never satisfactorily explained. Sheffer speculated at the time that, with some 20 to 40 enemy planes in the air, possibly one had made a chance sighting of the American plane's engine exhaust, which could have provided a point of aim to shoot O'Hare down.

BOMBARDMENT OF NAURU ISLAND
December 8, 1943

On December 8, 1943, in an effort to reduce enemy air capabilities in the area, NORTH CAROLINA and five other fast battleships — WASHINGTON, SOUTH DAKOTA, INDIANA, MASSACHUSETTS and ALABAMA, under Rear Admiral Willis A. Lee — carried out a bombardment of the Japanese airfield and other military installations on Nauru Island, 400 miles southwest of Tarawa. Since this was the second anniversary (east longitude date) of the Japanese attack on Pearl Harbor, Admiral Lee saw it as payback time.

NORTH CAROLINA fires the first 16-inch salvo of World War II into Japanese-held territory, Nauru Island, December 8, 1943.

Admiral Raymond A. Spruance
Commander 5th Fleet

Admiral William F. Halsey
Commander 3rd Fleet

Vice Admiral Marc A. Mitscher
Commander Task Force 58

Vice Admiral John S. McCain
Commander Task Force 38

The bombardment began, however, with an embarrassing misunderstanding of signals on the part of NORTH CAROLINA, last ship in the column. As the column approached the position from which firing was to begin, Admiral Lee ordered two flag hoist signals to be flown from WASHINGTON, his flagship at the head of the column. On the port yardarm a flag signal ordered "Commence Firing," the order to be carried out by all six battleships in one stupendous salvo the instant the flag hoist was "executed" (hauled down). On the starboard yardarm was another signal, merely ordering a minor adjustment of course, when hauled down. The ships had already loaded their guns, and all were ready to open fire the moment the order to fire was executed. Shortly before that was to happen, the course change signal was executed. Thereupon the Showboat's signal officer cried, "Execute!" prompting understandably eager Captain Frank P. Thomas to shout, "Commence firing!" Instantly NORTH CAROLINA, alone, let go with her broadside, sending nine huge shells whistling toward Nauru. Up ahead on the bridges of the other battleships, all eyes scowled rearward, as if to say, "Which one of you guys belched in church?"

Admiral Lee was not pleased, but since no harm was done, no serious consequences ensued. The way the gaffe was later explained by the Showboat's cocky sailors was: "We fired the first 16-inch salvo of World War II into Japanese-held territory!" Ammunition expended by NORTH CAROLINA in this unusually light bombardment was 135 rounds of 16-inch, 403 of 5-inch.

INITIAL FORMATION OF TASK FORCE 38/58
January 20, 1944

Following the recovery of the Gilberts at the end of 1943, newly constructed ships had reinforced the U.S. Pacific Fleet to such an extent as to reverse the odds over the Japanese. On January 20, 1944, NORTH CAROLINA, together with seven other fast battleships, 12 fast carriers, six cruisers and 34 destroyers, assembled secretly at remote Funafuti Atoll in the Ellice Islands to form what was to become the most powerful and most famous of World War II naval striking forces, the "fast carrier task force," also known as Task Force 38 or 58. Newly constructed aircraft carriers now added to that force included INTREPID (CV-11), LANGLEY II (CVL-27) and CABOT (CVL-28). New battleships were IOWA (BB-61) and NEW JERSEY (BB-62). Older battleships now added to those supporting the amphibious force were COLORADO (BB-45) and MARYLAND (BB-46).

The fast carrier task force was to spearhead the U.S. offensive across the central Pacific to Japan. The force was designated Task Force 38 or 58, depending on which admiral was in command. Vice Admiral John S. McCain commanded it as Task Force 38, while Vice Admiral Marc A. Mitscher headed it as Task Force 58. Over them in command of the Third Fleet and Fifth Fleets, respectively, were Admirals William F. Halsey and Raymond A. Spruance. Under the fleet commanders were hundreds of ships in addition to those of Task Force 38/58. These included transports with their embarked troops and their escorts, oil tankers, ammunition ships, cargo ships, refrigerator ships, mine sweepers, land-based search aircraft, and others. However, both Admirals Halsey and Spruance usually chose to sail with their strong right arm, Task Force 38 or 58; Halsey in battleship NEW JERSEY, Spruance in heavy cruiser INDIANAPOLIS (CA-35).

Both the planning and execution of the U.S. strategy of back-to-back campaigns across the central Pacific demanded intense, exhausting attention for months at a time. Thus, Admiral Nimitz appointed these admirals and their staffs to plan and execute alternating campaigns. Halsey, McCain and their staffs carried out one campaign while Spruance, Mitscher and their staffs were ashore at Pearl Harbor planning the next. Their roles reversed upon completion of each campaign. This pattern repeated itself again and again as our island-hopping strategy across the Pacific was carried out. The leaders changed, but the ships and their crews were the same.

Both Spruance and Halsey were military leaders of the highest order, but they differed markedly in personality and in the methods by which they exercised command. Spruance was a cold calculator, a brilliant strategist who took no chances. Halsey was an audacious swashbuckler, a fearless gambler. Spruance's operation plans were huge printed volumes, every minor detail spelled out with infinite care. Halsey's operation plans were much shorter, occasionally set forth in terse classified radio messages, as opposed to Spruance's weighty tomes. Spruance rarely changed his plans, while Halsey was much more flexible; quick to change course when he sensed an opportunity to surprise the enemy. Although Spruance had skillfully directed our forces in the Battle of Midway, he was not a naval aviator, his prior naval experience having been primarily with cruisers and battleships. Hence, he relied on his aviator subordinates to advise him on the intricacies of carrier flight operations. Halsey was an experienced naval aviator who had commanded SARATOGA before the war and had successfully led carrier task forces during the first several months of fighting. Halsey dominated McCain, while Spruance relied heavily on the advice of Mitscher.

Ships of Task Force 38/58 turn together into the wind preparatory to launching aircraft.

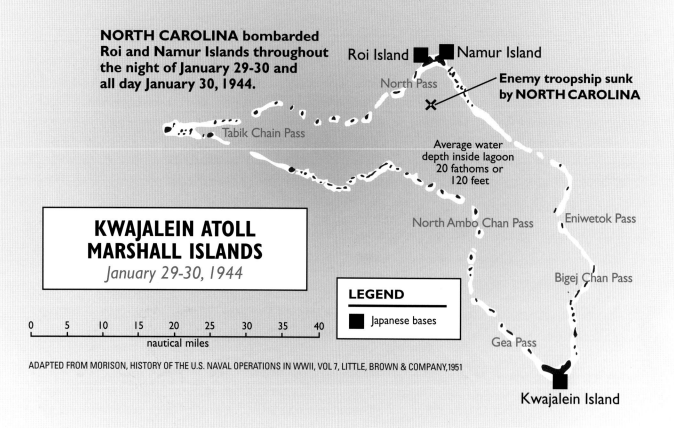

NORTH CAROLINA bombarded Roi and Namur Islands throughout the night of January 29-30 and all day January 30, 1944.

Roi Island   Namur Island

North Pass

Enemy troopship sunk by **NORTH CAROLINA**

Tabik Chain Pass

Average water depth inside lagoon 20 fathoms or 120 feet

KWAJALEIN ATOLL MARSHALL ISLANDS
January 29-30, 1944

North Ambo Chan Pass   Eniwetok Pass

Bigej Chan Pass

LEGEND

■ Japanese bases

Gea Pass

0 5 10 15 20 25 30 35 40
nautical miles

ADAPTED FROM MORISON, HISTORY OF THE U.S. NAVAL OPERATIONS IN WWII, VOL 7, LITTLE, BROWN & COMPANY,1951

Kwajalein Island

During 1942 and much of 1943, a carrier task force usually consisted of only one aircraft carrier protected by a meager screen of three or four cruisers and five or six destroyers. By early 1944, with the United States launching new warships at an amazing rate, Task Force 38/58 normally consisted of four or five task groups. Each group contained three or four carriers, together with many more escorts. When at sea in their usual circular cruising dispositions, the several task groups were in separate formations operating within sight of, or at least within voice radio range (roughly 10-15 nautical miles) of each other. The carriers formed the nucleus of each task group formation and were normally surrounded by two concentric circles of supporting ships. Battleships and cruisers comprised the inner circle, destroyers the outer. That way the ships of each task group were positioned to provide air defense in depth, the destroyers to detect and attack submarines before they could reach effective torpedo range on the larger ships. Should enemy surface units threaten the force, the battleships and cruisers could quickly deploy to engage them, while the more vulnerable carriers withdrew. The whole task force normally advanced in a body, but individual task groups were free to maneuver independently, which they repeatedly did while their carriers turned into the wind to launch or recover aircraft.

INVASION OF THE MARSHALL ISLANDS
January 29-February 5, 1944

The Marshall Islands included several atolls which the Japanese had secretly fortified before the war, and on which they built military airfields. There were many similar positions throughout the central Pacific. Our offensive could not advance into the western Pacific until these threats to our flanks and rear had been eliminated or neutralized. The strongest enemy position in the Marshalls was Kwajalein, one of the largest coral atolls in the world. This was to be the first and primary objective of the Marshalls invasion, with assault landings on January 31 and February 1 to be carried out by the 4th Marine Division and the Army's 7th Infantry Division.

In air operations during the last three days of January, Task Force 58 accomplished virtually the complete destruction of enemy aircraft and shipping in the Marshalls, helping to clear the way for the landings. The primary role of NORTH CAROLINA, aside from guarding the carriers, was the bombardment of Roi and Namur Islands at the northern tip of Kwajalein. She carried out this task throughout the night of January 29-30, and conducted a second bombardment throughout the day of the 30th, when other battleships joined her. Giant furrows made by the

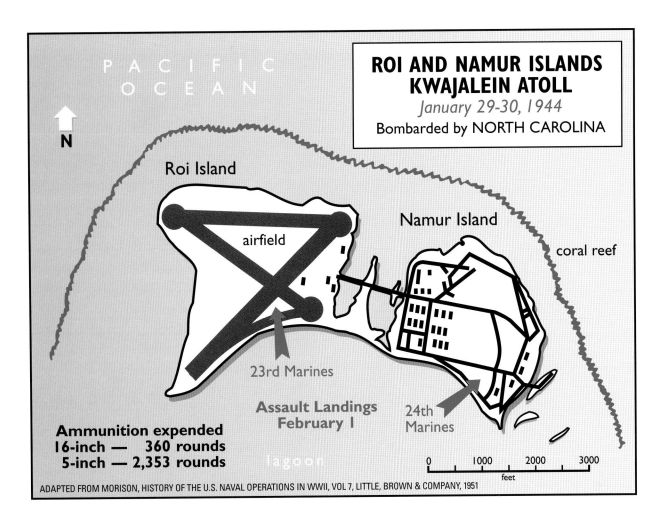

ROI AND NAMUR ISLANDS
KWAJALEIN ATOLL
January 29-30, 1944
Bombarded by NORTH CAROLINA

PACIFIC OCEAN

N

Roi Island

airfield

Namur Island

coral reef

23rd Marines

Assault Landings
February 1

24th
Marines

Ammunition expended
16-inch — 360 rounds
5-inch — 2,353 rounds

lagoon

0   1000   2000   3000
feet

ADAPTED FROM MORISON, HISTORY OF THE U.S. NAVAL OPERATIONS IN WWII, VOL 7, LITTLE, BROWN & COMPANY, 1951

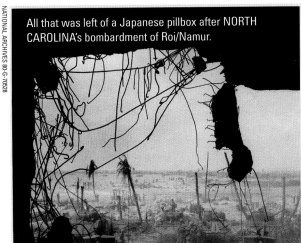

All that was left of a Japanese pillbox after NORTH CAROLINA's bombardment of Roi/Namur.

Fires burning on Roi following Showboat bombardment.

Showboat's 16-inch projectiles with time-delay fuzes extensively plowed up the enemy airfield, mystifying both the Japanese defenders and later the American landing force. Hangars and barracks were flattened, ammunition dumps blown up, blockhouses and pillboxes destroyed and the defending Japanese troops harassed and demoralized. NORTH CAROLINA fired a total of 360 rounds of 16-inch and 2,353 rounds of 5-inch ammunition in less than 24 hours — an exhausting experience for the entire crew.

A valuable extra prize fell to the American side when Japanese freighter EIKO MARU, sighted in Kwajalein's lagoon shortly before commencement of the bombardment, was sunk by the Showboat's gunfire. From the sunken wreck of this ship the Navy later salvaged up-to-date navigational charts covering the sea approaches and anchorages of many Japanese-held islands in the Pacific. These charts proved invaluable in subsequent operations where accurate navigational data would otherwise have been lacking.

On February 4, Task Force 58 anchored for the first time in the beautiful wide lagoon of Majuro Atoll, taken from the Japanese without opposition coincident with the seizure of Kwajalein. Majuro provided

"On April 6, 1944, during a second visit to Majuro by the fast carrier task force, I reported to NORTH CAROLINA for duty. I was then a 23-year-old lieutenant with three years' prior naval service, mostly in the Pacific. An interview that day with the executive officer, Commander Joe W. Stryker, led to my appointment as the ship's combat intelligence officer, with additional duty as assistant officer in charge of the combat information center. In the former capacity, it was my duty to keep the captain informed of significant intelligence regarding enemy forces capable of posing a threat to our ship and task force. Most of such intelligence reached us via encrypted radio messages, which arrived many times daily at all hours. Frequent among them were reports of the sighting of enemy fleet units sent from our submarines patrolling Japanese waters.

Since we carried no flag officer [admiral] during most of my tour, I was given Flag Plot, located on the 03 level directly below the pilothouse, to serve as my office. Only the captain, executive officer, navigator and I possessed keys to the space, which was always kept locked to protect the considerable volume of secret and top secret information in my custody. Most of my routine efforts involved maintaining a large chart of the western Pacific on which I kept track of the ships of the Japanese Navy, as well as the locations of friendly forces within 500 miles of our own position. In addition, for the convenience of the captain and navigator, I maintained in a small steel cabinet in the charthouse a mini-plot of enemy and friendly activity in our own general vicinity. After I had been on board several months I was assigned additional duty as custodian of our operation orders and as briefer of the ship's officers and senior enlisted men on NORTH CAROLINA's role in each impending operation. In other words, it was my job to know what was going on. I thought it was the best job on the ship."

— Author

Photograph of the author while on leave from NORTH CAROLINA in September 1944. The shotgun was for an impending hunting expedition in California's Mojave Desert.

the fast carrier task force with an excellent anchorage from which operations were conducted over the next several months, following the invasion of the Marshalls. From February through April 1944 the force swept back and forth across the central Pacific striking with impunity at military objectives deep inside what the Japanese had previously regarded as their own private domain. The enemy's main bastion at Truk was plastered repeatedly, as were Japanese airfields and bases on Guam, Saipan, Tinian, Palau, Yap, Woleai and other islands. During this three-month period, over 50 Japanese ships were sunk and hundreds of aircraft destroyed, mostly by our carrier planes. Meanwhile, major enemy naval units that had been based at Truk were withdrawn to the safer waters of the Philippines.

After firing 2,353 rounds of 5-inch ammunition at enemy installations on Roi and Namur Islands, the exhausted 5-inch fire control team poses for a photograph at its battle station in Sky Control.

One of the Showboat's 16-inch salvos straddles Japanese freighter EIKO MARU in Kwajalein Lagoon.

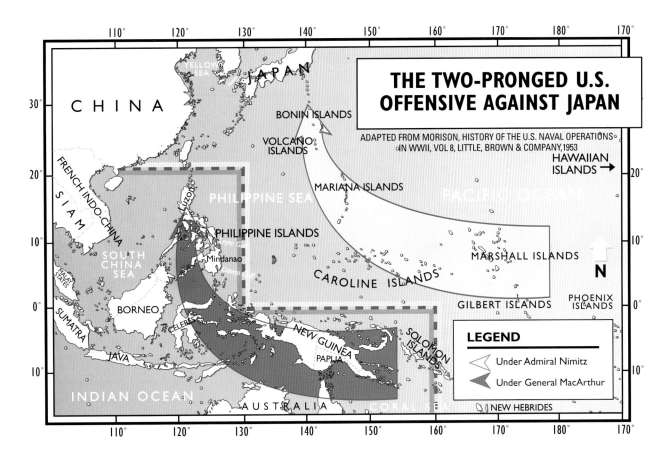

THE TWO-PRONGED U.S. OFFENSIVE AGAINST JAPAN

ADAPTED FROM MORISON, HISTORY OF THE U.S. NAVAL OPERATIONS IN WWII, VOL 8, LITTLE, BROWN & COMPANY, 1953

LEGEND

Under Admiral Nimitz

Under General MacArthur

NEW HEBRIDES

THE TWO-PRONGED OFFENSIVE AGAINST JAPAN

By early 1944, the U.S. joint chiefs of staff in Washington had decreed that our war effort against Japan would be built around a two-pronged offensive: one under Admiral Nimitz across the central Pacific, the other under U.S. Army General Douglas MacArthur advancing to the Philippines along the north coast of New Guinea. These two efforts were to be mutually supporting and were intended to keep the enemy guessing as to where the next blow would fall. As a part of this plan, from April 20 to 24, Task Force 58 carried out air strikes in support of forces under General MacArthur in landings on the north coast of New Guinea at Hollandia, Aitape, Tanahmerah Bay and Humboldt Bay. As usual, the Showboat was there.

RESCUE OF DOWNED AVIATORS OFF TRUK
April 30, 1944

During a strike on the enemy's main mid-Pacific naval base of Truk, April 30, Lieutenant John A. Burns, the pilot of a NORTH CAROLINA OS2U Kingfisher, fearlessly landed his plane in choppy seas east of the atoll and rescued the remarkable total of 10 Navy aviators who had been shot down by the intense Japanese antiaircraft fire. The plane could not take off, of course, with such a heavy load; so Burns taxied it out to sea, with drenched pilots perched on the wings and in rubber rafts towed astern. All were delivered to a rescue submarine, USS TANG (SS-306). Burns and his radioman, Aubrey J. Gill, then also boarded the sub, which sank the waterlogged Kingfisher with gunfire so it would not fall into enemy hands. For this heroic act Burns was awarded the Navy Cross.

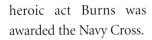

(Left) Overloaded Showboat Kingfisher rescues 10 downed aviators off Truk, April 30, 1944. Photograph taken from rescue submarine USS TANG.

Lieutenant John A. Burns, Kingfisher rescue pilot.

BOMBARDMENT OF PONAPE ISLAND
May 1, 1944

Seven fast battleships, NORTH CAROLINA, SOUTH DAKOTA, INDIANA, MASSACHUSETTS, ALABAMA, IOWA and NEW JERSEY, again under command of Admiral Lee, were detached from Task Force 58 on the morning of May 1, 1944, with orders to bombard Japanese military installations on the island of Ponape, largest of the Carolines, located 360 miles east of Truk. A rugged and heavily forested island, not an atoll, Ponape is 19 miles in diameter with a highest elevation of 2,500 feet. Ponape possessed a good harbor where the Japanese had built a seaplane base, with an airfield nearby and another airfield under construction. The main purpose of the bombardment was to destroy the capacity of the island to support air operations against American forces. After 70 minutes of bombardment, Admiral Lee decided that his mission was accomplished and ordered his ships to cease firing and withdraw. Ammunition expended by NORTH CAROLINA: 54 rounds of 16-inch, 131 of 5-inch.

INVASION OF THE MARIANAS
June 1944

After another hurried visit to Pearl Harbor in May, this time for rudder repairs, NORTH CAROLINA rejoined Task Force 58 in early June preparatory to the invasion of Saipan and Tinian and the recovery of Guam. The latter, with its excellent harbor and airfield, was the primary naval objective; but Saipan and Tinian were needed, too, as bases for future heavy bomber operations against the mainland of Japan. As usual Task Force 58 struck first, helping clear the way for the amphibious forces and assault troops. These were to include the 2nd, 3rd and 4th Marine Divisions; the 1st Provisional Marine Brigade; plus the 27th and 77th Infantry Divisions of the U.S. Army. Initial landings on Saipan were to be carried out on June 15; on Guam, July 21; and on Tinian, July 24. The Showboat was to take part in the first of these operations, but not the latter two.

On June 13, two days prior to the assault landings on Saipan, NORTH CAROLINA and six other fast battleships subjected the island to a preliminary

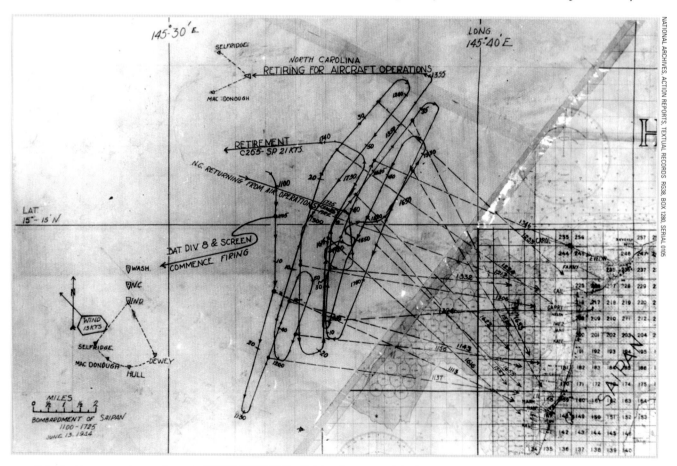

This chart is a copy of an enclosure to NORTH CAROLINA's official action report of the Saipan bombardment. In the center is the zigzagging track of the ship as it steamed back and forth during the 85-minute bombardment. At lower right is the shoreline of Saipan, on which a grid is super-imposed for the purpose of indicating target locations. Diagonal lines from the ship's positions to locations ashore represent main battery salvos. Ranges averaged 15,000 yards. The long, straight diagonal line extending from top right to bottom center is simply transparent adhesive tape used to attach two chart sections together.

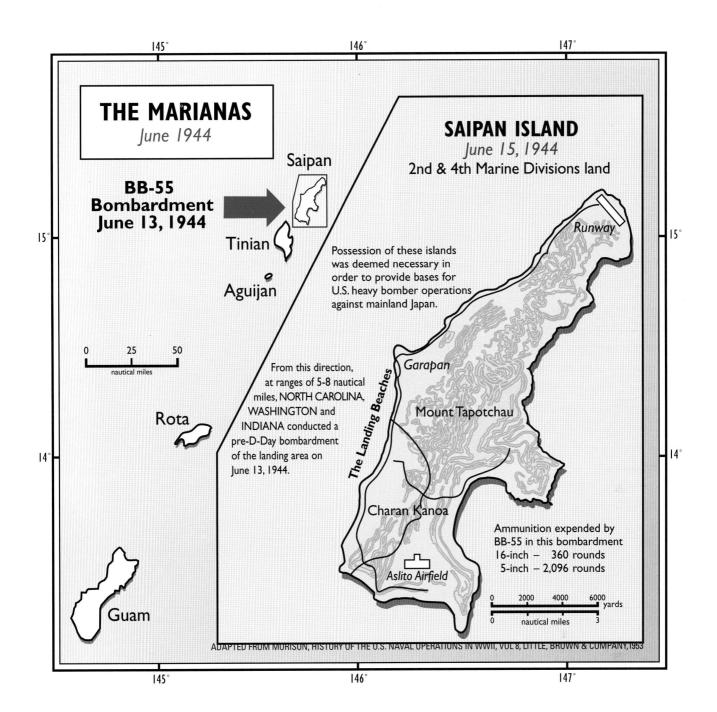

THE MARIANAS
June 1944

**BB-55
Bombardment
June 13, 1944**

Saipan

Tinian

Aguijan

0   25   50
nautical miles

Rota

Guam

SAIPAN ISLAND
June 15, 1944
2nd & 4th Marine Divisions land

Runway

Possession of these islands
was deemed necessary in
order to provide bases for
U.S. heavy bomber operations
against mainland Japan.

From this direction,
at ranges of 5-8 nautical
miles, NORTH CAROLINA,
WASHINGTON and
INDIANA conducted a
pre-D-Day bombardment
of the landing area on
June 13, 1944.

The Landing Beaches

Garapan

Mount Tapotchau

Charan Kanoa

Aslito Airfield

Ammunition expended by
BB-55 in this bombardment
16-inch —   360 rounds
5-inch — 2,096 rounds

0   2000   4000   6000
yards
0   nautical miles   3

ADAPTED FROM MORISON, HISTORY OF THE U.S. NAVAL OPERATIONS IN WWII, VOL 8, LITTLE, BROWN & COMPANY,1953

bombardment. NORTH CAROLINA, WASHING-
TON and INDIANA fired at ranges between 16,000
and 10,000 yards into the western side of the island,
where the landings were to take place. The main
purpose was to cover minesweeping operations
being conducted in shallower water closer to shore,
in order to make way for the amphibious force.
Under cover of the battleships' guns, the
minesweeping operation was successfully accomplished by ascertaining that no mines had actually
been laid off the landing beaches. Ammunition
expended by NORTH CAROLINA: 360 rounds of
16-inch, 2,096 of 5-inch.

With the coast of Saipan visible in the background,
NORTH CAROLINA reverses course preparatory to
resuming the bombardment.

The arrival of American invasion forces off the Marianas triggered a violent enemy reaction. The Japanese perceived at once the seriousness of this threat, not only to their extended island empire and its supply lines, but also to Japan itself. An all-out counter-attack was ordered with all available IJN combatant ships directed to deploy from the Philippines, preparatory to a decisive fleet engagement in the waters between the Marianas and the Philippines.

The main naval units committed by Japan to this effort consisted of five carriers with 473 aircraft; five battleships, including giants YAMATO and MUSASHI; 13 cruisers, 28 destroyers and 25 submarines. In command of the enemy fleet was Admiral Jisaburo Ozawa, one of the IJN's most experienced strategists. Opposing this armada, Task Force 58 then totaled 15 carriers with 956 aircraft, seven fast battleships, 21 cruisers and 69 destroyers. In addition, 28 American submarines patrolled the general area of impending combat. The American force clearly had the advantage in numbers, but this was partly offset by Japan's shore-based air power,

Admiral Jisaburo Ozawa, who commanded the Japanese Fleet in the Battle of the Philippine Sea.

which could be staged into the area to operate from fields on Guam, Yap and Palau.

Of particular concern to the Americans at this time were the combat capabilities of super battleships YAMATO and MUSASHI — largest, most heavily armed and most massively armored battleships ever built by any nation. Details, not fully revealed to the American side until after the war, were as shown in the following table, comparing YAMATO with the three classes of U.S. fast battleships:

COMPARISON: U.S. FAST BATTLESHIPS VS. YAMATO

	NORTH CAROLINA -class	SOUTH DAKOTA -class*	IOWA -class	YAMATO -class
STANDARD DISPLACEMENT	35,000 tons	35,000 tons	45,000 tons	64,000 tons
FULL LOAD DISPLACEMENT	42,000 tons	42,000 tons	57,500 tons	72,809 tons
LENGTH	729 feet	680 feet	887 feet	863 feet
BEAM	108 feet	108 feet	108 feet	127.5 feet
DRAFT	34.5 feet	36 feet	36 feet	35.62 feet
SHAFT HORSEPOWER	115,000	115,000	212,000	150,000
SPEED	26.5 knots	27 knots	33+ knots	27.5 knots
MAIN SIDE ARMOR	11.7 inches	11.5 inches	12.1 inches	16.14 inches
MAIN BATTERY	9 16-inch/45	9 16-inch/45	9 16-inch/50	9 18.1-inch/45
HEAVIEST MAIN BATTERY SHELL WEIGHT	2,700 pounds	2,700 pounds	2,700 pounds	3,219 pounds
MUZZLE VELOCITY in feet per second	2,300	2,300	2,500	2,559
RANGE	36,900 yards	36,900 yards	42,345 yards	45,275 yards
SECONDARY BATTERY	20 5-inch/38	20 5-inch/38*	20 5-inch/38	12 6.1-inch/55 12 5-inch/40

*SOUTH DAKOTA herself, configured as a force flagship, had only 16-5"/38 in order to accommodate a senior admiral and larger staff.

Japanese super battleship YAMATO during sea trials in 1941. This ship and her sister, MUSASHI, were the largest, most heavily armed battleships ever built by any navy.

FIRE CONTROL RADAR

Japanese optical range finders for gunfire control were superior to those of the Americans, but the IJN was far behind in the development and use of radar. Although dedicated gunfire control radar was under development in Japan late in World War II, such equipment is not known to have been installed operationally on any IJN ships. The nearest Japanese equivalent to shipboard fire control radar was the Type 22 surface search radar mounted on YAMATO during a January-April 1944 refit. This radar, never intended for gunfire control, provided a maximum detection range on battleships of 35,000 yards, with a range accuracy of ± 765 yards and a bearing accuracy of ± 5 degrees. In contrast, at a range of 37,000 yards the Mark 8 main battery fire control radars mounted on U.S. battleships provided range accuracy of ± 15 yards and bearing accuracy of 2 mils (a little over one-tenth of 1 degree). These wide differences meant that American battleships would possess a potentially decisive advantage over the Japanese in the event of a surface action at long range in low daytime visibility or at night.

BATTLE OF THE PHILIPPINE SEA
June 19-21, 1944

On the morning of June 18, three days after the initial landings on Saipan and one day before the impending sea battle was to begin, the four carrier task groups then comprising Task Force 58 assembled in a defensive position west of the Marianas. As first priority, they were under strict orders from Admiral Spruance to insure the protection of our invasion

The battle line is formed, with WASHINGTON leading, NORTH CAROLINA second, SOUTH DAKOTA third, cruisers follow. Four more fast battleships joined the column shortly after this photograph was taken.

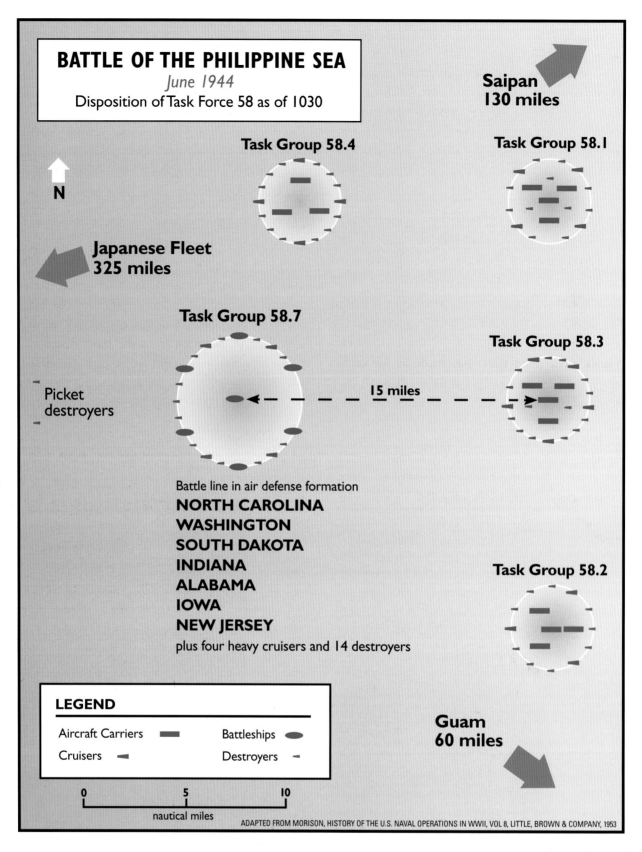

BATTLE OF THE PHILIPPINE SEA
June 1944
Disposition of Task Force 58 as of 1030

Saipan
130 miles

N

Task Group 58.4

Task Group 58.1

Japanese Fleet
325 miles

Task Group 58.7

Task Group 58.3

15 miles

Picket
destroyers

Battle line in air defense formation
NORTH CAROLINA
WASHINGTON
SOUTH DAKOTA
INDIANA
ALABAMA
IOWA
NEW JERSEY
plus four heavy cruisers and 14 destroyers

Task Group 58.2

LEGEND

Aircraft Carriers	▬	Battleships	●
Cruisers	◄	Destroyers	–

Guam
60 miles

0   5   10
nautical miles

ADAPTED FROM MORISON, HISTORY OF THE U.S. NAVAL OPERATIONS IN WWII, VOL 8, LITTLE, BROWN & COMPANY, 1953

force, then engaged in a furious struggle for Saipan. Anticipating that a major surface action could develop in addition to a carrier air battle, the battle line was formed — one of the rare occasions on which this occurred during World War II in the Pacific. In a battle line, battleships literally formed a line or column, best suited to bring the most guns to bear when engaging enemy surface combatants. Vulnerable aircraft carriers with their protective screen of destroyers and cruisers were to stay well behind the battle line. This line included NORTH CAROLINA, WASHINGTON, SOUTH DAKOTA, INDIANA, ALABAMA, IOWA and NEW JERSEY, accompanied by four heavy cruisers and 14 destroyers.

This "Surface Action Group," designated Task Group 58.7, took station ahead of of Task Force 58 and 15 miles to the west, the direction from which the enemy was expected to attack. Fighter aircraft from

Task Group 58.4 provided cover over the battle line. With the wise and experienced Vice Admiral Lee in command, and with our battleships able to fire a combined, radar-controlled broadside of 85 tons, the men of the Showboat eagerly awaited the fray. But alas, that kind of battle did not materialize. Instead, what occurred was the greatest carrier air battle of the war.

The fighting on the first day, June 19, sometimes referred to as "The Marianas Turkey Shoot," took place at long range with the opposing fleets separated during most of the action by more than 300 nautical miles. The shooting began around mid-morning with the first of a daylong series of attacks against Task Force 58 by Japanese land-based and carrier-based planes. The main effort was made by the carrier planes, which attacked in four successive waves totaling 373 aircraft. With the approach of the first wave, Admiral Lee ordered his ships into a circular formation to provide best air defense. That first day of fighting was almost entirely defensive on the part of the Americans because the Japanese aircraft — unburdened by gas-guzzling armor to protect the pilot (as were U.S. Navy aircraft) — had a greater radius of action than ours, and Admiral Ozawa shrewdly kept his ships beyond American attack range.

Our fighter planes, under radar control of fighter director officers on board the ships of the task force, including NORTH CAROLINA, intercepted each attacking wave, shooting down most of the enemy aircraft before they reached the ships of the force. Those reaching the ships of Task Group 58.7 received a murderous reception from the most destructive mass of naval antiaircraft guns ever assembled. According to an official report of the action, "the battleships, cruisers and destroyers ahead put up a

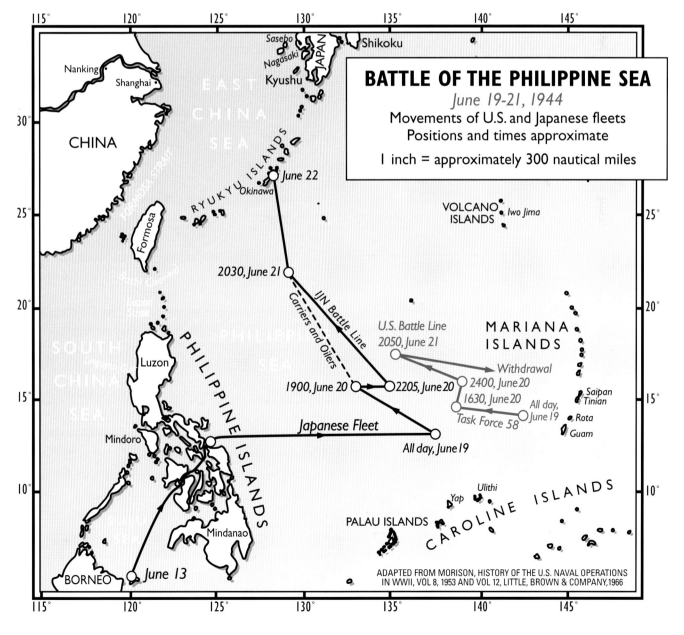

BATTLE OF THE PHILIPPINE SEA
June 19-21, 1944
Movements of U.S. and Japanese fleets
Positions and times approximate

1 inch = approximately 300 nautical miles

ADAPTED FROM MORISON, HISTORY OF THE U.S. NAVAL OPERATIONS
IN WWII, VOL 8, 1953 AND VOL 12, LITTLE, BROWN & COMPANY, 1966

tremendous barrage which, together with the burning planes all around the horizon, created a most awesome spectacle."

An enemy torpedo plane succeeded in crashing into INDIANA at her waterline, but the torpedo failed to explode. Another plane dropped a 500-pound bomb on Turret II of SOUTH DAKOTA. The explosion did no damage to the turret, but killed 27 men and wounded 23 others at nearby exposed battle stations. Otherwise, Task Group 58.7 was unscathed.

After an overnight lull, occasional air attacks on Task Force 58 resumed on the 20th, but with the Japanese gradually retiring westward, keeping their distance from the Americans. Late that afternoon, after an American search plane located the enemy fleet, Admiral Spruance ordered a long-range twilight air attack by Task Force 58 planes. This was a bold move, but it meant that the pilots would have to return to their carriers long after dark, dangerously low on fuel. The strike achieved substantial success, in that one enemy aircraft carrier was sunk, along with two oil tankers, while four other carriers, two other tankers, a battleship and a cruiser were damaged.

The willingness ...

of these courageous young airmen to undertake this mission, regardless of the risks involved, constituted one of the most heroic actions of World War II. They well knew that they might not have enough fuel for the long return flight, but they carried out their orders. Especially daunting for some of the younger pilots was the fact that they had never before landed on a carrier flight deck at night. These lads rank with the bravest of the brave.

Task Force 58 paid dearly, however, for these gains. The returning pilots, exhausted after battling enemy fighters and gunfire at the end of the longest and most risky flight most of them would ever make, now had to wing their way back to their parent carriers on a very black night with fuel tanks running dangerously low. Some of the pilots were wounded, and most were so fatigued that they had to fight to stay awake. Late that night, as they began to approach the task force, Admiral Mitscher endeared himself to them forever by ordering a radical departure from the normal wartime practice of showing no lights at night. NORTH CAROLINA was one of several ships he ordered to turn on one of their giant 36-inch searchlights. With the beam aimed straight up, its purpose was to serve as a beacon for our returning planes. The lights helped, but at least 100 pilots did not make it to their carriers and were compelled to "ditch" in the water and await rescue by our ships. Of those who ditched, 84 pilots and 76 aircrewmen were rescued, while 16 pilots and 33 crewmen were lost.

After dark on the 20th, the commanders of both sides considered closing with battle lines for a decisive surface engagement. For this purpose, at 1900 (7:00 p.m.) major surface units of the Japanese fleet, including super battleships YAMATO and MUSASHI, actually commenced a high-speed run toward the American fleet (see chart). Shortly after 2200, however, complying with orders from IJN headquarters in Tokyo, the Japanese retreated without having made contact with the Americans. The reason is not clear, but was probably that the enemy destroyers were low on fuel, their tankers sunk.

Meanwhile, Admiral Spruance and his subordinates debated the desirability of sending the American battle line in hot pursuit. Spruance delayed his decision while Task Force 58 carriers recovered the aircraft that had executed the night attack. This lost much ground on the retreating enemy fleet, since the Americans' course for recovery had to be into the wind, which was from the east. Apparent indecision continued through the night, and it was not until 1050 on the 21st that the U.S. battle line was detached for the chase. A further delay was then necessary to fuel destroyers. This took nearly three more precious hours, from noon until 1500, while Ozawa's ships steamed away at 22 knots. By then halfway to

Okinawa, there was no hope of overtaking them. Task Force 58 retired to the vicinity of the Marianas, and the battle was over.

The men of the Showboat were bitterly disappointed not to engage the enemy directly with gunfire, feeling that an opportunity to crush the Japanese fleet once and for all had been lost. Most other participants in the battle shared the disappointment. Strong disapproval of Admiral Spruance's delay in closing with the enemy fleet was widespread, even among other flag officers of Task Force 58. Admiral Spruance, himself, conceded after the war that a more decisive outcome might have been achieved had he followed up his victory of June 19 by aggressively pursuing the Japanese fleet and forcing a showdown fight. He countered this argument, however, by pointing out that until late on the afternoon of the 20th he had been unsure of the location of the enemy fleet. He argued that protecting the amphibious ships and troops then fighting a desperate battle for control of Saipan was his primary responsibility. He was concerned that the Japanese fleet might be split, with one force acting to decoy him away from Saipan, allowing another to outflank him and disrupt the landing operation. The argument will doubtless continue as long as there are professional naval tacticians and armchair strategists to debate it.

Regardless of one's point of view, the outcome of the battle — the virtual elimination of Japan's once formidable carrier air power — was an overwhelming victory for the United States. The Japanese lost three aircraft carriers (two to U.S. submarines) and 476 aircraft, of which about 50 were shore-based. Most significant, they lost 445 carrier aviators. American losses for the three days of fighting totaled 130 aircraft and 76 aviators, with no ships lost. This battle greatly reduced the offensive power of the Japanese Navy for the remainder of the war. Such heavy attrition of irreplaceable flying personnel left the surviving Japanese carriers almost useless, while the lack of seaborne air cover severely limited the radius of action of what was left of the enemy fleet.

OVERHAUL AT PUGET SOUND NAVY YARD
July-September 1944

The morale of the Showboat's crew, never low, surged upward following the great victory off the Marianas. It shot to a new high when news came of a trip "Stateside." In early July NORTH CAROLINA was detached from Task Force 58 and departed for a long-needed shipyard overhaul at the Puget Sound Navy Yard, Bremerton, Washington. This gave most of the officers and men their first opportunity since the ship's arrival in the Pacific two years earlier to go home and visit their families. All hands were granted 25 days leave, half the crew to be away at a time.

Showboat sailors prepare to go on well-earned leave while the ship undergoes major overhaul at Puget Sound Navy Yard.

Weddings

The possibility of a lengthy war with the threat of death caused countless American couples to "rush to the altar." The ship's weekly newspaper, TARHEEL, was filled with congratulations to numerous newlyweds. Estimates nationwide reached over 1,000 brides a day in the first months after the attack on Pearl Harbor. By the end of the 1940s proportionately more women were married than at any other time in the century.

Many crewmembers married before the ship left for the war and especially in 1944 when the ship returned to Bremerton, Washington, for a 60-day overhaul. It was the first trip home after a two-year tour of duty in the South Pacific. The crewmembers and their wives in these stories represent a small sample of the officers and crew that were married during the war years.

Tay & Edward Cope, Electrician's Mate First Class

"I met my husband, Edward, when I was eight years old and in third grade. Ted was 10 and in fifth grade. For me, it was love at first sight. I don't think Ted noticed me, although we lived on neighboring streets, until later on in that year when we had our school picnic in June. I ran down a long hill and to my surprise, he caught me at the bottom and kissed me. My first kiss!"

In spite of the kiss, the couple did not start dating until 1940. Engaged in May 1942, they planned a June wedding, but NORTH CAROLINA left in June for the Pacific fleet. Their June wedding was postponed for over 27 months!

On August 5, 1944, Tay Cope had returned from a voice lesson in New York City and called her mother for a ride home from the Trenton Railroad Station. *"She informed me that 'my Ted' was home and on his way to see me, that day. When he walked into my home, it was one of the most wonderful days of my life."*

Tay and Ted Cope married on August 9, 1944, at 9 a.m. on the lawn of Tay's parish church. Tay traveled with Ted to Bremerton, Washington, where the ship was being overhauled. After the ship left, Tay returned home to await Ted's homecoming.

Carol & Joe Mikitka, Metalsmith First Class

While in Brooklyn, New York, on Thanksgiving Day 1941, Joe accidentally bumped into a young lady on the corner of Clinton and Loraine streets. Sparks flew! For the remainder of his leave, Joe and Carol Mikitka enjoyed several dates. The two corresponded faithfully over the next three years.

On May 3, 1943, a package from Hawaii arrived for Carol containing an engagement ring with a note asking, "Will you marry me?" The couple wed on August 13, 1944, at the Dutch Reform Church of Flatbush in Brooklyn, New York. Carol's father, a Seabee in the Navy, could not get leave. He left without permission (AWOL) to give the bride away.

After the wedding, the Mikitkas boarded a train to Bremerton, Washington, where NORTH CAROLINA continued her stay in port for another five weeks. Carol stayed with Joe in Bremerton until the ship departed. This was the first time away from home for 18-year-old Carol. When Joe left, Carol returned home and waited for Joe's return in July 1945.

Eileen & Francis O'Brien, Machinist's Mate Second Class

Eileen and Francis O'Brien grew up on nearby Minnesota farms. The two did not meet until one night at a community dance. After that night, Francis and Eileen started dating.

When Francis joined the Navy in 1944 and came aboard NORTH CAROLINA, the two exchanged letters every day. One day something more than a letter arrived for Eileen. It was a diamond engagement ring from Hawaii!

The couple decided to have the wedding when Francis was on leave. They were married on May 7, 1947, at St. John's Catholic Church in Rochester, Minnesota.

Carol & Peter Polk, Junior Officer, Second Division

Stanford University students Carol and Peter Polk met on a blind date. When Peter left Stanford University to pursue his studies at Colorado and then Columbia, the two faithfully kept in touch.

Carol was a junior in college when Peter finally returned to Stanford in 1943. Peter was commissioned an officer in the United States Navy in February 1944 and joined NORTH CAROLINA later that year. They made a pact to each other — whenever and wherever the ship landed in the United States, they would get married. NORTH CAROLINA ended up in Boston, Massachusetts, on October 17, 1945. Three days later the couple held a naval wedding in the Unitarian Church on Beacon Street with the ship's chaplain conducting the service. Unfortunately, short notice prevented family from attending, but Peter's fellow officers witnessed the occasion. Their families gave the newlyweds a reception upon their return to the West Coast.

Jean & Paul Wieser, Boatswain's Mate First Class

Jean Coddington and Paul Wieser grew up in the town of Linden, New Jersey, with only a picket fence separating their two houses. While the two had dated a couple of times prior to Paul's joining the Navy in 1941, it was the exchange of letters that fostered their relationship and love.

When NORTH CAROLINA came to Pearl Harbor for repairs, Paul purchased Jean's engagement and wedding rings at the Naval base. He sent the two rings to his older brother and asked him to propose to Jean on Paul's behalf.

NORTH CAROLINA arrived in Bremerton, Washington, July 1944. Paul seized the opportunity and joined Jean in marriage on August 16, 1944, at St. Elizabeth's Church in Linden, New Jersey.

The newlyweds honeymooned in New York City. After a three-night stay at the Hotel Imperial, the couple headed out for Washington. Jean and Paul were able to spend another 30 days together before NORTH CAROLINA returned to the South Pacific. Jean returned home and lived with her mother until Paul's discharge in December 1946.

Norma & Stanley Shefveland, Fire Controlman Third Class

Norma Peterson and Stan Shefveland both grew up in the town of Clarkfield, Minnesota, where their paths crossed at Clarkfield High School. In the fall of 1939, Norma started high school where Stan was working part time as a hall monitor to earn extra money for his education. Norma recalls distinctly, *"I had my eye on him from the beginning."*

Norma graduated from high school in 1943 and began working as the "ration girl" selling gasoline ration stamps to farmers in western Minnesota. Norma and Stan both ate at the same restaurant daily, but it took a horror movie to bring them together. *"One evening I went to a show in town there and happened to sit alongside him. It turned out to be kind of a scary show, so we started holding hands. I saw him the next noon again at lunch and he had enjoyed the idea and we became better acquainted and started having dates."*

Stan left for boot camp right after Christmas in early 1944. He was assigned to the NORTH CAROLINA in May 1944. Through newspapers and radio, Norma kept informed of the latest developments in the war. They also kept in touch by writing letters, which Norma received almost daily.

When NORTH CAROLINA docked in Bremerton, Washington, Stan returned to Clarkfield and proposed to Norma on September 1, 1944. After the war, the couple was married on November 18, 1945 and honeymooned in Minneapolis.

After a complete overhaul, drydocking and installation of a new combat information center, the ship rejoined the fast carriers at Ulithi Atoll, November 5, 1944. This brought her back to the combat area just a few days too late to take part in the late October battles of Leyte Gulf and Samar, in which Japanese super battleship MUSASHI was sunk by carrier aircraft of Task Force 38.

SUPPORTING OPERATIONS IN THE PHILIPPINES
November-December 1944

During this period the main offensive operations of our fleet in the western Pacific were again under command of Admiral Halsey, with Vice Admiral McCain commanding the fast carriers. The force operated primarily in the Philippine Sea, supporting forces of General MacArthur fighting to recover the Philippines. On November 25, in the first of a long series of suicide attacks against our ships, Japanese "kamikaze" pilots crashed their planes into carriers ESSEX (CV-9), INTREPID (CV-11), HANCOCK (CV-19) and CABOT (CVL-28). These attacks came as a shocking surprise to most Americans.

Such tactics were far more difficult to defend against than conventional bombing, torpedo or strafing attacks. The pilot usually came down out of the sun or out of cloud cover in a very steep dive at terrific speed, headed straight for his intended victim. Usually there was little or no delay for evasive maneuvers. In the final seconds of the dive, even a direct hit by a 5-inch projectile might not prevent what was left of the plane from crashing into its target.

Life aboard...

"At 1256 [November 25] a Jap single-engine plane crashed into the port gun gallery of the ESSEX from an almost vertical dive. There was an intense, brilliant red flash of flame rising half again as high as the carrier's mast and seeming to spread out the entire width of the flight deck. ESSEX was about 3,700 yards away on a parallel course, broad on our starboard quarter. Immediately fire broke out in the hangar deck, under the flight deck. The fire was practically out in 15 minutes, and shortly thereafter planes were taking off. Several minutes later a second enemy plane came streaking over the formation at about 3,000-foot altitude. Smoke was streaming from its starboard wing as the Jap wove and twisted, trying to escape the storm of fire coming up at him from all the ships. He crossed over our stern from starboard to port, turned and seemed to be heading for us, then twisted around and headed back toward ESSEX and SANTA FE, on our starboard quarter. He finally dove vertically into the water, halfway between SANTA FE and ESSEX, with a billowing cloud of black smoke and a flash of deep red flame."

— Charles Paty, Jr., Radioman Second Class

Later in the war a frequently used variation in tactics was for the pilot to approach the force at very low altitude in order to avoid radar detection, then leap-frog over the screening ships before crashing a major vessel. This created an additional danger for our ships because of the spray of "friendly" gunfire in the heat of battle. Upon crashing a ship, the kamikaze delivered a duel death load: his bomb load exploded and his gasoline tanks ruptured, creating an instant bloody inferno amid structural shambles.

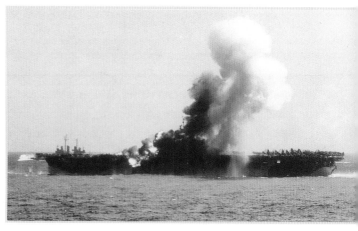

NATIONAL ARCHIVES 80-G-270738

At left a kamikaze (suicide pilot) dives on carrier ESSEX; the crash and explosion at right. This incident, which took place November 25, 1944, in the Philippine Sea, marked the beginning of a long series of such attacks on our ships. Photographs taken from NORTH CAROLINA.

Photographs taken December 13 show NORTH CAROLINA crashing through immense swells then racing across the Philippine Sea from east to west. Obviously a major storm was approaching from the east, but no one knew where its center was or where it was headed. Five days later its center slammed into Task Force 38.

A TYPHOON HUMBLES TASK FORCE 38
December 18, 1944

War was not the only mortal danger threatening our ships, as the crew of the Showboat was to learn on December 18 when a violent typhoon collided with Task Force 38. The task force was in the Philippine Sea attempting to fuel destroyers preparatory to launching air strikes in support of American landings on Mindoro Island in the central Philippines. Wartime weather observations on which to base forecasts were far from adequate, and the typhoon caught Task Force 38 by surprise.

Around mid-morning December 18 barometric pressure began to fall sharply. By early afternoon it had plunged below 27 inches, out of sight on the gauges. As the typhoon approached Task Force 38, an endless procession of immense swells rolled toward the force from the east, moving at a speed estimated at 30 knots. On they came, one after another with the military precision of a vast army, their ranks stretching north and south as far as the eye could see. Crests were nearly 1,000 feet apart. Troughs between them were so deep that 300-foot destroyers almost dropped out of sight in them. Winds rapidly built up to over 100 knots with gusts much stronger. As the eye of the typhoon drew closer, the wind gradually backed toward the north, superimposing north-to-south cross-swells on those

coming from the east, resulting in chaotically violent seas. Torrential rain combined with spray, foam and solid sheets of brine torn by the wind from the crests of waves soon reduced visibility to only a few yards.

During the most severe part of the storm, the course of NORTH CAROLINA's task group was generally toward the south and southwest. This enabled the ships to run with the sea most of the time. For the Showboat, the result was to minimize the amount of water taken on deck, and to reduce "pounding." Pounding was the violent impact and shudder felt all over the ship when the bow, after rising on one giant wave, crashed down into the next. The storm center passed 10-15 miles north of the ship at about 1550. At that time the eye of the typhoon was clearly visible on radar scopes as a brightly illuminated "doughnut," 12-15 miles in diameter.

Average roll recorded by NORTH CAROLINA was 10 degrees, but ship motion varied as the task group commander ordered course changes, mainly in an effort to reduce danger to the smaller ships. On a few occasions NORTH CAROLINA rolled as much as 43 degrees to each side, which meant that the crew could walk on the bulkheads almost as easily as on the decks. There were 70-foot seas. Lookouts on watch high in the tower foremast endured a dizzying swoop from one side to the other, occasionally as much as 90 feet, enough to make the toughest old salt seasick.

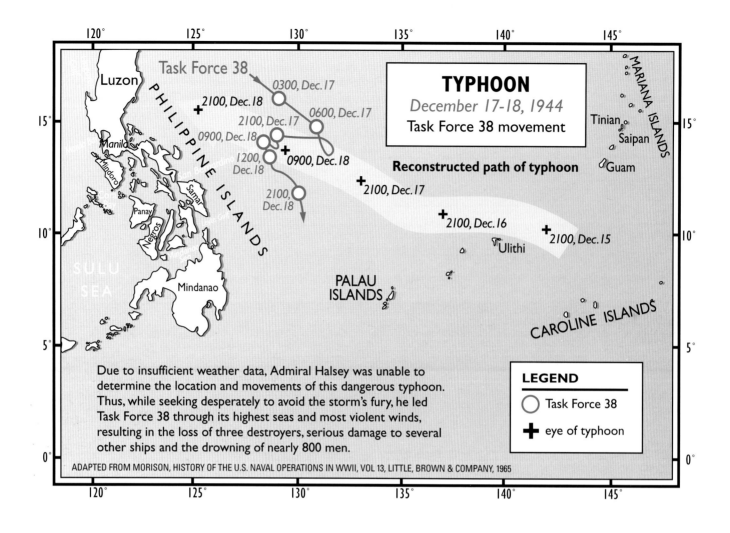

TYPHOON
December 17-18, 1944
Task Force 38 movement

Reconstructed path of typhoon

Task Force 38 · 0300, Dec. 17

2100, Dec. 18

2100, Dec. 17 · 0600, Dec. 17

0900, Dec. 18

1200, Dec. 18 · 0900, Dec. 18

2100, Dec. 18

2100, Dec. 17

2100, Dec. 16

Ulithi · 2100, Dec. 15

PALAU ISLANDS

Luzon

PHILIPPINE ISLANDS

Manila

Mindoro

Samar

Panay

Negros

Mindanao

SULU SEA

Tinian · Saipan · Guam

MARIANA ISLANDS

CAROLINE ISLANDS

Due to insufficient weather data, Admiral Halsey was unable to determine the location and movements of this dangerous typhoon. Thus, while seeking desperately to avoid the storm's fury, he led Task Force 38 through its highest seas and most violent winds, resulting in the loss of three destroyers, serious damage to several other ships and the drowning of nearly 800 men.

ADAPTED FROM MORISON, HISTORY OF THE U.S. NAVAL OPERATIONS IN WWII, VOL 13, LITTLE, BROWN & COMPANY, 1965

LEGEND
◯ Task Force 38
✛ eye of typhoon

Life aboard...

"At the height of the typhoon I deliberately stepped out into the fiercest weather I've ever witnessed to experience it first hand. I did this on the fore-and-aft catwalk above the signal bridge, nearly 50 feet above the normal waterline. My most vivid memory is of the fearsome sound of the wind as it screamed and roared — yes, roared — through the guy wires and antennas overhead. Gusts were so strong that I felt compelled to grip the steel handrail with all my strength to keep from being blown bodily away. Flying salt spray stung my face like sleet. All the buttons on my khaki shirt were quickly torn off. Crests of some of the immense waves loomed well above my head before the great ship staggered upward to ride over them. I watched in awe as the sea surged over the decks below me, crashing and foaming around the guns. Tons of white water were flung into the air, only to vanish instantly into the storm's whirling gray fury. I could take it for only about a minute before I was driven back into the shelter of the charthouse."

— Author

"The scariest time of my life was the typhoon.... We were fueling destroyers, and the seas were getting really rough. We fueled them as long as we could, and then it started to get dangerous. The captain ordered us to just cut the ropes and get out of there as it was getting worse by the second. We just left the fuel hoses on the deck and everyone went below decks.

"While playing pinochle, one of our head men of the division walks by and tells about 15 of us to get our life jackets on. We were going topside! This I will never, ever forget. No Japanese plane ever scared me as much as this. Three of us went up to the very tip of the bow. The others were spread out along the number one turret and were going to tie down the fueling lines. At the bow, before we even touched the lines, the ship went up on a swell and we knew we were going to take on a good bit of water, so we grabbed onto whatever we could find. We went down and about three feet of ocean hit us and sent us sprawling. We got up and got back to position when we started to go up on a swell again, this time WAY up and when we started to head back down I knew this was going to be really bad. I grabbed a

Light aircraft carrier LANGLEY (CVL-27) wallows in heavy seas after the eye of the typhoon has passed.

A destroyer drops almost out of sight in a trough after the eye of the typhoon has passed.

cable that ran from a 40-mm mount down into the deck, and when we went down I pulled the whole thing out and I just remember being washed down the deck towards the number one turret and hitting all these obstacles under all this water, and when I came to a stop I was under the spray shield of the 16-inch guns.

"The ship then lurched to port and I was heading out over the side and all I could see was the top lifeline. I put my arms straight down as far as I could and when I felt the top and middle lines I held on and just hung there like a shirt on a line until all that water went on through. Had those lines broken I would have died because I wasn't a good swimmer and in that kind of a sea they wouldn't have been able to pick up anyone anyway. Another man was hanging onto the lifeline as well, but he was hanging on the outside with a broken leg. But we didn't lose a single man in all of this. We were banged up but very lucky. We all went to sick bay to get fixed up. For the first and only time we were all given a shot of brandy."

— Robert Palomaris, Gunner's Mate First Class

The typhoon caused only superficial damage to NORTH CAROLINA, her only serious casualty being the loss of her aircraft, which were totalled and had to be replaced. On board some of the smaller ships, invisible in the typhoon, it was a different story, revealed only in fragments through desperate radio reports. From several of the light carriers came word of aircraft breaking loose on the hangar decks, crashing back and forth as the ships rolled, rupturing their gas tanks and starting terrible fires. From the destroyers came frantic reports of rolling 60, 70 and more degrees; of hanging there helpless for minutes at a time. Later it was learned that three of the destroyers had rolled all the way over on their beam-ends, where they lay pinned flat to the sea by the wind, as mountainous waves rolled over them. The sea poured into their smokestacks, putting out the fires in their boilers and leaving them with no hope of staying afloat. With that, their radios suddenly went silent, the reason dreadfully clear. All three destroyers, HULL (DD-350), MONAGHAN (DD-354) and SPENCE (DD-512) went down, taking with them nearly 800 men. Thus was proud Task Force 38 reminded of the awesome power of the sea.

ULITHI ATOLL, ADVANCED FLEET BASE

By late 1944, U.S. Navy Construction Battalions (Seabees) had developed a base at Ulithi Atoll in the western Carolines, which served as the main advanced base supporting operations of our Navy in the western Pacific until the end of the war. It was to this base that the fast carrier task force retired after scouring the sea for typhoon survivors. We arrived there December 24 for a gloomy Christmas, in view of all the lives so recently lost.

Ulithi is 900 nautical miles from Iwo Jima, 1,200 from Okinawa, 360 from Guam and 1,300 from Tokyo. Thus, it was ideally located to provide logistics support to the fleet. The atoll was occupied by U.S. forces, unopposed, September 20, 1944. It offered a relatively safe anchorage for the upkeep and provisioning of the ships, plus wide sandy beaches under coconut palms for crew relaxation and recreation. The wide lagoon, with water depths averaging around 120 feet, provided anchorage berths for 625 ships, from the largest aircraft carriers and battleships down to the smallest ocean-going amphibious types. Falalop Island was big enough to allow construction of a 3,500-foot airstrip. Asor was the site of the base headquarters, port director's office, radio station,

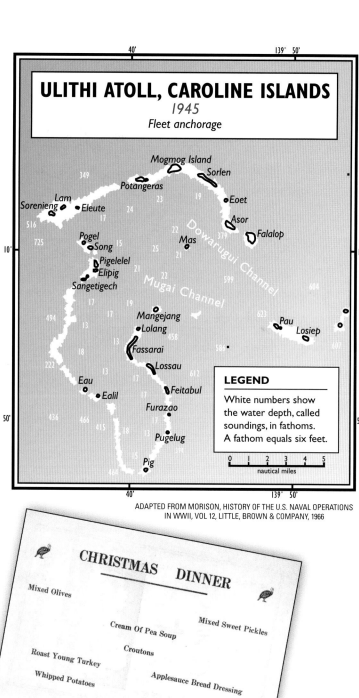

ADAPTED FROM MORISON, HISTORY OF THE U.S. NAVAL OPERATIONS IN WWII, VOL 12, LITTLE, BROWN & COMPANY, 1966

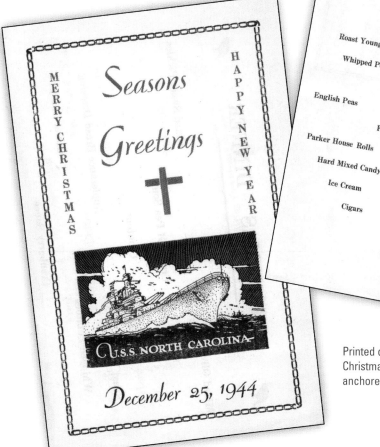

Printed dinner menu for all messes, Christmas 1944, while the ship was anchored in Ulithi lagoon.

Mogmog, Recreation Island, Ulithi Atoll

The beach (top) offered a place where war-weary men of the fleet could enjoy the water in healthy exercise while officers (bottom) and enlisted men (above) relaxed and blew off steam in separate areas under the palms.

evaporator plant, small boat landing and cemetery. Sorlen was equipped with a shop for maintenance of small craft.

Mogmog Island was devoted to recreation, with separate areas for officers and enlisted men. The island's facilities, built by the 88th Naval Construction Battalion, included a 1,200-seat theater and a 500-seat chapel. Ball fields, bars, soft drink stands, heads (toilets) and coral-cleared beaches accommodated up to 8,000 enlisted men and 1,000 officers per day. After weeks of the danger and stress of combat operations at sea, Mogmog provided a much needed refuge where the exhausted crews of our ships could relax and blow off steam. During NORTH CAROLINA's several visits to Ulithi, the ship's Mogmog liberty parties averaged 30 officers and 350 enlisted men per day.

Life aboard...

"Mogmog was an uninhabited island with a few coconut palms, some underbrush and lots of sand and beach. The island's highest elevation was six feet above sea level, and it was so small that you could walk completely around it in 10 minutes. We could strip down to our skivvies and swim in the surf, get in a crap game or into fights [which were plentiful], or just lounge around and relax, which most of us did. We were allowed three bottles of beer each. Since I didn't care too much for beer, I think I drank one and gave two away."

— William Fleishman, Water Tender Second Class

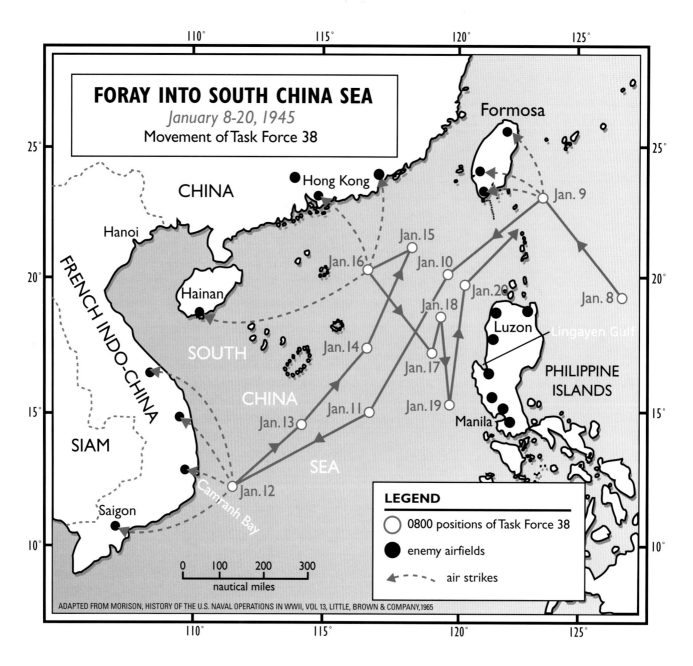

FORAY INTO SOUTH CHINA SEA
January 8-20, 1945
Movement of Task Force 38

CHINA

Formosa

Hanoi

Hong Kong

25°

FRENCH INDO-CHINA

Hainan

Jan. 9

Jan. 15

Jan. 16

Jan. 10

20°

Jan. 20

SOUTH

Jan. 18

Jan. 8

Luzon

Lingayen Gulf

Jan. 14

CHINA

Jan. 17

PHILIPPINE
ISLANDS

15°

Jan. 13

Jan. 11

Jan. 19

SIAM

SEA

Manila

Saigon

Camranh Bay

Jan. 12

LEGEND

○ 0800 positions of Task Force 38

● enemy airfields

◄ - - - air strikes

0   100   200   300
nautical miles

ADAPTED FROM MORISON, HISTORY OF THE U.S. NAVAL OPERATIONS IN WWII, VOL 13, LITTLE, BROWN & COMPANY,1965

DARING FORAY INTO THE SOUTH CHINA SEA
January 10-20, 1945

For Task Force 38, the year 1945 began with a bold move on the part of Admiral Halsey, as he led the force on a wide-ranging foray into the South China Sea. Except for submarines, no American or Allied warships had dared venture there since Japan drove the British, French, Dutch and Americans out of southeast Asia three years earlier. The operation was risky in view of the land-based aircraft, including kamikazes, which the enemy could send out to attack Task Force 38 in that confined body of relatively shallow, reef-filled water. Moreover, one purpose of the operation was to provoke enemy attacks on Task Force 38 in order to relieve pressure on American naval and ground forces under General MacArthur, then carrying out a major amphibious operation in Lingayen Gulf, on the west coast of Luzon. Admiral

Halsey had yearned for months to undertake the operation, as he believed that several of the remaining combatant ships of the Japanese Navy, including two battleships, were holed up in Camranh Bay, one of the largest naturally protected anchorages in the world, on the coast of French Indo-China (now Vietnam).

To kick off the operation, a surprise air attack on Camranh Bay was to take place January 12, followed, it was hoped, by a battle line engagement with enemy surface units. Thereafter, Halsey's plan was to attack Japanese merchant shipping, aircraft and airfields from Saigon north along the coast of mainland Asia as far as Hong Kong, while protecting Task Force 38 from enemy air attack with an especially strong fighter defense.

As it happened, bad weather on the western side of the South China Sea limited offensive air operations of Task Force 38, while good weather over Lingayen

January 8, 1945: "Luzon is a bloody battlefield. The enemy is fighting to the death. So far, our task force has had no attacks, but the hunt for big game may start in two or three days. The safety of our ships depends on the alertness of all hands. On your toes and give them all you've got."

January 11, 1945: "We have sighted one enemy battleship, a number of destroyers and destroyer escorts about 400 miles to the southwest and we are heading in that direction. Also a number of cargo ships have been sighted off the coast of French Indo-China. The enemy probably does not know that we are in this area. We are to strike at these targets tomorrow. Tomorrow may be our golden opportunity. You all know what to do. Give them hell and God bless you."

— Excerpts from diary of William Fleishman, Water Tender Second Class

PHOTOGRAPH NATIONAL ARCHIVES 208 PU88-2b

Gulf resulted in extremely heavy American losses to kamikazes in that area. A particular disappointment to the strike aviators of Task Force 38 was to find no major Japanese fleet units in Camranh Bay, as all had been withdrawn southward to Lingga Roads near Singapore. After attacks through January 16 against targets along the coasts of French Indo-China and China, including Hong Kong, the weather became unfavorable for flight operations and no further air strikes could be carried out. About this time, Japan's radio propagandist, Tokyo Rose — a turncoat Japanese-American woman — broadcasted from Tokyo: "We don't know how you got in there, but how the hell do you think you're going to get out?"

Well, after a three-day delay for fueling in rough seas, the admiral got his ships out easily enough on January 20, and nobody tried to stop them. The foray was at least a limited success, with one cruiser, 44 Japanese merchant ships and minor naval vessels sunk, and over 100 enemy aircraft shot down in the air or destroyed on the ground. Loss of 12 oil tankers was especially damaging to the enemy cause, as Japan was totally dependent on oil from the Dutch East Indies to fuel what was left of its war machine. Admiral Halsey later declared this operation "...one of the heaviest blows to Japanese shipping of any day of the war."

Life aboard...

"January 30, 1945 - Tuesday. We are...in the harbor of Ulithi in the biggest congregation of ships that was ever in one place in history. We are doing minor repairs to the ship and loading stores for our next trip out."

"February 3, 1945 - Saturday. We have started to take off 16-inch armor piercing shells and have been working all night on them and we are bringing on 16-inch bombardment shells so I guess the Japs are really going to catch hell the next time we go to sea."

"February 4, 1945 - Sunday. We are still bringing on 16-inch shells and I think we are supposed to bring on 900 rounds, so that will mean that we have about two more days work on the 16-inch, and when we get through with that we have to bring on 2,000 rounds of 5-inch shells. If only the people back home could see how these fellows work when they are in port and fight when they are at sea, they wouldn't believe it."

"February 5, 1945 - Monday. We are still bringing on ammunition.... We sure must be going to blow the hell out of things, or they wouldn't load all the ammunition on the ship like they have been in the last two days."

— Excerpts from diary of Joseph Halas, Seaman First Class

NATIONAL ARCHIVES 80-G-314506

A turret crew prepares to lower a 16-inch projectile through a main deck hatch to magazine stowage, four decks below.

PREPARATIONS FOR THE BOMBARDMENT OF IWO JIMA

While at Ulithi during the first nine days of February 1945, Admiral Spruance again replaced Admiral Halsey in command of what then became the Fifth Fleet, with Vice Admiral Mitscher relieving Vice Admiral McCain in command of the fast carriers, now Task Force 58. At the same time, a significant change was ordered in the main battery ammunition load carried in the magazines of our battleships. This was dictated by the types of projectiles that would be most effective for the impending bombardment of Iwo Jima, together with the now reduced likelihood of a surface engagement with enemy battleships.

The 16-inch magazines of NORTH CAROLINA were intended to carry a total of 1,200 rounds, including powder and projectiles. Actually, due to structural anomalies, only 1,188 rounds could be accommodated. Prior to 1945, the priority was ship-versus-ship action, so the ship normally carried two-thirds armor piercing type projectiles. Before departing Ulithi on February 10 for the Iwo Jima operation, the priority reversed such that the magazines stocked 873 high capacity (bombardment) projectiles and only 315 armor piercing ones. The load of 5-inch ammunition of various types totaled 12,800 rounds.

Aerial view of Task Force 58 at high speed.

NATIONAL ARCHIVES 80-G-427931

TASK FORCE 58 STRIKES TOKYO
February 16-17, 1945

Three days before the assault landing on Iwo Jima was to begin, Task Force 58 carried out a surprise air strike on the Tokyo area for the purpose of reducing the enemy's ability to launch air attacks against our Iwo Jima invasion force. Task Force 58 was at the peak of its awesome power with 116 fast ships, including 16 aircraft carriers, eight battleships, one battle cruiser, 14 heavy and light cruisers and 77 destroyers. Over 1,000 planes could be put in the air at one time, and the combined ships' crews and aviation personnel numbered over 100,000 men. The task force was divided into five task groups, with three or four carriers in each. Steaming at 25 knots in a column of task groups the formation, including picket destroyers, was 96 miles long as it churned toward Japan.

For the crew of NORTH CAROLINA the high-speed approach to the launch area, roughly 120 miles southeast of Tokyo, was a memorable experience. This was the first time since the war began that any ships of our Navy, other than submarines, had approached that close to the Japanese mainland. Even though the enemy's navy was no longer a match for ours, it still had thousands of shore-based aircraft to send against us as kamikazes, along with the super battleship YAMATO, a few cruisers, destroyers, submarines and high-speed torpedo boats.

In Tokyo, with the first light of a gray dawn, air raid sirens wailed as hundreds of U.S. Navy fighters suddenly zoomed down out of the clouds to strafe and rocket airfields surrounding the city. Later in the morning a few Japanese fighters rose to meet them, and flak soon peppered the sky, but most defenders seemed to have been taken by surprise. Thus began a day and a half of strikes which, despite bad weather, cost Japan over 500 aircraft — losses which Tokyo Rose was never heard to report. Our own losses were 88 planes, but not one enemy plane attacked the ships of Task Force 58.

"Unable to sleep on the night before our Tokyo attack, I remember lying awake on my canvas cot in Flag Plot listening by radio to Tokyo Rose as she sweet-talked us 'Yanks.' She warned us that night that our girlfriends in the states were playing around with other men, so maybe we'd better desert and go home before it was too late. I recall later in the night stepping out on the darkened signal bridge, where I was surprised to see the western sky luridly aglow from an erupting volcano on one of Japan's small islands south of Tokyo Bay.

"An hour before sunrise, as we raced toward launch position, on every ship the general alarm began its jarring clang! clang! clang! alerting those hundred thousand men to prepare for action. Below decks, in the dim red light of battle lanterns, gun crews, signalmen and lookouts bound for exposed battle stations topside fumbled into foul weather clothing before donning life jackets and steel helmets. Long used to fighting in the tropics, they were startled by the biting cold wind and flurries of snow that greeted our first venture into the latitude of central Japan in winter.

"Through the darkness and flying spray of that foul night, pinpoint spurts of flame suddenly began to appear on the flight decks of the carriers as hundreds of aircraft engines coughed, sputtered and roared into the steady drone of warm-up. Then, as though steered by a single helmsman, the entire force of 116 ships turned together into the wind and 16 carriers began launching 'Hellcat' and 'Corsair' fighters. Short bursts of machine gun fire rattled in the darkness overhead, as pilots tested their guns while they climbed. Some were to serve as combat air patrol defending our ships, but most formed into tight formations and streaked toward the enemy coast."

— Author

BOMBARDMENT OF IWO JIMA
February 19-22, 1945

Iwo Jima is a small, relatively flat volcanic island located about halfway between Saipan and Tokyo. In early 1945, the island's terrain and location made it an objective of vital importance to American forces closing in on Japan. The U.S. Army Air Corps, as the Air Force was then known, badly needed an airfield exactly where Iwo Jima was located to serve three purposes: first, as a haven for damaged B-29 heavy bombers returning to the Marianas after missions over the Japanese mainland; second, as a base for fighters to escort those bombers; and third, as a base for air-sea rescue operations.

Needing Iwo Jima was one thing; wresting it from the 22,000 tough Japanese soldiers and naval gunners who held it was another. They had sworn to their emperor to defend it to the death, and nearly all of them did. The four-square-mile island bristled with weapons of all types and was honeycombed with caves and tunnels. All of this was to make Iwo Jima the bloodiest Pacific battlefield of all, before Okinawa.

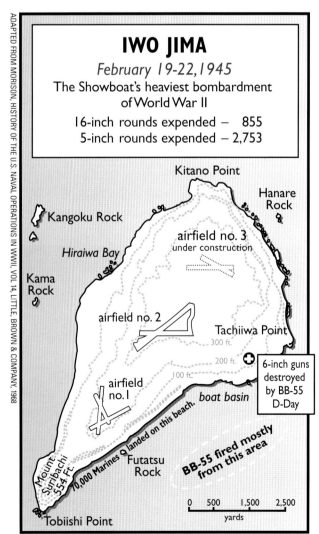

ADAPTED FROM MORISON, HISTORY OF THE U.S. NAVAL OPERATIONS IN WWII, VOL. 14, LITTLE, BROWN & COMPANY, 1968

IWO JIMA

February 19-22, 1945

The Showboat's heaviest bombardment of World War II

16-inch rounds expended — 855
5-inch rounds expended — 2,753

Kitano Point

Hanare Rock

Kangoku Rock

airfield no. 3
under construction

Hiraiwa Bay

Kama Rock

airfield no. 2

Tachiiwa Point

300 ft.

200 ft.

100 ft.

6-inch guns destroyed by BB-55 D-Day

airfield no. 1

boat basin

10,000 Marines landed on this beach.

Mount Suribachi 554 Ft.

Futatsu Rock

BB-55 fired mostly from this area

Tobiishi Point

0   500   1,500   2,500
yards

D-Day, H-hour at Iwo Jima. The Showboat was just off the picture at right, firing at enemy defense works on the right flank of the beach.

When over 70,000 men of the 3rd, 4th and 5th Marine Divisions began their assault on February 19, they were supported by the heaviest naval bombardment in history. This was carried out by NORTH CAROLINA along with seven other battleships, five heavy cruisers, three light cruisers and 10 destroyers. On D-Day the Showboat alone fired 806 rounds of 16-inch, mostly in direct support of the landing force. Positioned on the right flank of the assault, the ship was charged primarily with firing ahead of and to the right of the marines, both at pre-designated targets and against "on call" targets, when so requested by the troops ashore.

First priority, before the ship moved in to close range, was given to destroying a battery of 6-inch coastal defense guns (see chart), which two days before had scored six hits on heavy cruiser PENSACOLA, killing 17 and wounding 119 of her crew. NORTH CAROLINA opened main battery fire on this target at 0701 from 11,500 yards. Eight armor piercing rounds and 14 high capacity rounds were expended,

leaving nothing but smoke, debris and a crater of smoldering earth the size of a football field where the enemy guns had been. Thereafter, at ranges down to 4,600 yards, other early targets included blockhouses, gun emplacements, pillboxes and the mouths of caves concealing enemy troops. Crewmembers on board the Showboat noted scattered splashes in the sea around the ship, apparently from small caliber weaponry, but no hits were reported and no one was injured.

NORTH CAROLINA was on the firing line four consecutive days. The initially clear and bright D-Day weather deteriorated during the remaining three days. Intermittent rain reduced visibility, often to near zero, and made accurate firing much more difficult. Nevertheless, the marines ashore repeatedly called on the Showboat's guns for help, often on targets dangerously close to their own front. It was partly for this reason that most of the firing by NORTH CAROLINA after D-Day was with 5-inch guns, rather than 16-inch. Altogether, the ship fired

855 rounds of 16-inch and 2,753 rounds of 5-inch, in the heaviest bombardment the Showboat ever fired.

Because the enemy defensive system on Iwo Jima included troop shelters below ground to depths of 25 feet or more, and because strong points on the surface had been painstakingly concealed, naval gunfire was effective in most cases only when delivered with pinpoint accuracy under control from shore by observers in close proximity to the target. NORTH CAROLINA repeatedly provided such fire. Enemy fire pinned down the troops on many occasions, preventing them from advancing without the aid of the Navy's guns. Every marine who fought at Iwo Jima came to have a deep and abiding affection for battleships.

Japanese air opposition at Iwo Jima, sporadic during the days, filled the nights with horror as swarms of enemy planes came down from the north to harass our ships and their exhausted crews. One small carrier, BISMARCK SEA (CVE-95), received such severe damage that her magazines blew up and she was lost. In two waves, 11 fiercely aggressive kamikazes attacked SARATOGA, setting her ablaze and knocking her out of action for over three months.

More than 7,500 Americans were killed in action during the Iwo Jima campaign, with nearly 20,000 more wounded. Japanese losses included nearly 21,000 dead and 1,083 taken prisoner. Although the struggle for Iwo Jima was extremely costly, the value of the island's airfields was amply proven during the final months of the war, when some 2,400 emergency landings were made there by damaged planes, which might not otherwise have survived.

Life aboard...

"I had a wonderful view [from Batt Two] of the whole show, which was really a thriller. The surrounding ocean was swarming with every kind of ship you could think of. In the dim light of the early morning the flashes of guns, bursting shells and the brilliant glare of star shells silhouetted the rugged contour of the land in a gigantic fireworks display.... I watched our first salvo arc over to Iwo and send a geyser of dust and debris hundreds of feet into the air. The din was terrific, and as the scheduled hour for the assault approached, it rose in a crescendo until it was just one continuous roar. The island disappeared almost entirely in a fog of smoke and dust through which the twinkle of bursting shells could barely be seen. A steady procession of large and small bombers droned over the target, each contributing his bit to the holocaust. It looked as though nothing above or below that piece of earth could live through such a pounding."

— Commander Harold Harnly,
Executive Officer

No one on board NORTH CAROLINA would have traded places with these brave marines. Of the 70,000 who fought on Iwo Jima, over 7,500 lost their lives, while 20,000 more were wounded. Mount Suribachi, an extinct volcano crater, looms in the background.

LIFE ON THE FIRING SHIP DURING A SHORE BOMBARDMENT

Contrary to the way naval shore bombardment has been depicted on television and in motion pictures — usually as though it were one continuous rapid-fire barrage — firing such as that of NORTH CAROLINA at Iwo Jima was relatively slow and deliberate. Ships in the firing line, unless being engaged by shore batteries, usually steamed very slowly back and forth, firing first to one side before reversing course to fire to the other. After each salvo there was a pause to reload and await the observed correction spot. The pause was usually a brief one of not more than the 30 seconds required to reload, but was sometimes as long as several minutes when shifting targets. Usually the salvos were fired in a fairly steady, semi-rhythmic cadence, speeding up when orders were given to "fire for effect."

Those who have ever been on the receiving end of naval gunfire have usually attested that nothing in their experience was more terrifying. The mere sound of those huge projectiles screaming over one's head like a flock of wailing banshees is singularly unnerving. No member of the Showboat's crew would have traded places with those being fired upon, and few would have swapped with the marines ashore. However, being on the firing end was no picnic either. In fact, the strain of an all-day fire support mission was incredibly exhausting.

For those topside, on the bridge, the signal bridge, elsewhere in the open, or even inside the superstructure, the thunderous blast of the 16-inch guns struck the chest with the blow of a baseball bat. The sharp crack of the short-barreled 5-inch gun was skull splitting, even more painful to endure. Like waiting for the other shoe to drop, the next main battery salvo could not be anticipated. No matter how one might brace his body to protect himself, there was no way to avoid the bruises inflicted on elbows, knees, hips and shins, as the entire ship lurched in angry recoil with every main battery salvo. Dust and debris burst from cracks and corners, lagging (thermal padding) flew from piping and insulation tore loose from the overhead. Every object not bolted or welded in place bounced or ricocheted as though kicked by gremlins.

With every salvo, solid sheets of flame, followed by great clouds of gas and smoke, erupted from the gun muzzles, often as not to be carried by the wind back across the ship's upper works, enveloping men at exposed stations. At the end of such a day, all hands suffered from throbbing headaches, and many were virtually deaf. (Many remained hearing-impaired for the rest of their lives.) Eyes smarted from the pall of smoke. Each man's entire body was grimy with the abrasive residue of burned gunpowder. Lines formed at sick bay for treatment of powder burns, cuts, bruises and worse injuries. All of this could be, and was, endured. But it was like being on the receiving end of a heavy artillery barrage, with only the possibility of being hit not present. There was no pleasure whatever in it, only the grim satisfaction of helping the marines win the battle ashore.

THE ORDEAL OF USS FRANKLIN
March 19, 1945

During the three-month period of February through April 1945, the fast carriers launched repeated air strikes on airfields, shipping and port facilities in southern Japan, aimed mainly at destroying the last major remnants of the Japanese Navy. The enemy reacted with a frenzied increase in air attacks against our ships, including hundreds by kamikazes. Despite desperate efforts by our fighter pilots and ships' gunners, several carriers of the task force were hit. The most devastating and tragic of all such episodes was experienced by USS FRANKLIN (CV-13).

FRANKLIN was attacked early on the morning of March 19 while Task Force 58 steamed off the east coast of Kyushu conducting strikes against shipping and port facilities in Japan's Inland Sea. Planes that had participated in the first strike of the day were returning to their carriers. Approaching with them was a single enemy plane taking advantage of the concealment afforded by a partial low overcast and the radar clutter created by our own planes. Although the Showboat's air search radar operator, Everett R. Beaver, detected the approaching "bogey" and all ships were warned, strict orders to "hold fire" remained in effect due to the large number of friendly aircraft circling in low clouds overhead.

With FRANKLIN launching her second strike of the day, the enemy pilot succeeded in reaching a position above her, diving on her out of the cloud cover and dropping two bombs amidst the heavily armed and fully gassed planes crowding the carrier's flight deck. "Big Ben" immediately burst into flames from stem to stern. Thunderous explosions erupted fore and aft. By the hundreds, men were blown over or compelled to jump over the side. Over 1,700 men were soon visible as a trail of bobbing heads in the wake of the stricken ship, some dead and some terribly wounded. NORTH CAROLINA, steaming at high speed directly astern of the carrier, was forced to swerve sharply to port in order to avoid plowing through these men. As the Showboat steamed past, her crew showered the sea with their own life jackets, life rafts, empty powder cases, spud crates and anything else that would float. Destroyers quickly closed in for the rescue. When the losses were finally tallied up, 724 men of FRANKLIN's crew were killed or missing, 265 wounded. This was the single worst combat disaster witnessed during the entire war from the decks of NORTH CAROLINA.

Carrier FRANKLIN lists to starboard, her crew desperately fighting fires, after being bombed March 19, 1945.

Life aboard...

"It was the 0400 to 0800 watch. I picked up a bogey to the west of us, somewhere around 40 miles. I reported it to our combat information watch officer, who reported it to the bridge and the flagship. Apparently no other ship could pick it up. I had a good track. We kept reporting this bogey to the flagship and yet no one ordered the fleet to go to air defense. Finally, one of the destroyers visually sighted the aircraft and reported it as a Japanese plane. Of course, then we went to air defense."

— Everett Beaver, Radarman Second Class

"...I rushed to my battle station on the bow, uncovered my gun, put a magazine in it, had it cocked and ready to fire, but I couldn't fire because the USS FRANKLIN was dead ahead of us. This plane came in dead ahead of the FRANKLIN and I watched the whole thing. He came right on down over the carrier, whose flight deck was loaded with planes, and dropped two bombs. They just absolutely annihilated everything. After dropping the two bombs he kept heading straight at us and he came up right over our radar. Some of the guys who were in Sky Control said he came so close they could have stuck a broom right up in his prop. Then he went right down over the water and started 'hedge-hopping' his way out of the fleet. Of course once one is in a fleet he is pretty much on a suicide mission, and he was shot down by one of our combat air patrols. At about this time the FRANKLIN had pulled out of its line in front of us, on fire and things going off, guys in the water. I never saw so many sailors in the water, some dead, some alive and hollering, and we started throwing everything we could get our hands on: life jackets and rafts, shark repellents. This went on for a long time and we felt sure the ship was gone, but the captain took a lot of his crew off and took that thing back, smoking, to Pearl Harbor."

— Robert Palomaris, Gunner's Mate First Class

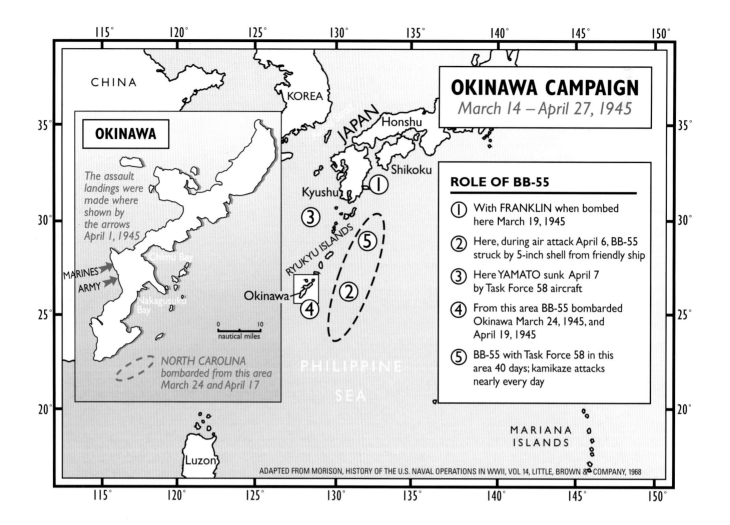

OKINAWA CAMPAIGN
March 14 – April 27, 1945

OKINAWA

The assault landings were made where shown by the arrows April 1, 1945

MARINES
ARMY

Chimu Bay
Nakagusuku Bay

0   10
nautical miles

NORTH CAROLINA bombarded from this area March 24 and April 17

CHINA

KOREA

JAPAN

Honshu

Shikoku

Kyushu

RYUKYU ISLANDS

Okinawa

PHILIPPINE SEA

MARIANA ISLANDS

Luzon

ROLE OF BB-55

① With FRANKLIN when bombed here March 19, 1945

② Here, during air attack April 6, BB-55 struck by 5-inch shell from friendly ship

③ Here YAMATO sunk April 7 by Task Force 58 aircraft

④ From this area BB-55 bombarded Okinawa March 24, 1945, and April 19, 1945

⑤ BB-55 with Task Force 58 in this area 40 days; kamikaze attacks nearly every day

ADAPTED FROM MORISON, HISTORY OF THE U.S. NAVAL OPERATIONS IN WWII, VOL 14, LITTLE, BROWN & COMPANY, 1968

BOMBARDMENTS OF OKINAWA
March 24 and April 17, 1945

Coincident with the air offensive of Task Force 58 against mainland Japan, American amphibious forces were closing in for the invasion of Okinawa. The 1st, 2nd and 6th Marine Divisions, together with the Army's 7th, 27th, 77th and 96th Divisions were employed in this operation, the last of the major island assaults of the Pacific war. Okinawa's proximity to the Home Islands of Japan, together with its airfields and anchorages, made it the best choice to support the planned invasion of Kyushu, scheduled to commence November 1, 1945. Task Force 58, under command of Admirals Spruance and Mitscher, covered the Okinawa operation from beginning to end, providing air support and fighter defense.

NORTH CAROLINA, in company with other fast battleships, conducted a pre-invasion bombardment of Okinawa from very long ranges on March 24, and fired again in support of a feint landing on the night of April 17. The total expenditure of ammunition in these two bombardments was 359 rounds of 16-inch. No 5-inch was fired due to the long range. "Love

Day," the incongruous name chosen for the date of the initial American assault landing on the west coast beaches of Okinawa, was April 1.

For the first bombardment, the Showboat, after launching one of her Kingfisher float planes, commenced firing shortly after 9:00 a.m., first at a pillbox, then at an artillery emplacement. The pilot of the Kingfisher was Lieutenant Almon P. Oliver. Using binoculars from a position above the target area, Oliver was responsible to report the results of our gunfire, provide corrections in aim and inform the ship of any targets of opportunity. After the third salvo, he reported that he had sighted what he believed would be an appropriate target. He called it an "antique fort." It was located on a hilltop near the center of the Showboat's assigned target area, at a range of about 10 nautical miles from the ship. Lieutenant Commander Widmer C. Hansen, main battery control officer, from his perch in the director atop the foremast, peered in that direction through the director's high-powered optics. He made out massive stone walls comprising what appeared to be the southeast corner of a fortress-like compound, partly obscured by dense woods. The target was

NORTH CAROLINA bombards Okinawa, March 24, 1945. In photograph below, note six 16-inch projectiles the camera caught in flight at upper left. With a range of nearly 20,000 yards to the target, the six projectiles were in flight 23 seconds before impacting the target, as shown in photograph at right, taken by pilot Oliver.

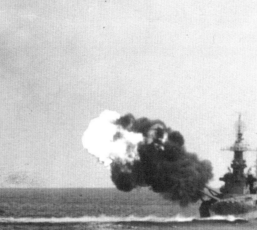

(Left) Aerial photograph of Shuri Castle taken from Showboat Kingfisher by pilot Oliver during March 24 bombardment. Note gunfire damage to inner building (circled).

immediately taken under fire at a range of 19,970 yards. A corner of the inner building wall was soon seen to be damaged by one of our salvos. Thereupon, according to pilot Oliver, a number of people, most appearing to be women dressed in black, suddenly emerged from the structure and ran for the cover of nearby woods. This led Oliver to radio the ship that he feared we might be firing on a target which, for humanitarian reasons, should be off limits. The Showboat's captain, now Oswald S. Colclough, immediately ordered cease firing, and the guns were shifted to other targets.

What we did not know then was that we had pounded on the door of the main command center for all Japanese ground forces defending Okinawa. That "antique fort" was actually ancient Shuri Castle, a compound of sturdy buildings occupying several acres of land, surrounded by massive stone walls and a mote. Early in the 15th century under orders of their king, 10,000 Okinawans had labored eight years to build the elaborate oriental citadel. It had then served over 500 years as the island's seat of government. Thus, it was unfortunate that such a treasure should have been a target for our guns; but war is war, and at that time we had no knowledge either of Shuri's history or of its military use by the Japanese Army. Here it must be noted that such military use by the Japanese Army was in no way the work of the innocent native Okinawan people.

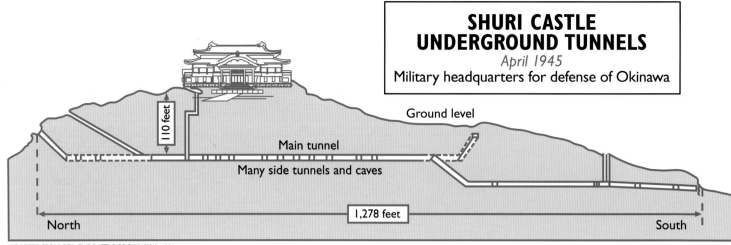

SHURI CASTLE
UNDERGROUND TUNNELS
April 1945
Military headquarters for defense of Okinawa

Ground level

110 feet

Main tunnel

Many side tunnels and caves

1,278 feet

North

South

ADAPTED FROM OTA, THE BATTLE OF OKINAWA, 1984

What made Shuri Castle strong in 1945 was not the ramparts and buttresses of stone visible above ground, but the extensive honeycomb of tunnels and caves which the Japanese had bored into the volcanic earth to depths of more than 100 feet beneath the castle, thus making the headquarters impervious to our gunfire. Two months of the most violent land warfare, supported by repeated aerial and naval bombardments, were to take place on Okinawa before troops of the 1st Marine Division would finally fight their way into the rubble and begin sealing the entrances to the underground works. After World War II the aboveground parts of Shuri Castle were completely restored almost exactly as originally built.

THE KAMIKAZES

During most of the Okinawa campaign the ships of Task Force 58 operated in an area 70-100 nautical miles east of the island, providing fighter protection for the ships of the expeditionary force (amphibious force) as they landed and supported the invading American troops. In addition to a desperately stubborn defense ashore, the Japanese reaction to the invasion took the form of a steadily increasing offensive by suicide pilots crashing into our ships.

The Japanese word kamikaze, or "divine wind," dates from the year 1281, when Mongols under Kublai Khan attempted to invade Japan, but were thwarted by a wind said to have been sent from heaven. That wind, actually a typhoon, destroyed the invasion fleet and saved Japan. Hoping to achieve the same happy outcome in the waning months of World War II, kamikaze operation "Ten Go" was launched in deadly earnest during the weeks following our April 1

landings on Okinawa. The attacks came sporadically, at all hours, sometimes by single planes or in twos and threes; other times in swarms of a dozen or more. As mentioned before, some attackers approached at very high altitude before diving at terrific speed to crash like thunderbolts into our ships. Many more streaked in at wave-top level to avoid radar detection, often surprising our gunners only seconds before impact. Low fliers posed an extra problem because our ships risked spraying each other with gunfire in the heat of battle. Aircraft carriers were most often targeted, but no ship type was immune. In all of 1945, five of the older battleships were crashed. For obvious reasons, the aiming point for most attacks was the target ship's bridge, a fact that did not escape the notice of those of us whose battle stations were in the combat information center (CIC), directly under the pilothouse.

Life aboard...

"During this air attack which lasted 14 minutes, enough sweat came from those of us in this upper [5-inch] handling room that my shoes were just sloshing in sweat. I didn't think of it until after the battle was over. I looked on the deck and as the ship rolled you could see the sweat rolling from one side of the room to the other. Now this is the honest truth if I've ever told it. I reckon half of it was my sweat...."

— Willie Jones, Gunner's Mate First Class

This photograph, dating from the Gilberts Campaign, shows how flak peppered the sky during a concerted air attack on Task Force 58. Similar scenes occurred day after day during the kamikaze attacks of the Okinawa Campaign.

"FRIENDLY" SHELL HIT ON NORTH CAROLINA
April 6, 1945

April 6 produced a particularly fierce level of kamikaze attacks. An estimated 182 planes in 22 groups attacked the expeditionary force off the west coast of Okinawa. Of these, 55 were destroyed by our fighters, 35 by ships' antiaircraft fire and 24 by actual crashes into our ships. Task Force 58 claimed to have destroyed 249 attacking planes that day. Since the Japanese themselves counted 355 kamikazes committed to the April 6 attacks, American estimates were not far off the mark. Expeditionary force losses that day alone included three destroyer types, one tank landing ship (LST) and two ammunition ships sunk; and 10 ships, including eight destroyer types, severly damaged with many casualties. As for Task Force 58, no ships were hit, but three carriers, two cruisers and two destroyers were narrowly missed by kamikazes. At least 30 kamikazes were shot down over the task force.

The following edited excerpts from the Showboat's War Diary and Deck Log of April 6, 1945, give an idea of what a trying day that was for the ship's company:

0000 — As the day began, all eight boilers were on the line, meaning that power was available for the ship's maximum speed of 26+ knots. The ship was darkened and in Readiness Condition III, meaning that one-third of the guns were manned.

NORTH CAROLINA was a unit of Task Group 58.3, consisting of three large carriers, two light carriers, three battleships, four light cruisers and 12 destroyers.

Along with the rest of Task Force 58, this task group was zig-zagging at 17 knots in an area about 100 nautical miles due east of Okinawa. The weather was cool, with cumulus and altostratus clouds covering 8/10 of the sky. Wind was from the north at 16 knots, air temperature 66 degrees.

0246 — Unidentified aircraft reported bearing 270 degrees true, distance 37 miles. Set Condition I (battle stations) in the antiaircraft battery. This involved about half the ship's company: all 5-inch, 40-mm and 20-mm guns, plus Sky Control, the AA (antiaircraft) directors, Plot and CIC.

0310 — Radar screen clear. Secured from Condition I and returned to Condition III in the AA battery.

0430 — Unidentified aircraft reported bearing 300 degrees true, distance 27 miles. Set Condition I in the AA battery.

0447 — Radar screen clear, set AA Condition 1-Easy (stand easy at the guns).

0456 — Enemy planes approaching. Set Condition 1 in the AA battery.

0515 — General Quarters (GQ; battle stations for all hands) for routine one-hour dawn alert.

0603 — Enemy plane reported shot down bearing 315 degrees true, distance 32 miles.

0612 — Sunrise. Secured from GQ, with Condition I remaining in AA battery.

0624 — Secured from Condition I in AA battery. Back to Condition III.

0817 — Enemy planes approaching. Set Condition I in the AA battery.

0844 — Set Condition I-Easy in the AA battery.

1221 — Unidentified aircraft reported in the vicinity.

1223 — Sky Control reported firing by other ships off port quarter. Set Condition I in the AA battery.

1225 — NORTH CAROLINA commenced firing to port at enemy aircraft, which crashed into the sea 2,000 yards off port bow, narrowly missing aircraft carrier CABOT.

1301 — Enemy aircraft reported bearing 105 degrees true, distance 7 miles.

1302 — NORTH CAROLINA commenced firing to port at second enemy plane, which crashed into the sea 2,000 yards off the starboard quarter.

1304 — NORTH CAROLINA opened fire on third plane, which crashed into the sea 2,000 yards ahead, close aboard CABOT.

1305 — NORTH CAROLINA accidentally struck by friendly fire; a 5-inch/38 caliber AA Common projectile, which impacted the base of the port 5-inch battery director, Sky II, killing three men, wounding 44 in nearby areas and disabling the director.

1628 — One of NORTH CAROLINA's OS2U Kingfisher aircraft capsized and was lost while taxiing alongside preparatory to being hoisted aboard. The pilot was rescued, but the rear seat man was lost.

Shell hole accidentally made in trunk of Sky II by a 5-inch projectile fired at a low-flying kamikaze by one of our own ships. The hole is visible between the two men on the scaffold.

Life aboard...

"My battle station was in Batt Two. We had been firing for the last several minutes when all of a sudden I heard this loud bang, and a large black cloud of smoke enveloped the tower. Instantly I heard what sounded like someone throwing a handful of marbles against the tower. I was sitting inside, but I saw one guy fall over. I looked out on the platform outside [Stryker's bridge] and everybody was looking down. I ran out to see, thinking we had been hit by a bomb. Down below men were lying everywhere — on the signal bridge, around the 40-mm gun mount and director and in several other locations. Blood was running across the deck. I then saw the hole in the director base and it was obvious we had been hit by a 5-inch from one of our own ships."

— Charles Paty, Jr.,
Radioman Second Class

WE BURY OUR DEAD

The day after the shell hit, the bodies of our three dead shipmates were sewed into canvas shrouds, each one weighted at the foot with two 5-inch projectiles. They were then buried at sea with the Navy's traditional solemn service, in a position about 100 miles east of Okinawa. Shortly before taps that night, the voice of our senior chaplain, Commander Emil Redman, came over the 1MC (public address) system with this prayer: *"Heavenly Father, today we committed to the deep the bodies of three of our shipmates who gave their lives so that others might live. We are particularly mindful at this time of their loved ones at home. Sustain them in their sorrow. Help them to understand that those they love gave their lives for their protection and care. Be with all the officers and men of this ship. Give us heart and mind to serve Thee and our country willingly and faithfully...."*

SUICIDE MISSION OF BATTLESHIP YAMATO
April 7, 1945

After dark April 6, the last seaworthy ships of the Imperial Japanese Navy, giant battleship YAMATO with nine escorts, slipped quietly out of Japan's Inland Sea with orders to engage our invasion forces at Okinawa in a fight to the finish. YAMATO's orders were to destroy the Americans' Okinawa invasion fleet, following which the great ship was to be beached and serve thereafter as a fortress. The force sailed with barely enough fuel to carry out these orders. U.S. submarines shadowed them throughout the night of April 6, keeping Commander Task Force

Burial at sea. The bodies of the dead, sewed into canvas shrouds weighted at the foot by two 5-inch projectiles, were buried at sea 100 miles east of Okinawa on the afternoon of April 7. The service was twice interrupted by kamikaze attacks.

58, Admiral Raymond A. Spruance, posted on their movements. Our carrier search planes spotted the monster early April 7, after it had rounded southern Kyushu in a westerly direction before turning south toward Okinawa. Carriers of Task Force 58 immediately launched the first of a series of attacks by torpedo planes, dive-bombers and fighters. They soon overwhelmed the enemy force, sinking the battleship and five other ships. Only four badly damaged destroyers limped back to Japan. Of

This photograph, actually dating from 1941, shows how the 72,000-ton Japanese battleship YAMATO must have looked as it charged south toward Okinawa at 22 knots on the morning of April 7, 1945, in a hopeless attempt to halt the American invasion of the island.

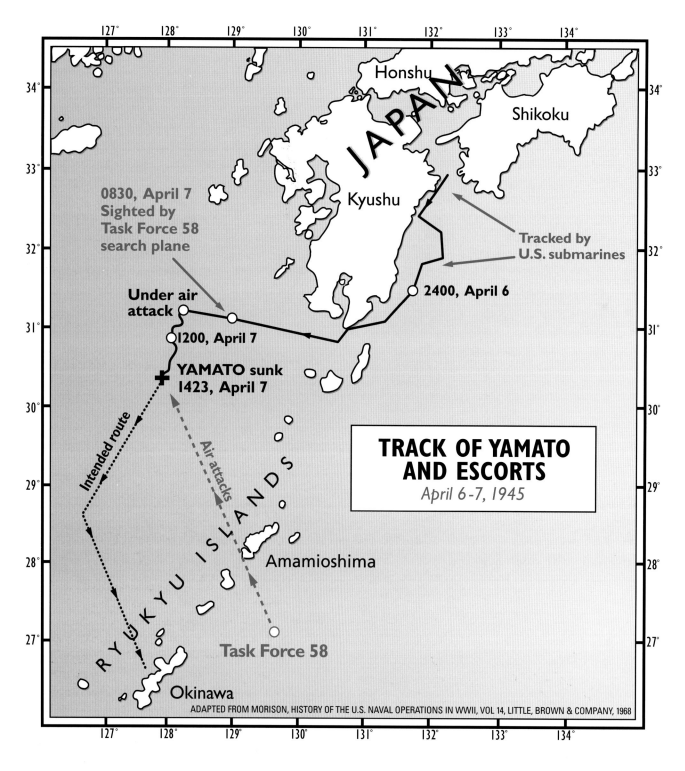

**TRACK OF YAMATO
AND ESCORTS**
April 6-7, 1945

0830, April 7
Sighted by
Task Force 58
search plane

Tracked by
U.S. submarines

2400, April 6

**Under air
attack**

1200, April 7

**YAMATO sunk
1423, April 7**

Honshu

Shikoku

JAPAN

Kyushu

Intended route

Air attacks

RYUKYU ISLANDS

Amamioshima

Task Force 58

Okinawa

ADAPTED FROM MORISON, HISTORY OF THE U.S. NAVAL OPERATIONS IN WWII, VOL 14, LITTLE, BROWN & COMPANY, 1968

YAMATO's crew of over 3,200, all but 23 officers and 246 enlisted men went down with the ship. This action was greeted with mixed emotions by the crew of NORTH CAROLINA: satisfaction that their ultimate adversary had been sunk, disappointment that they had again been denied an opportunity to prove their worth in ship-to-ship combat and a mixture of disbelief and admiration over the courage of the enemy for daring to fight against such overwhelming odds.

NATIONAL ARCHIVES 80-G-281699

Super battleship YAMATO under air attack in Sibuyan Sea (central Philippines), November 25, 1944, during Battle of Samar. Note bomb explosion forward of Turret I.

BATTLESHIP NORTH CAROLINA

136

BATTLESHIP COLLECTION 82.10

Scores of empty 5-inch powder cases litter the 01 level amidships attesting to the ferocity of the ship's defense against a kamikaze attack. Empties were saved and sent back to the United States for refilling.

FORTY DAYS AND NIGHTS IN THE CRUCIBLE THAT WAS OKINAWA

NORTH CAROLINA fought from mid-March to the end of April 1945 in the fiery crucible created by the kamikazes at Okinawa. In addition to bombarding the island twice, the Showboat opened fire on attacking enemy aircraft almost daily and often at night, shooting down or assisting in the destruction of at least 14 planes. Our gunners saved several carriers, as well as the Showboat, herself, from suicide crashes. During the Okinawa campaign alone, no fewer than 1,465 Japanese pilots went to their death in this manner. The American toll, heaviest of the war in the Pacific, was some 120 ships hit, of which 29 were sunk. Navy men killed or missing totaled 3,048, with 6,035 wounded.

REFLECTIONS ON THE KAMIKAZE PHENOMENON

The kamikaze brought to the war an entirely new dimension, at first incomprehensible to the crew of NORTH CAROLINA. Deeply rooted Judeo-Christian reverence for human life makes it difficult for most Americans to understand how any modern society could deliberately regiment mass suicide by large numbers of its people. Western civilization has always respected the courage of individuals who sacrifice

Life aboard...

"I never did get scared at the time because we were all well trained. We knew our jobs and we did them. It was just automatic. You didn't question. You didn't have time to get scared. You were doing a job. After it was over and you could think about it a little bit, you could say, 'Man, what could have happened?' At the time you were actually engaged in action, you didn't think about things like that. You just did what you were to do. I knew I had good shipmates. They were trained and they knew what to do and they did it."

— Donald Rogers, Boatswain's Mate Second Class

"The fact is that you are concentrating, and the adrenaline is running like mad at that moment when you are in combat. It's exciting, and you just have to be so damned alert."

— Lieutenant (jg) Ralph Sheffer, Fighter Director Officer

"It got very personal. There was no question in my mind who they were aiming at. Every bomb or torpedo was aimed at my precious butt."

— Donald Wickham, Musician Second Class

"For those who lived through those endless days and weeks off Okinawa, memories linger like a hideous nightmare of war's ravages: the unexpected suddenness of the violence, the grim faces of the gunners, a sky filled with shell bursts and crisscrossed with tracer streaks, flaming planes diving into the sea, ships burning and exploding, wounded men struggling to survive in the sea, our own returning planes — always less in number than went out — circling to land on damaged carriers. These were the visible scenes of war. Not so obvious were the effects on the inner man. On May 1, when NORTH CAROLINA was at last on her way back to Pearl Harbor for repairs to her battle damage, she carried as passengers 250 survivors from ships that had been crashed by kamikazes. In outward appearance all seemed normal. Then at sunset the first day out came the clang! clang! clang! of the general alarm, calling our crew to battle stations for the usual evening stand-to; not an emergency, mere routine. The reactions of the passengers were dumbfounding. They fell apart. Some dived under tables, others screamed incoherently or dashed about aimlessly. All were casualties of war no less than those who had stopped a bullet."

— Commander Kemp Tolley, Navigator

"If anyone wasn't scared, they're crazy!"

— Louis Favereaux, Electrician's Mate Third Class

"I cannot deny the fear that gripped me and others in the CIC during a kamikaze attack. We could see nothing, so all we knew was what we could hear. First warning of a kamikaze attack was usually the sudden, ear-splitting crack of a single 5-inch gun. Opening range could be anywhere from 12,000 yards down to perhaps half that distance, depending on how much warning preceded the attack. Two or three more hesitant rounds might follow, as the gunners limbered up. Then, in a thunderous crescendo, all ten 5-inch guns on the ship's engaged side would open fire, leaving no doubt that the shooting was deadly serious.

The sound of the rapid-firing 5-inchers was deafening, even for those of us inside the CIC. Nothing else could be heard. Unable to banter or commiserate with each other, as men in combat are prone to do, each man could only withdraw into himself, relying on his own resources of courage. With the threat of a fiery death suddenly staring us in the face, staying cool required the utmost willpower. With the task force steaming at high speed, the entire ship vibrated and rattled in time with the churning propellers. This, along with the usual violent evasive maneuvers, added suspense and urgency to the unseen danger screaming toward us from above. As the range closed, the 40-mm guns opened up with a steady ka-boom! ka-boom! ka-boom! more felt than heard above the sounds of the 5-inch. This meant that the pilot was within a couple of miles of us and well into his dive. Finally, with only seconds left before the crash, as many as 50 short-range 20-mm guns began their fierce popping stacatto. At that moment, even the most stoic of the listeners would grit his teeth, shut his eyes and pray. In these circumstances it seemed to me that courage was nothing more — and nothing less — than the willpower to shut off all thought of what might happen, to force your mind to concentrate solely on what had to be done and to do it."

— Author

their lives in defense of their loved ones or who fight to the death with their backs to the wall in a just cause. But for a whole people to resort to or condone the behavior of lemmings, drowning themselves en masse for a lost cause, is beyond Western understanding. Off Okinawa, however, the Showboat's gunners quickly realized that they did not have to understand the kamikaze menace to deal with it. It simply demanded the same grim response as always in mortal combat — *you must kill your enemy before he kills you.*

On May 24, while NORTH CAROLINA was at Pearl Harbor undergoing repairs, her old comrade in arms ENTERPRISE was crashed by a kamikaze off Kyushu. Shortly after first light that morning, a swarm of 26 Japanese planes suddenly attacked. Six were shot down by antiaircraft fire and 19 by the combat air patrol, but the one survivor crashed into ENTERPRISE, just abaft her forward elevator, blowing a hole and causing a huge bulge in her flight deck. The bomb exploded deep within the ship, killing 13 men and wounding 68. The gallant old carrier, veteran of more World War II combat than any other ship of the U.S. Navy, underwent three months of repairs at the Puget Sound Navy Yard, but by the time she was back at Pearl Harbor ready to rejoin the fleet the Japanese had surrendered.

SHOWDOWN WITH JAPAN
July – September 1945

In early July, following repairs to the damaged director at Pearl Harbor, NORTH CAROLINA rejoined her task force, now Task Force 38, for further offensive operations against mainland Japan. Added now to the carrier strikes that had been conducted off and on since February was a series of shore bombardments on mainland Japan by battleships, cruisers and destroyers.

On the afternoon of July 17 NORTH CAROLINA, together with five other fast battleships, including the British KING GEORGE V, began their approach to a position off the east coast of Honshu, about 80 miles northeast of Tokyo. Their mission was a night bombardment of an area known as the Hitachi Industrial Complex. This complex included six major industrial plants producing arms, steel, electrical machinery and copper products. The area was of enough strategic importance to Japan's war effort that American intelligence experts expected it to be well defended. In fact, it had been anticipated that, as the battleships approached the coast for their bombardment, high-speed suicide boats carrying explosives might be sent out to meet them. This concern was widely circulated among the crew of the Showboat, and the speculation it generated created a high degree of apprehension.

The battleships opened fire at midnight. There was steady rain throughout the bombardment and visibility was less than two miles. The average distance of the ships from the shoreline was 28,000 yards, or about 14 nautical miles. Ranges to the targets varied from 35,000 yards down to 23,000 yards. The ships were navigated entirely by radar, so the aim of the guns was equally dependent thereon. U.S. battleships fired a total of 1,238 16-inch rounds. In post-war assessment, the damage resulting from this bombardment could not be isolated from that inflicted by two preceding raids by heavy bombers; but the cumulative effect was to cut production almost to zero and to interrupt rail service, electricity and water supply.

Apprehensions of a possible Japanese counterattack proved to have been unfounded, as indicated by the following entry in the Showboat's official War Diary: "No enemy reaction whatever was manifested before, during or after the bombardment."

This telling incident was evidence that the Japanese had been reduced to relative impotence in terms of their abililty to wage war outside of the Japanese Home Islands; but their capacity and will to defend themselves against invasion remained most formidable. As of early August 1945, according to naval historian Samuel Eliot Morison, "Although 2,550 kamikaze planes had been expended, 5,350 were still left, together with as many more ready for orthodox use. Some 7,000 planes were under repair or in storage and 5,000 young men were training for the Kamikaze Corps." Admiral Nimitz and General MacArthur, then readying forces for a massive invasion of Japan in November, anticipated a savage struggle against almost an entire nation of suicidal fanatics. Combined losses, it was feared, could well mount into millions of lives. Then came the explosions of atomic bombs over Hiroshima and

Nagasaki, August 6 and 9, and Japan's political leaders, armed with Emperor Hirohito's reluctant acquiescence, overruled their still defiant military leaders in accepting Allied surrender terms. On August 15, ships of the Third Fleet received word that Japan had agreed to surrender. Thereupon Admiral Halsey issued orders that any Japanese planes threatening the fleet were to be shot down "in a friendly fashion."

EPILOGUE TO WAR'S END

For the crew of NORTH CAROLINA, the war's end came almost as an anticlimax. It wound down, rather than halting all at once. In early August, Task Force 38 was inexplicably ordered to cease air operations over southern Japan and withdraw 300 miles seaward.

On board the Showboat this produced a wide range of speculation as to the reason. One rumor had it that American forces on Okinawa were preparing to launch against Japan a massive barrage of the powerful German-type V-2 rockets, with the possibility of wild shots making it prudent to withdraw the fleet.

Then came the spine-tingling news of the atomic bombs dropped on Hiroshima, August 6, and on Nagasaki, August 9. With that came the realization that apparently operations had been suspended temporarily in order to assure for Task Force 38 a wide margin of safety surrounding the first operational use of man's most awesome creation.

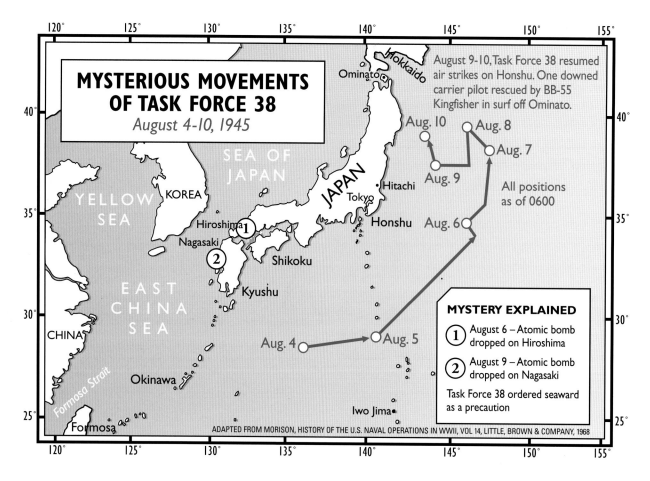

MYSTERIOUS MOVEMENTS OF TASK FORCE 38
August 4-10, 1945

August 9-10, Task Force 38 resumed air strikes on Honshu. One downed carrier pilot rescued by BB-55 Kingfisher in surf off Ominato.

All positions as of 0600

MYSTERY EXPLAINED

① August 6 – Atomic bomb dropped on Hiroshima

② August 9 – Atomic bomb dropped on Nagasaki

Task Force 38 ordered seaward as a precaution

ADAPTED FROM MORISON, HISTORY OF THE U.S. NAVAL OPERATIONS IN WWII, VOL 14, LITTLE, BROWN & COMPANY, 1968

ANOTHER HEROIC AIR-SEA RESCUE

On August 9, Task Force 38 resumed offensive air operations against northern Japan, including attacks on the Ominato Naval Air Station, near the northern tip of Honshu. When one of the attacking carrier planes was shot down, the pilot, Lt(jg) Vernon T. Coumbre, was forced to ditch in Mutsu Wan (Bay). He paddled his inflatable rubber raft five miles to the eastern shore of the bay, where he spent a sleepless night hiding in a sparse clump of trees. The next morning two OS2U Kingfisher pilots from NORTH CAROLINA were called upon to attempt rescue. They found Coumbre on the beach where indicated on the chart, at right, waving frantically to attract their attention. With the wind blowing steadily from the west at 25-30 knots, pounding the beach with a violent surf, landing a seaplane there would be extremely risky. Adding to the danger, enemy gun batteries to the north were within range.

Landing safely in the bay outside the breakers, a first attempt to reach Coumbre by one of the Kingfishers met disaster when the pilot, Lt. Ralph J. Jacobs, was thrown from his plane by a violent wave as he attempted to toss a line to Coumbre. Thereupon

his un-manned Kingfisher, chased by a hail of enemy shell splashes, raced crazily out into the bay because Jacobs, when thrown from the plane, had accidentally kicked the throttle wide open.

The second rescue pilot, Lt(jg) Almon P. Oliver, circling low over the scene, was astonished to see that the first plane's cockpit was empty and there were two men on the beach, waving frantically for his attention. Now it was all up to Oliver, who braved a harrowing landing through the splashes of what he estimated as 3-inch and 5-inch shells. Keeping his Kingfisher on a westerly heading into the wind and

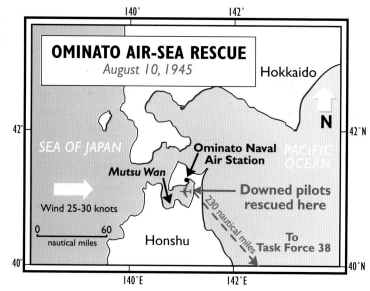

OMINATO AIR-SEA RESCUE
August 10, 1945

Hokkaido

N

SEA OF JAPAN

PACIFIC OCEAN

Ominato Naval Air Station

Mutsu Wan

Downed pilots rescued here

Wind 25-30 knots

0 ____ 60
nautical miles

Honshu

220 nautical miles

To Task Force 38

applying engine power as necessary to maintain control, he allowed the plane to "sail" (his word) backwards through the breakers far enough so that the stern of his main float actually grounded on the beach. There the two downed pilots crammed themselves into the plane's rear cockpit, designed to be snugly occupied by only one man. Still under intense fire, Oliver powered his way through the surf, forced his overloaded plane into the air and returned safely 230 miles to the Showboat. Upon being hoisted aboard, his plane's fuel gauge registered almost empty.

Although the mission was near the extreme range of their aircraft, both Jacobs and Oliver volunteered for the task, knowing they would be fired upon and that their chances of returning were slim — but they brought back their man. This incident, along with the rescue of 10 downed airman off Truk, April 30, 1944, credit NORTH CAROLINA pilots with two of the most heroic air-sea rescues in naval history.

Captain B. Hall Hanlon, NORTH CAROLINA's Commanding Officer, reads citations for the award of Distinguished Flying Crosses to (2nd and 3rd from left) Lieutenant Ralph J. Jacobs and Lieutenant (jg) Almon P. Oliver for their daring rescue of a downed pilot near Ominato, Japan, August 10, 1945. At far left is 1945 Executive Officer, Commander Harold S. Harnly; Navigator, Commander Kemp Tolley is at Captain Hanlon's right shoulder; Gunnery Officer, Commander Thomas H. Morton, at Hanlon's left shoulder.

Lieutenant Jacobs, left, and Lieutenant (jg) Oliver, right, wearing Air Medals (temporarily substituted for Distinguished Flying Crosses because the latter were out of stock in the fleet).

THE WAR ENDS, AT LAST

Three weeks were to pass before Japan's formal surrender, and in that gray interim between war and peace mixed feelings of hope and caution prevailed on board NORTH CAROLINA. Blue skies and almost a flat calm sea helped sustain the sense that peace was in the air, but there was no relaxation of vigilance at the guns. As Navigator Kemp Tolley put it, "With the Japanese, one could always expect the unexpected." However, the surrender documents were duly signed on board battleship MISSOURI in Tokyo Bay on September 2, 1945. On that day the Showboat's Captain B. Hall Hanlon was finally able to announce to the crew over the 1MC that the war was officially over.

Japanese Foreign Minister Mamoru Shigemitsu signs surrender terms on board battleship MISSOURI, September 2, 1945. Spectators included dozens of admirals and generals representing the Allies. Behind Shigemitsu, the Japanese delegation consisted of General Yoshijiro Umezu, Chief of the Army General Staff, plus three representatives each from the Foreign Office, the Army and Navy. With backs to the camera facing Shigemitsu at the table are, right to left, General Douglas MacArthur and Lieutenant General Richard K. Sutherland, MacArthur's chief of staff. Admiral Chester W. Nimitz, present but not in the photograph, signed later for the United States.

Life aboard...

"I was below decks when Captain Hanlon announced the war was over, and I can still to this day remember him saying 'Now here this, this is the captain' and then he went into telling us. Boy, you talk about a roar that went up! I think the whole ship jumped about two feet out of the water!"

— Robert Palomaris, Gunner's Mate First Class

"We got word over the public address system that the Japanese had surrendered, the war was over, and you could have heard us back in New York City screaming out there in the Pacific."

— Paul Wieser, Boatswain's Mate First Class

"It was like the reprieve of a death sentence, a deliverance, a time to be deeply thankful, and we were. Beyond that, I was so drained in every way after those four long years of war, that entering Tokyo Bay didn't matter very much. All I really cared about was, thank God, it's over and we can go home." [Author's note: this from a man who had survived the sinking of two destroyers in the Guadalcanal campaign before serving three full years in the Showboat.]

— Lieutenant (jg) Ralph Sheffer, Fighter Director Officer

SUMMARY OF THE WAR RECORD OF NORTH CAROLINA

The contribution of NORTH CAROLINA to victory in the Pacific during World War II is incalculable, and certainly cannot be isolated from that of all the other worthy participants in that war; but here are a few pertinent facts.

As the first of the fast battleships to join the United States Fleet in the World War II era, NORTH CAROLINA necessarily coped first with all the tough new problems that invariably crop up in such a situation. Her officers and men successfully solved these problems and in so doing "wrote the book" for the nine new battleships that followed.

Earning 15 battle stars, the Showboat carried out nine shore bombardments, sank an enemy freighter, destroyed at least 24 enemy aircraft and assisted in shooting down many others. Most important, her antiaircraft gunners helped halt or frustrate scores of attacks on our aircraft carriers, saving them from untold damage and loss of life.

Transiting the Panama Canal on the way home.

The ship's fighter-director officers were responsible for many successful interceptions and shoot-downs of enemy aircraft. Her OS2U Kingfisher aircraft rescued 12 downed American aviators.

The Showboat steamed over 300,000 wartime miles, her crew enduring the hardships and dangers of service in the combat area for over three years. Few ships and few men in the history of the U.S. Navy have served as long in the presence of the enemy. The ship was in actual combat with enemy forces on more than 50 separate occasions. Although Japanese radio announcements claimed six times that the ship had been sunk, she survived at least seven near misses and close calls.

When victory finally came, NORTH CAROLINA had helped almost every step of the way from Guadalcanal to Tokyo Bay. Through it all, she lost only 10 men killed in action and 67 wounded. This relatively low number of casualties was due partly to chance and partly to the fact that the enemy considered carriers better targets than battleships. But there was also another reason: the officers and men of NORTH CAROLINA learned early in the war how to fight their ship with extraordinary skill, determination and effectiveness. It was they who gave their beloved Showboat her superb spirit and character, and it was they who made her one of the greatest fighting ships in the history of the United States Navy.

The traditional homeward bound pennant, flown on the ship's arrival at Boston, was nearly 200 feet long, enough to reach from the mainmast aft to the aircraft crane. Aerographer's balloons filled with helium were attached to keep the pennant airborne.

HOMEWARD BOUND TO A HERO'S WELCOME
September – October 1945

As part of the initial American occupation force placed ashore in Japan immediately following the surrender, NORTH CAROLINA contributed a detachment of about 100 men with six officers. This group was transferred to a smaller ship while the Showboat was still at sea on August 20 and was then put ashore at the Yokosuka Naval Base in Tokyo Bay. There they assisted in providing security for the base and were intended eventually to take over and operate American and Japanese harbor craft. Orders were changed, however, and the detachment returned to NORTH CAROLINA on September 5

"We recovered our people, steamed to Okinawa, embarked passengers and headed in formation for home, at last. After a brief stop at Pearl Harbor, we sailed down to the Panama Canal where sailors threw their hats to spectators gathered along the sides of the locks to see us into the Atlantic after three years in the Pacific."

— Lieutenant (jg) Tracy Wilder, F Division Officer

"The thing I remember most was the cool weather and how delicious it felt. After we came through the Panama Canal and started north up the coast, the weather cooled off day by day, and being late October, it felt good to shiver a little on deck."

— Richard McCullough, Radioman First Class

"Sailing into Boston Harbor, October 17, 1945, was an exciting experience, bands playing and lots of people waiting to greet us. I had heard many stories about how the people of Boston were not very fond of Navy men. However, I must say that they greeted us with open arms, and our six-week stay was very enjoyable. A large number of our crew was discharged the next day. For those of us who remained aboard, life also changed. The daily routine was much more relaxed. The crew had liberty every other night. We went into the city and saw movies and went to the USO Club on the Boston Common. All the residents were very friendly, and we were treated nicely."

— William Shelnutt, Seaman First Class

"We were given a tumultuous victory welcome. [After meeting his wife and parents at the train station], I took them in a cab to see the ship. As we passed the last building and turned toward the pier, there was the Showboat in all its grandeur and power. It took the cabbie's breath away. He gasped, 'Whatta canoe, whatta canoe!'"

— Lieutenant (jg) Tracy Wilder, F Division Officer

when the Showboat finally anchored in Tokyo Bay. On September 6 she headed for home, via Okinawa to take on passengers, then on to Hawaii and the Panama Canal.

After the longest and happiest voyage of her life, the ship arrived at Boston on October 17 for a hero's welcome, and the following message from the President of the United States: "No vessel of America's World War II battleship fleet served as long in combat or with greater distinction than the USS NORTH CAROLINA, from Guadalcanal to Tokyo Bay. The whole nation is proud of her." - Harry S. Truman.

A grand welcome from a Boston harbor tugboat.

Showboat's crew enjoys USO entertainment on the fantail.

The Showboat arrived at the mouth of the Cape Fear River, near Southport, North Carolina, on October 1, 1961. The next day she was towed 30 miles up the Cape Fear River to Wilmington with thousands of spectators lining the river. The photograph shows the ship near her final berth opposite downtown. Note the domed "igloos" installed to preserve her 40-mm guns while the ship was in the Reserve Fleet. The igloos were removed before the ship opened to public visitation.

POST-WAR SERVICE
November 1945 – June 1947

Due to post-war disarmament, the ship's remaining active service was short. Twice during the summer of 1946 she visited the Naval Academy at Annapolis to embark midshipmen for training cruises in the Caribbean. In October of that year she returned to her birthplace, the New York Navy Yard, for inactivation. She was decommissioned June 27, 1947, and placed in the "mothballed" Reserve Fleet at Bayonne, New Jersey. There she remained in obscurity for the next 14 years.

THE STATE OF NORTH CAROLINA SAVES ITS NAMESAKE

In 1960 when the Navy announced its intention to scrap the famous ship, two Wilmingtonians were first to propose her rescue. James S. Craig, Jr. conceived the idea, and Hugh Morton was prime mover of a plan to save her for posterity. With the endorsement of North Carolina Governor Luther Hodges and the help of many other prominent citizens of the state, a campaign was mounted to raise funds required to bring the ship to North Carolina and preserve her as a state war memorial.

The idea caught fire and thousands of citizens, including countless school children, contributed money. They raised $330,000 to have the ship moved to Wilmington and to prepare a suitable berth for her. In September 1961 she was towed from Bayonne down the East Coast to the Cape Fear River, and on October 2 was moored in her present berth across the river from downtown Wilmington. On April 29, 1962, NORTH CAROLINA was dedicated as a memorial to all the men and women of North Carolina who served in the United States Armed Forces during World War II, and to the memory of nearly 10,000 North Carolinians who gave their lives in that war.

ONE KID'S WAY OF HELPING RAISE THE MONEY

"I went to Plains Elementary School in White Plains, N.C., in early 1960. The teachers asked us kids to sell doughnuts to do our part in raising the money. I went around where I lived in the Haystack Road Community trying to sell doughnuts to our neighbors. Three dollars a box was the going price, quite high for that day and time. The people were not very interested in buying, so at the end of each day I would eat the dozen or so doughnuts and then go home. I was so happy to be doing my part, so full of sweets and head held so high. But I had a problem — no money. I mowed yards each Saturday to raise the money to take to school on Monday to cover the cost of the doughnuts I sold to myself which has been a very close kept secret that was not known by anyone until now. I finally gave up trying to sell them, so I just took them home each day where I got a quart of fresh milk and went down by the creek to a feast that will forever remain a fond and loving memory. I sold over three hundred dollars' worth of doughnuts to help raise money to save the mighty NORTH CAROLINA and I am happy to say that I was the proud owner and eater of each and every doughnut."

— Howard Hodges, White Plains, N.C.

Battleship NORTH CAROLINA today in her permanent berth in the Cape Fear River opposite downtown Wilmington, North Carolina.

BATTLESHIP NORTH CAROLINA TODAY

Six times the Japanese claimed to have sent her to the bottom of the sea, but the gallant lady and her crew survived every onslaught. With a fire in her magazines due to the torpedoing, she was spared from disaster only by the quick thinking of her crew, who turned on the sprinkling system barely in time to prevent a terrible explosion. Doomed for the scrap heap, she was saved again by the good people of the state whose proud name she had carried into battle. And thus the immortal Showboat lives on and will continue to do so for hundreds of years as a symbol of courage and sacrifice — an inspiration to millions of Americans of future generations.

Today NORTH CAROLINA is preserved and maintained almost exactly as she was in her awesome prime during World War II. Thus, she is an authentic fighting battleship of her era and is one of the few surviving units of the most powerful naval striking force ever assembled up to her time.

Berthed permanently across from historic downtown Wilmington, the ship is open to visitors every day of the year. The self-guided tour offers portions of nine levels for exploration at each visitor's own pace. Most spaces are authentically restored, and many offer interpretive signage, photographs and other aids to enhance understanding. The tour correctly leaves visitors with the impression that the ship was a floating city in addition to being a famous fighting warship.

On the tour are the crew's living quarters, officers' staterooms, medical and dental facilities, galley, butcher shop, bakery, barber shop, post office, soda fountain, convenience store, print shop, dark room, laundry, shoe repair shop, tailor shop and chapel. The tour includes the bridge and charthouse, one of four engine rooms, combat information center, admiral's and captain's cabins, radio central, the coding room, damage control spaces, the rudder spaces and the computer rooms that aimed the 16-inch and 5-inch guns. All four types of guns — the 16-inch, 5-inch, 40-mm, and 20-mm — are available for close-up inspection. Additional highlights of the tour are the OS2U Kingfisher floatplane, one of a handful in existence; the 120-plus-piece silver service from the Armored Cruiser NORTH CAROLINA; original artwork; and models of naval vessels named NORTH CAROLINA. Restored to her wartime appearance, Battleship NORTH CAROLINA stands as an enduring tribute to the valor of her wartime crew.

Life aboard...

"It's a spiritual feeling. I had it then as well as now, about the ship and the Navy. I don't think you ever lose it. If I were young, I would go back to sea again. I walked a lighter step. I had a smile on my face. I think my shoulders were squared back more. My head was held high and my hat was cocked. I was cocky. I was a battleship sailor. We were the first. I think that is what it is. Being the first of the new line of battle lions. When I walk up that gangway and I salute the colors, believe it or not, I am 17 years old again. I swear to you, I am a kid again. If I keep going, I will bring up tears. You can go home. They say that you can't go home. But you can go home. I am home. I don't know that I will ever have another opportunity to come here, but I am home now."

— Reunion attendee Jackson Belford,
Signalman Third Class

"It is part of the age-old lore of the sea that those beautiful white gulls you see gliding so gracefully over the seascapes of the world are the souls of dead sailors haunting the places they loved most during their lifetimes. So if some day you see a gull soaring back and forth in the winds around Batt Two, just throw him a fish and call him Joe."

— Commander Joe Stryker; 1941-42 Navigator,
1943-44 Executive Officer, to whom this book is dedicated

The All-Service Color Guard renders honors during the national anthem for the ceremony commemorating the 50th anniversary of VJ Day, September 2, 1995, for which the battleship was one of five national sites for the remembrance.

Proud USS NORTH CAROLINA veteran, Gerald Lape, on VJ Day, September 2, 1995, wearing one of his original wartime jumpers (shirts).

NORTH CAROLINA'S CAPTAINS

During the course of her six-year naval career, NORTH CAROLINA had nine captains. They all graduated from the United States Naval Academy in Annapolis, Maryland. Commanding NORTH CAROLINA was a prestigious position and a stepping stone to admiral for all of her captains. All but one were promoted to admiral upon leaving the ship, and he was promoted later.

Olaf M. Hustvedt
April 9, 1941 -
October 23, 1941
Class of 1909

Oscar C. Badger
October 23, 1941 -
June 1, 1942
Class of 1911

George H. Fort
June 1, 1942 -
December 5, 1942
Class of 1912

Wilder D. Baker
December 5, 1942 -
May 27, 1943
Class of 1914

Frank P. Thomas
May 27, 1943 -
October 6, 1944
Class of 1914

Frank G. Fahrion
October 6, 1944 -
January 28, 1945
Class of 1917

Oswald S. Colclough
January 28, 1945 -
June 15, 1945
Class of 1920

B. Hall Hanlon
June 15, 1945 -
February 1, 1946
Class of 1921

Timothy J. O'Brien
February 1, 1946 -
June 27, 1947
Class of 1920

ASIATIC-PACIFIC CAMPAIGNS

NORTH CAROLINA served in every major naval offensive in the Pacific area of operations during World War II, earning 15 battle stars.

★ **Landings on Guadalcanal and Tulagi**	August 7-9, 1942
★ **Capture and Defense of Guadalcanal**	August 16, 1942 – February 8, 1943
★ **Battle of the Eastern Solomons**	August 23-24, 1942
★ **New Georgia Group Operations** New Guinea, Rendova, Vangunu invasion	June 30 – August 31, 1943
★ **Gilbert Islands Operation** Tarawa and Makin	November 19 – December 8, 1943
★ **Bismark Archipelago Operations** Kavieng strike	December 25, 1943
★ **Marshall Islands Operation** Invasion of Kwajalein and Majuro Atoll	January 29 – February 8, 1944
★ **Task Force Strikes** Truk Marianas Palau, Yap, Ulithi and Woleai Truk, Satawan and Ponape	 February 16-17, 1944 February 21-22, 1944 March 30 – April 1, 1944 April 29 – May 1, 1944
★ **Western New Guinea Operations** Hollandia	April 21-24, 1944
★ **Marianas Operation** Invasion of Saipan Battle of the Philippine Sea	 June 11-24, 1944 June 19-20, 1944
★ **Leyte Operation** Attacks on Luzon	November 13-14, 19-25, 1944; December 14-16, 1944
★ **Luzon Operation** Luzon Formosa China coast Nansei Shoto	 January 6-7, 1945 January 3-4, 9, 15 and 21, 1945 January 12 and 16, 1945 January 22, 1945
★ **Iwo Jima Operation** Invasion, assault and occupation of Iwo Jima Raids against Honshu and Nansei Shoto in support	February 15 – March 1, 1945
★ **Okinawa Operation** Invasion, assault and occupation of Okinawa Capture of the Kerama Islands Raids against Kyushu and Inland Sea targets	March 17 – April 27, 1945
★ **Third Fleet Operations** Bombardment of and air strikes on Japanese Home Islands	July 10 – August 15, 1945

GENERAL DATA

Name and hull number	NORTH CAROLINA (BB-55)
Builder	New York Navy Yard, Brooklyn, New York
Laid down	October 27, 1937
Launched	June 13, 1940
Commissioned	April 9, 1941

Disposition	Transferred to state of North Carolina	September 6, 1961
	Opened to the public	October 14, 1961
	Dedicated as state's WWII memorial	April 29, 1962

Displacement, 1942	Standard load, everything but fuel and water	36,600 tons
	Full load	44,800 tons

Dimensions	Overall length	729 feet
	Waterline length	713 feet
	Maximum beam	108 feet
	Mean (average) draft at 42,329 tons	32 feet
	Maximum draft	36 feet

Complement, approximate	Officers	141 men
	Enlisted	2,115 men
	Marines, enlisted plus three officers	85 men

ARMAMENT in gun barrels

	Antiaircraft Battery				Secondary Battery	Main Battery
	.50-caliber	1.1-inch/75-caliber	20-mm/70-caliber	40-mm/56-caliber	5-inch/38-caliber Mark 12	16-inch/45-caliber Mark 6
	single mounts	four quadruple mounts	single & twin mounts	15 quadruple mounts	10 twin mounts	three 3-gun turrets
Apr 1941	12	16	none	none	20	9
Dec 1941	12	16	40	none	20	9
Jun 1942	28	16	40	none	20	9
Nov 1942	none	none	46	40	20	9
Nov 1943	none	none	46	60	20	9
Mar 1944	none	none	53	60	20	9
Dec 1944	none	none	48	60	20	9
Jun 1945	none	none	36	60	20	9

ARMOR PROTECTION

Belt Armor Top of belt has 12 inches of armor, inclined at 15 degrees, tapering to 6.6 inches at lower edge. Armor is mounted onto .75 inches STS (Special Treatment Steel) for support. Belt does not extend to lower sides.

Deck Armor

LEVEL	CENTERLINE	OUTBOARD
Main Deck	1.45 inches	1.45 inches
Second Deck	1.4 to 3.6 inches*	1.4 to 4.1 inches*
Third Deck	.62 inches	.75 inches

* thicker armor provided to compartments with vital equipment

ARMOR PROTECTION

Turret Armor	Face plates	16 inches
	Sides	9.8 inches
	Back plates	11.8 inches
	Roof plates	7 inches
Secondary Battery Armor	Gun mounts	1.95 inches
	Magazines	1.95 inches
Conning Tower Armor	Centerline sides	14.7 inches
	Beam sides	16 inches
	Roof plates	7 inches
	Bottom plates	3.9 inches
	Communications tube	14 inches

MACHINERY

Boilers

Eight Babcock & Wilcox three-drum, express-type boilers fitted with two furnaces and double uptakes

575 pounds per square inch pressure
850 degrees Fahrenheit water temperature

Turbines

Four sets of General Electric geared turbines

High-pressure impulse steam passes through 12 stages at 5,904 revolutions per minute maximum

Low pressure impulse steam passes through six stages at 4,937 revolutions per minute maximum

Astern (reverse) impulse passes through three stages at 3,299 revolutions per minute maximum

Shaft horsepower

Ahead	121,000 horsepower
Astern	32,000 horsepower

Maximum speed

28 knots at 199 revolutions per minute

Generators

Four ship's service turbogenerators producing 1,250 kilowatts of electrical power
Four ship's service diesel generators producing 850 kilowatts of electrical power
Two emergency diesel generators producing 250 kilowatts of electrical power

Propellers

Two four-bladed 15 feet, 4 inches in diameter mounted inboard
Two four-bladed 16 feet, 7.5 inches in diameter mounted outboard

Rudders

Two balanced streamlined type with train limits of 36.5 degrees to either port or starboard

TANK CAPACITIES

Fuel oil	1,985,314 gallons
Diesel oil	212,619 gallons
Gasoline	8,478 gallons
Reserve feed water for boilers	110,478 gallons
Potable (fresh) water	163,525 gallons

BIBLIOGRAPHY

Boyd, Carl and Akihiko Yoshida. *The Japanese Submarine Force in World War II.* Annapolis, Md.: Naval Institute Press, 1995.

Calhoun, C. Raymond, CAPT, USN (Ret). *Typhoon: The Other Enemy.* Annapolis, Md.: Naval Institute Press, 1981.

Carpenter, Dorr and Norman Polmar. *Submarines of the Imperial Japanese Navy.* Annapolis, Md.: Naval Institute Press, 1986.

Celustka, Robert J., LT(jg), USN. "Report from Officer of the Deck to Commanding Officer; Subject: Torpedo Action, September 17, 1942." Battleship NORTH CAROLINA Collection, Wilmington, N.C.

Cohen, David E. "The Mk. XIV Torpedo: Lessons for Today." *Naval History* 6, no. 4 (winter 1992): 34-36.

Dulin, Robert O., Jr. and William H. Garzke, Jr. *Battleships: United States Battleships in World War II.* Annapolis, Md.: Naval Institute Press, 1976.

Dull, Paul S. *A Battle History of the Imperial Japanese Navy, 1941-1945.* Annapolis, Md.: Naval Institute Press, 1978.

Fahey, James C. *The Ships and Aircraft of the United States Fleet.* Annapolis, Md.: Naval Institute Press, 1973.

Feifer, George. *Tennozan: The Battle of Okinawa and the Atomic Bomb.* New York: Ticknor and Fields, 1992.

Friedman, Norman. *Naval Radar.* Annapolis, Md.: Naval Institute Press, 1981.

----------- *U. S. Battleships: An Illustrated Design History.* Annapolis, Md.: Naval Institute Press, 1985.

Garzke, William H., Jr. and Robert O. Dulin, Jr. *Battleships: Axis and Neutral Battleships in World War II.* Annapolis, Md.: Naval Institute Press, 1985.

Hodges, Peter. *The Big Gun: Battleship Main Armament, 1860-1945.* Annapolis, Md.: Naval Institute Press, 1981.

Holcombe, A. Robert, Jr. "The Evolution of Confederate Ironclad Design." Master's thesis, East Carolina University, Greenville, N.C., 1993.

Hood, Maurice C. IV, LT(jg), USNR. "U.S.S. North Carolina Battleship Organization and Instructions for the Combat Information Center," Rev. ed. San Diego, Ca., January 2002.

Layton, Edwin T., RADM, USN (Ret), CAPT Roger Pineau, USNR (Ret), and John Costello. *"And I Was There" — Pearl Harbor and Midway — Breaking the Secrets.* New York: William Morrow and Company, Inc., 1985.

Lott, Arnold S., LCDR, USN (Ret) and Robert F. Sumrall, HTC, USNR. *Ship's Data 1: USS NORTH CAROLINA (BB55).* Wilmington, N.C.: USS NORTH CAROLINA Battleship Commission, 1982.

Mitsuru, Yoshida. *Requiem for Battleship YAMATO.* Annapolis, Md.: Naval Institute Press, 1999.

Morison, Samuel Eliot, RADM, USN (Ret). *History of the United States Naval Operations in World War II.* Vol. 3, 1948. Vol. 4, 1949. Vol. 5, 1949. Vol. 6, 1950. Vol. 7, 1951. Vol. 8, 1953. Vol. 12, 1958. Vol. 13, 1965. Vol. 14, 1968. Boston, Ma.: Little, Brown and Company.

Naval History Division. *American Ships-of-the-Line.* Washington, D.C.: Navy Department, 1970.

Newhart, Max R. *American Battleships: A Pictorial History of BB-1 to BB-71 with Prototypes of Maine and Texas.* Missoula, Mont.: Pictorial Histories Publishing Company, 1995.

Noel, John V., Jr., CAPT, USN (Ret) and Edward L. Beach, CAPT, USN (Ret). *Naval Terms Dictionary.* 5th ed. Annapolis, Md.: Naval Institute Press, 1988.

Ota, Masahide. *The Battle of Okinawa.* Okinawa, Japan: Kume Publishing Company, 1984.

Paty, Charles M., Jr. "BB55 Crew," Rev. ed. Charlotte, N.C., Vol. 1, June 2002.

-------- and Sue K. Paty. "BB55 Crew," Charlotte, N.C., Vol. 2, 2001.

-------- "BB55 Day by Day," Rev. ed. Charlotte, N.C., March 2004.

Polk, Orval H., LCDR, USNR, LT Ernest H. Dunlap, Jr., USN, and LT Frank L. Seyl, USNR. *Naval Ordnance and Gunnery, NAVPERS 16116.* N.p.: Bureau of Naval Personnel, 1944.

Potter, E. B. *Bull Halsey.* Annapolis, Md.: Naval Institute Press, 1985.

---------. *Nimitz.* Annapolis, Md.: Naval Institute Press, 1976.

--------. *Sea Power: A Naval History.* Englewood Cliffs, N.J.: Prentice-Hall, Inc., 1960.

Prados, John. *Combined Fleet Decoded: The Secret History of American Intelligence and the Japanese Navy in World War II.* New York: Random House, 1995.

Rohwer, Jurgen. *Axis Submarine Successes of World War II: German, Italian and Japanese Submarine Successes, 1939-1945.* Annapolis, Md.: Naval Institute Press, 1999.

Roscoe, Theodore. *United States Destroyer Operations in World War II.* Annapolis, Md.: Naval Institute Press, 1953.

--------. *United States Submarine Operations in World War II.* Annapolis, Md.: Naval Institute Press, 1949.

Skulski, Janusz. *The Battleship YAMATO.* Annapolis, Md.: Naval Institute Press, 2000.

Stafford, Edward P. *The Big E: The Story of the USS ENTERPRISE.* New York: Dell Publishing, 1964.

Stryker, Joe W., RADM, USN (Ret). Personal Journal. Joe W. Stryker Papers. Battleship NORTH CAROLINA Collection, Wilmington, N.C.

The United States Naval Institute. *The Bluejacket's Manual.* 14th ed. Annapolis, Md.: Naval Institute Press, 1950.

United States Naval Academy. *Naval Ordnance and Gunnery, NAVPERS 16116-B.* Washington, D.C.: Bureau of Naval Personnel, 1950.

USS NORTH CAROLINA. *Action Reports,* August 24, 1942- August 10, 1945. Battleship NORTH CAROLINA Collection, Wilmington, N.C.

---------. *Deck Log,* April 9, 1941 — September 2, 1945. Battleship NORTH CAROLINA Collection, Wilmington, N.C.

---------. *War Diary,* December 7, 1941- September 2, 1945. Battleship NORTH CAROLINA Collection, Wilmington, N.C.

Wheeler, Keith and the editors of Time-Life Books. *The Road to Tokyo.* Vol. 19 of World War II. Alexandria, Va.: Time-Life Books, Inc., 1979.

Y'Blood, William T. *Red Sun Setting: The Battle of the Philippine Sea.* Annapolis, Md.: Naval Institute Press, 1981.

INDEX

Page numbers in italics refer to illustrations

Lingga Roads, Japanese fleet at, 123
LISCOME BAY (Aircraft carrier CVE-56), 99
London Naval Treaty (1936), 3; violations of, 10
Lookouts, *66*
Lott, Arnold S., v
Luzon: Halsey on, 123; MacArthur at, 122

MacArthur, General Douglas, 105; at Japanese surrender, *142*; at Luzon, 122; recovery of Philippines, 116
Mail, censoring of, 59
Mail call, 57, 58, 95
Majuro Atoll, Task Force 58 at, 103–4
Makin Atoll, recovery of, 97, 98
Malaya, Japanese invasion of, 76
Marianas, *107*; invasion of, 106–8; Japanese counterattack at, 108; Task Force 58 at, 113
Marines, 43, *43*; 1st Division, 132; 2nd Division, 98, 106; 3rd Division, 106, 126; 4th Division, 106, 126; 5th Division, 126; in Gilbert Islands recovery, 98; at Guadalcanal, 79, 82; at Iwo Jima, 126, *127*; at Okinawa, 132; 1st Provisional Brigade, 106; 7th Regiment, 82; Tulagi landing, 79
Marko, Paul, 54
Marshall Islands: Japanese airfield at, 99; Task Force 58 in, 102
MARYLAND (Battleship BB-46), in Task Force 38/58, 100
Masie, James, 40, 98
Mason, James M., *46*
MASSACHUSETTS (Battleship BB-59), 4; in Gilbert Islands' recovery, 98; Nauru bombardment, 99; Ponape bombardment, 106; in Solomons Campaign, 97
Mast (court), 56, 58
Material conditions: Y, 55; Z, 53, 54
McCain, Vice Admiral John S., 100, *100*, 101, 116
McCullough, Richard, 86, 144
Means, Eldon E., ii, 134
Merchant ships, Allied: torpedoing of, 93
MERRIMACK (ironclad), 1
Message delivery systems. *See* Communications systems
"Mess Gear" (bugle call), 60
Midway Island, Battle of: U.S. losses in, 77, 78
Mikitka, Carol and Joe, 114
Minvielle, Paul H., *43*, 95
MISSISSIPPI (Battleship BB-41), 76; in Gilbert Islands' recovery, 98;
MISSOURI (Battleship BB-63), 4; surrender aboard, 142
Mitscher, Vice Admiral Marc A., *100*, 100, 101, 112; in Iwo Jima Campaign, 124; in Okinawa Campaign, 130
Mitsubishi "Zero" fighter planes, 48; in Eastern Solomons Campaign, 80
Miyazawa, Juichiro, 90
Mogmog Island (Ulithi Atoll), *121*, 121
MONAGHAN (Destroyer DD-354), 119
MONITOR (ironclad), 1
MONTEREY (Aircraft carrier CVL-26), 98
Moore, Lieutenant Arthur, Jr., *60*

Morison, Samuel Eliot: *History of United States Naval Operations in World War II*, vi, 88; on kamikazes, 139
Morton, Commander Thomas H., *60, 141*
Morton, Hugh, 145
Mount Suribachi (Iwo Jima), *127*
Murmansk, Allied convoys to, 76
Murray, Rear Admiral George D., 85, 87
MUSASHI (Japanese Battleship), 10; in Battle of Philippine Sea, 112; in Marianas operation, 108; at Truk, 98
Mussolini, Benito, 31
MUSTIN (Destroyer DD-413), 84

Nagasaki, bombing of, 139
Namur Island (Kwajalein Atoll), 103; NORTH CAROLINA's bombardment of, 102, *102*
Nauru Island: bombardment of, *99*, 99–100; Japanese airfield at, 99; Japanese invasion of, 76
Naval Academy (Annapolis, MD), 42
Naval Academy, Japanese (Etajima, Japan), 91
Naval architects, battleship designs of, 2
Naval warfare (World War II), 1; ship-to-ship, 17
Navy, Imperial Japanese (IJN), 76; at Camranh Bay, 122–23; destruction of records, 87–88; fighting ability of, 79; at Lingga Roads, 123; navigational charts of, 103; at The Philippines, 104; at Truk, 98, 104
Navy, U. S.: African Americans in, 42; Construction Battalions, 120; cryptologists, 77; General Board, 3; punishment in, 56, 58; reservists, 42; uniforms, 63
Navy Time, 53, 54
Nelson, Ingwald N., ii
Neumann, Leo, 62
New Guinea, landings on, 105
NEW JERSEY (Battleship BB-62), v, 4; in Battle of Philippine Sea, 110, *110*; bombardment of Ponape Island, 106; in Task Force 38/58, 100, 101
NEW MEXICO (Battleship BB-40), 76; in Gilbert Islands' recovery, 98
New York City, liberty in, 40
New York Navy Yard, 6, 34; building ways at, 6
Nimitz, Admiral Chester W., 97, *97*, 101, 105
NORTHAMPTON (Cruiser CA-26), 78
NORTH CAROLINA (Armored Cruiser ACR-12), 1–2, *2*; silver service of, 147
NORTH CAROLINA (Battleship 52, uncompleted), 2
NORTH CAROLINA (Battleship BB-55)
    Action Reports, vi
    air attacks on, 27, 99
    aircraft, *28*, 29–30; crew of, 29; fragility of, 30; fuel for, 10; landing, *28*, 29–30; launch of, *28*, 29; during shore bombardment, 30
    armament, 150; Browning machine guns (.50 caliber), 25; guns (1.1-inch), 25, *25*; guns (20-mm), 25-27, 75; guns (40-mm), 25-27, 94; guns (5-inch), *20*, 20–21, 23, 54, 67, 126–27, 128; guns (16-inch), 10-11, *11, 13, 14*, 103, 126, 128; powder bags, 12, *13*; projectiles, 12, *13*, 15, 20, 26, 91
    armor of, 3, 6, 7–8, 92, 150–51